SELLING
REAL ESTATE
WITHOUT
PAYING TAXES

SECOND EDITION

Richard T. Williamson, Esq.

KAPLAN PUBLISHING

Vice President and Publisher: Maureen McMahon
Editorial Director: Jennifer Farthing
Acquisitions Editor: Victoria Smith
Development Editor: Joshua Martino
Production Editor: Dave Shaw
Production Artist: John Christensen

© 2007 by Richard T. Williamson, Esq.

Published by Kaplan Publishing,
a division of Kaplan, Inc.

Printed in the United States of America

07 08 09   10 9 8 7 6 5 4 3 2 1

Kaplan Publishing books are available at special quantity discounts to use for sales promotions, employee premiums, or educational purposes. Please call our Special Sales Department to order or for more information at 800-621-9621, ext. 4444, e-mail kaplanpubsales@kaplan.com, or write to Kaplan Publishing, 30 South Wacker Drive, Suite 2500, Chicago, IL 60606-7481.

DEDICATION

To Michelle, my wife, soul mate, and best friend

To Christina, a truly exceptional human being who possesses
a rare combination of intellect, beauty, and selflessness

To Rebecca, a 12-year-old who keeps me young and reminds
me how important it is to make time for play

CONTENTS

15. WORKING WITH ADVISORS 191

APPENDIX 197

This is the second edition of *Selling Real Estate without Paying Taxes*. A lot has changed since the first edition was written. The capital gains tax rate has changed, estate tax exemptions have changed, holding requirements in some tax planning techniques have changed, and the IRS has clarified some of the ambiguities that existed then. In addition, some of the lesser-known tax strategies in the first edition have become more mainstream. This second edition contains updates for the changes that have taken place as well as topics that have become important in capital gains tax planning.

One thing that has not changed since the first edition is that no one likes to write checks to the IRS. This is especially true when it comes to writing *large* checks for capital gains taxes. Unfortunately, capital gains taxes are a reality most investors have to face. However, there are alternatives. If you know how, there are ways to defer taxes and, in some cases, even completely eliminate them. The best part is, you don't have to be a Yale accountant or a Harvard lawyer to understand the alternatives available and how they work.

Selling Real Estate without Paying Taxes: A Guide to Capital Gains Tax Alternatives was designed and written for ordinary real estate investors and real estate agents. Although this book covers some very complicated areas of tax law, great effort was made to keep the explanations and examples straightforward and easy to understand. This book is not intended as a replacement for the situation-specific advice and guidance of accountants and attorneys but rather as an overview and guide to the various capital gains tax alternatives available.

In 20 years of advising real estate investors, I have been asked the same questions and have seen the same mistakes made again and again. Usually, the problem is that an investor simply does not know how a particular tax-deferral method works or that there are other alternatives available. Some of the everyday concepts in this book such as installment sales and 1031 exchanges may seem well known, and you may be tempted to skip over those sections. I encourage you not to. In the beginning chapters, an effort was made not only to cover the basics for the true novice but also to really focus on the areas and issues where most investors and real estate agents either make mistakes or miss opportunities. You also will find that some of the basic tax-deferral tools can be used in ways you may not have previously considered.

At the other end of the spectrum, this book contains some sophisticated tax-deferral methods that will probably be unfamiliar to you and may seem a bit complicated. In these chapters, an effort was made to make the reading easy by sticking to an overview of the concept and giving lots of examples, so you can see how each of the tax alternatives works in everyday situations.

Whether you are a new property investor or a seasoned real estate professional, this book will show you tax-deferral methods and techniques you probably have never seen before. This book is only a starting place in capital gains tax strategy. It may answer a lot of your questions, but it may also raise a lot of new ones. That's okay, because getting good advice almost always starts with knowing the right questions to ask.

ACKNOWLEDGMENTS

This book could never have become a reality without the encouragement and assistance of people around me. First, I would like to thank my wife and my daughter for tolerating all the nights and weekends I spent working on the book.

In writing this book, I was fortunate in having the assistance and input from a number of professionals. I would like to give credit and my sincere thanks to the following people:

- **Michelle Williamson,** a real estate investor in Long Beach, California. Michelle spent long hours editing and proofreading. Her suggestions and feedback were very helpful in keeping me from straying too far into lawyerlike technical explanations.

- **Ed Dowd,** a real estate broker and longtime investment property specialist with Coldwell Banker Coastal Alliance Real Estate in Long Beach, California. Ed's enthusiasm and encouragement helped keep me motivated. His contributions and wealth of real-world experience gave substance to many of the situational examples in this book.

- **Matthew Crammer,** an accountant and financial planner with Crammer Accountancy in Downey, California. Matthew was very generous with his time in reading the rough draft of the manuscript and making suggestions for improving the accounting examples and explanations. He also contributed his accounting expertise by providing the completed IRS-form illustrations for situational examples scattered throughout the book.

- **Anette E. Kerr,** my legal assistant, the keeper of my schedule, the protector of my time, and my own version of a trusted Radar O'Riley.

CHAPTER ONE

Introduction

The investment real estate market in America is booming as never before. More and more, the market has surged as people decide that real estate should be a significant portion of their investment and retirement planning. The conventional investment wisdom of mutual funds and stocks seems less palatable to the average person.

Higher real estate demand is the result of more potential buyers in the market, and for every investment property buyer there has to be a corresponding investment property seller. Many of the investors who bought properties in the 1980s and 1990s are finding high prices from the current demand simply too favorable to ignore. Their biggest problem is how to deal with the taxes.

Every time a piece of real estate changes hands, tax consequences emerge. The two primary tax considerations are capital gains and recapture of depreciation. Between the two, state and federal taxes can be as much as a full one-third of the profit on the sale of a property. Not surprisingly, investment property sellers are less than enthusiastic about writing large checks to the IRS. As a result, everyone selling investment property inevitably asks, Is there any way to avoid these taxes? The answer is yes.

The fact is that capital gains taxes *can* be legally deferred or eliminated. In this book you are going to get a nontechnical, straightforward look at the possible ways to avoid taxes when selling real estate. From the simple to the sophisticated, I explore the various capital gains tax-deferral and elimination methods, discuss the pros and cons of each, and offer examples of how each method works in everyday practice.

When the average person thinks of taxes, he or she usually thinks of *income* taxes. However, the tax system in the United States is not based on taxing income; instead, our tax system is based on taxing *increases in wealth*. The subtle difference in this terminology is very important, because taxing all forms of wealth increases allows the IRS to tax things other than just the earnings we take home. So in addition to income taxes, we also have taxes on gifts, interest income, debt forgiveness, capital gains, and even on death (estate taxes). All of these represent increases in wealth according to the IRS and, as such, are taxed in one manner or another.

Both income taxes and gift taxes are scaled to essentially provide that the more you make or give, the higher the percentage of taxes you pay. Likewise, estate taxes as a percentage are higher in larger estates. Taxing debt forgiveness is an odd concept but necessary in the eye of the IRS. If debt forgiveness were not taxed, companies could circumvent *income* taxes by simply paying wages to their employees with "loans" each month and then forgiving the debts at the end of the year.

That's a simple example of tax-planning creativity, but it makes the point that the IRS needs to focus on increases in wealth instead of merely income. The focus of this book will be on capital gains taxes. Capital gains are actually given preferential tax treatment by the basing of the applicable tax on a flat rate. At the time of this writing, the long-term federal capital gains tax rate is 15 percent. Okay, it's not quite that simple. In real estate investment tax considerations, there is also a recapture of depreciation rate at 25 percent and state capital gains taxes to take into account. Then there is the lower 5 percent capital gains rate for persons in the 15 percent income tax bracket. These rates are lower than in previous years; however, they are temporary because the legislation that lowered the rates to these levels was set to expire in 2009. I say "was set to expire" because in 2006 legislation was passed to extend the temporary reduction an additional two years. For the purposes of this book, I am going set aside this variability and just focus on the regular person in an ordinary real estate capital gains situation. So, for the regular person in a ordinary capital gains situation, the federal capital gains tax rate right now is 15 percent.

State taxes are another matter. Each state can make its own rules for taxing capital gains. Some states impose no state capital gains taxes, but most require that some tax liability is incurred on the sale of an appreciated property. In addition, each state has its own rules covering capital gains tax deferral. Most states mirror the federal taxation rules and guidelines, but not all do. The focus of this book is on federal taxation and those states, California for example, that mirror the federal rules. A state-by-state analysis is beyond the scope of this book, but I have included a list of the capital gains tax rates for the individual states in the appendix. Nevertheless, I suggest you see your local tax advisor regarding your state's tax treatment of capital gains on the sale or exchange of property.

As previously mentioned, true *income* tax is scaled to tax larger incomes at higher percentage rates. Capital gains tax, however, is currently based on a flat 15 percent rate. This is the lowest capital gains rate in almost 40 years. And unlike other types of taxes, capital gains taxes can be deferred indefinitely and, in some situations, eliminated completely. In the next section, I look at the types of wealth increases categorized as capital gains.

WHAT ARE CAPITAL GAINS?

The IRS considers just about everything you own and use for personal purposes or for investment a capital asset. Examples it gives are your home, household furnishings, and stocks or bonds held in your personal account. It divides capital gains into three foundational taxation categories: long-term, midterm, and short-term capital gains.

If you hold an asset for more than one year before you dispose of it, your capital gain is a long-term gain. If you hold it for one year or less, your capital gain is considered a short-term gain. And although that definition came directly from the IRS, the agency also says that the long-term capital gains rate is based on an 18-month holding period. When you sell a capital asset, the difference between the amount for which you sell it and your cost or adjusted basis is a capital gain or a capital loss. In the case of real estate investments, most people take depreciation and make improvements to the property over time so the basis of the property changes each year. In a normal property investment situation, two forces are at work creating a gain on the property (see Figure 1.1). First, appreciation increases the fair market value of the property; and, second, depreciation taken on the property over the years correspondingly reduces the property's basis and thus adds another component of taxable gain when the property is eventually sold.

FIGURE 1.1   Forces at Work Creating Taxable Gain

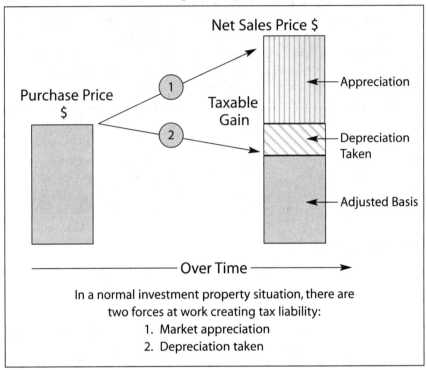

In a normal investment property situation, there are
two forces at work creating tax liability:
1. Market appreciation
2. Depreciation taken

CAPITAL GAINS TAXES ARE...GOOD?

Because the Alternative Is Bad

The idea of having the capital gains tax eliminated sounds appealing, but in reality it may not be. Remember that the focus of the IRS is to tax increases in wealth, not income. Right now, the capital gains rate set at a flat 15 percent is one of the lowest taxes available. If you had $100,000 of *income* in a year, your tax rate would be approximately 30 percent. A taxable *gift* of $100,000 would be taxed at approximately 35 percent. A taxable *estate* inheritance would be taxed at approximately 35 percent. So what's so bad about a 15 percent flat rate tax on capital gains? Naturally, *zero* tax on capital gains would be better, but it is unimaginable that the IRS and a constantly changing political climate in the country are going to completely eliminate the capital gains tax. To do so would allow this obvious increase in wealth to be taxed in some other way. At least there is some certainty now and the increase in wealth is taxed at the lowest available tax rate. So, from this perspective, the current capital gains tax is good because the alternative is sure to be less desirable.

Certainty Allows Planning

Another reason the current capital gains tax is good is because it permits planning. If you know that the taxable consequence of selling a capital asset is going to be the same now as it will be in the future, you are more able to achieve intelligent tax planning. Most capital assets have a built-in variable: the resale market. Real estate values have cycles just like any other investment. Anyone who has held real estate for more than ten years can tell you the market has highs and lows. The last thing an investment needs to compound its uncertainty and risk is a variable tax environment. In one worst-case scenario, politicians could eliminate the capital gains tax to get votes, but the next administration would decide that same increase in wealth should be taxed at the (higher) ordinary income tax rates. The last thing we need is politicians messing around with tax rates that are already the lowest they have been in a half century. Stability and certainty in an investment or business environment encourage additional investment by allowing intelligent growth planning.

Capital Gains Deferral as a Wealth-Building Tool

Almost any form of investment must be done with after-tax dollars. The capital gain you make from real estate investing, however, is the exception. You cannot sell 100 shares of Google stock in a high market and reinvest it in 100 shares of another stock without cashing out, paying the taxes due, and then buying the replacement stock with after-tax dollars. However, in real estate you can sell an investment property and buy another using the untaxed dollars from the returns on the first investment (a 1031 exchange, explained in detail in Chapter 8). This ability to defer all taxes on the investment returns has made more than a few people very wealthy.

There is no limit to the number of times you can use a 1031 exchange to trade up without incurring any tax liability. The key is that current IRS regulations allow this continuing deferral on capital gains but not on any other types of increases in wealth. The ability to defer capital gains in the now commonly known 1031 exchange was a hard-fought-for right that had to been pounded out in the courts and forced

Example: Paul is an insurance agent; he bought a triplex ten years ago for $200,000, and its current value is $420,000. Recently, he has considered opening his own insurance office and has found a perfect office building for sale at $600,000 that he wants to buy. Paul sells his triplex under the provisions of a 1031 tax-deferred exchange and purchases the office building replacement property. He is able to fully defer any capital gains tax or recapture of depreciation. Paul operates his insurance company for 15 years and is ready to retire. He would like to move to another state and buy an income-producing investment property there. The office building's value has grown to $900,000, and the 12-unit apartment building he would like to buy is priced at $950,000. Again, Paul uses a 1031 exchange to sell the office building, and he purchases the 12-unit apartment, completely deferring all capital gains and recapture of depreciation.

upon the IRS through legislative mandate over a period of 20 to 30 years. This wealth-building tool now works extremely well, and any changes in the capital gains tax rules can only harm wealth-building tools like 1031 exchanges.

If It Isn't Broken, Don't Fix It

In sum, the idea of eliminating the capital gains tax sounds great but at what real cost? It is unrealistic to think that the IRS's concept of taxing increases in wealth is going to carve out a major exception and allow significant income from capital investments to flow to individuals tax free. It may be a great promise in an election year, but anyone who looks past the political rhetoric will quickly see that it's not going to happen in the real world. Politicians may eliminate the capital gains tax as currently defined, but an increase in wealth is going to be taxed in some other way. When you consider that the present method of taxing capital gains is given preferential treatment by being a flat tax at the lowest rate, as noted earlier, any alternative is likely to be a step backward. Add to that the now-existing certainty for planning and the present ability to defer capital gains for wealth building and you start to appreciate the current capital gains tax environment.

DEFERRAL VERSUS ELIMINATION OF TAXES

If you are going to sell a capital asset at a gain, you have to make a choice: you can pay the taxes, defer the taxes, or eliminate the taxes. Each has its pros and cons, so the answer is not as easy as it may appear. You don't need a book to show you how to *pay* taxes, so presumably you are reading this to learn how to defer or eliminate taxes. Nevertheless, sometimes the option to just pay the taxes is a choice worth considering. If the gain is a small one and you are at a point in your life where the goal is to simplify, the choice of just paying the taxes may be a good one. If you are like most people, however, you are looking for alternatives.

Methods are available for both deferring and eliminating capital gains taxes, but each method comes at a cost and each has advantages and disadvantages. Most of the time, the decision comes down to "doing the math," but not always. For example, people can completely eliminate their capital gains taxes through a charitable remainder trust, but the property has to ultimately be given to the charity. Some people choose this alternative strictly for the personal financial benefits. Others may choose this same option, not for the financial benefits, but because they like the idea of giving Uncle Sam's money to their favorite charity. Likewise, deferral methods such as 1031 exchanges and private annuity trusts accomplish the goal of deferring the taxes but have costs and disadvantages that must be taken into account. And like the previous example, different people may use the same method of tax planning but for completely different reasons. The immediate short-term objective for all of these people is to *not* pay capital gains taxes, but which method is best depends on each person's specific long-term objectives.

2

What Are Your Objectives?

Many people start on a course of action without really setting any goals or objectives. This book is not about goal setting, so we are not going to spend any time on the "how-to" concepts of setting personal goals. However, you cannot properly evaluate which planning alternative will best suit your long-term needs if you have not already set long-term objectives. In the following sections, I review the most common of these objectives and touch on which of the four main methods of selling real estate and deferring or eliminating tax liability might be appropriate given the objective.

FOUR GOALS OF INVESTMENT OR REINVESTMENT

There are basically four stages of investment and reinvestment in the selling of real estate that may take place throughout a lifetime: (1) building wealth, (2) protecting assets, (3) creating a stream of income, and (4) estate planning.

Presuming a person has a normal life span and has invested well, he or she usually will have had objectives that fall into one or more of these four categories. Each stage has different levels of acceptable risk and different goals.

Building Wealth

If you think that the only objective anyone ever has for investing is building wealth, then you are not old enough or have not accumulated enough assets to start trying to balance the potential growth with the acceptable risk. When you are 25 years old, you have a lifetime to make up for a high-risk investment that goes bad. When you are 65, it would be hard to recover from that same bad investment. At a younger age, investors make financial decisions primarily based on growth and future return, but retirement-minded investors focus on income flow and stability.

Of the four main tools for selling real estate without paying taxes, only two will appeal to the investor who is aggressively trying to build wealth. The first and easiest to understand is the tax-deferred 1031 exchange. By using a tax-deferred exchange, property investors are able to continually step up their real estate investments. You may start with a rental house that you trade up to a four-unit building. Then some years later you may decide to trade up to a 20-unit apartment, and so on. All of these transactions will be protected from capital gains taxes if properly done by using the provisions of section 1031 of the Internal Revenue Code (hence, the nickname "1031 exchange"). There are, of course, certain restrictions and formalities that must be followed, but for the most part, 1031 exchanges are very common in real estate transactions.

The second method, a private annuity trust, also offers the potential for building wealth. For this tool to be appropriate, however, the goals must be long term and calculated to provide a return in the future. Placing a property into a private annuity trust removes the asset from the reach of the investor but allows the trust to invest the proceeds with a high degree of flexibility. The growth of wealth in this case is usually for retirement-oriented thinking, but the growth potential, when done properly, is hard to dispute. The other two options, installment sales and charitable remainder trusts, are not really suitable for growth-oriented investors because each locks in the proceeds from the sale, allowing little or no flexibility.

Protecting Assets

Everyone who invests money has some degree of desire to protect the asset. The desire to protect is simply another way of looking at an investor's acceptable level of risk. As mentioned previously, there are varying degrees of acceptable risk. The aggressive wealth-builder will take chances that an asset-protection-minded person would not. Most of the time, the asset protection person will simply opt not to sell, but sometimes a need arises to geographically relocate the investment or perhaps improve the quality of the property without expanding the investment or increasing the risk.

Many times, clients simply want different but similarly valued property in a different or "better" area. These clients have no real need to explore all the possible ways to defer the taxable gain because the short-term goal is a lateral move of the investment. The obvious choice is to do a 1031 exchange, selling (relinquishing) one property and purchasing (replacing it with) another. However, this is also a good time for clients, including you, to consider long-term objectives.

Retirement and estate planning considerations may make a private annuity trust more attractive than a straight 1031 exchange. With a private annuity trust you can still meet your short-term goal of selling one property, buying another, and deferring the taxes. But a private annuity trust, as a result of its characteristics, also allows planning for a guaranteed stream of retirement income and may mean huge estate tax savings because it removes the asset from your taxable estate. A private annuity trust also protects the investment from future creditors and personal or professional lawsuit liability. But on the negative side, a private annuity trust has more formalities, requires more planning, and commits the asset/investment to an irrevocable family trust.

Whether a 1031 exchange or private annuity trust is right for the asset-protection-minded person simply depends on each individual's set of circumstances and personal objectives.

Providing or Restructuring a Stream of Income

In some cases an investor has property that has been in the family for a long time. Perhaps it's a piece of vacant land, a rental house, or some other type of investment property. Many times it is producing little or no real income in relation to its current market value if it were to be sold.

Example: Mary is 70 years old and lives in northern California. Her mother passed away 20 years ago, leaving Mary a small house located in southern California. There is no mortgage on the house, and it is rented for $800 per month. After management fees, repairs, property taxes, and insurance, Mary's yearly income on the property is about $7,200. The current market value of the house is $220,000, so the stream of income on this asset is only about 3.3 percent.

If Mary in the previous example were trying to provide the best stream of income, the intelligent financial decision would be to sell the house and invest the money another way. However, Mary has had the house for 20 years, so having to pay taxes on her capital gain and recapture of depreciation will reduce proceeds in her situation by about 25 percent. For Mary, a better choice would be to defer her capital gains taxes through an installment sale, defer her taxes through a private annuity trust, or eliminate the tax liability through a charitable remainder trust. All three of these options dramatically improve Mary's stream of income. Which one is best depends on determining Mary's secondary goal. For example, if she is primarily interested in improving her income stream and only secondarily interested in removing the asset from her estate, a private annuity trust or charitable remainder trust might be best. If her secondary goal is to pass the remaining asset to her children, then an installment sale or private annuity trust might be best. And a charitable remainder trust might be best if the secondary goal was charitable giving.

Each person's situation is going to be slightly different based on his or her own specific needs and objectives. Mary was actually a real client. What did she do? She sold the property to a long-term investor by way of an installment sale. After receiving a 10 percent down payment that covered the expenses of the sale and the capital gains tax that would become due on the down payment, Mary carried a first mortgage of $198,000 at 7.5 percent amortized over 30 years and all due in 15 years. Mary no longer has tenant problems, repairs, property taxes, management fees, or insurance expenses. Her interest income from the asset is now approximately $14,850 per year (a 106 percent improvement), and she will still be able to leave a significant portion of the asset's value to her children when she dies.

Mary's choice was based primarily on her desire to restructure and improve her income stream, but her secondary goal was to provide for her children, which discounted the idea of a charitable remainder trust. And the private annuity trust option would have returned more of the principal and gain to her more quickly than she wanted, so the best choice for her needs was a straight installment sale.

Estate Planning

For some investors there comes a time when the most important factor guiding their investment or reinvestment decisions is estate planning. You don't have to be rich to do estate planning—just smart. Everyone dies; it's not a question of if you are going to die; it's a matter of when. Many investors reach a point where they decide to make changes in their investments so that their estate is more manageable for their heirs or is structured properly to minimize any potential estate taxes. Sometimes a high-maintenance property has to be exchanged for a low-maintenance one. Or perhaps a partnership interest in a property investment has to be divided to eliminate the potential for future disputes. Or maybe an investor wants to remove certain investments from her taxable estate through a charitable remainder trust or private annuity trust. Whatever the specific situation, there are savvy ways to restructure property investments so capital gains taxes can be deferred now and possibly eliminated completely for an investor's heirs.

MAKING THE RIGHT DECISIONS

Making the right decisions starts with identifying your objectives and then seeking good advice on how to meet them. It defies common sense, but many people do start on a course of action before they really know what they are trying to achieve. The best advisors in the world are useless if they don't really know what it is you want to accomplish.

3

How to Estimate *Your* Capital Gains Taxes

Before you can make any decisions about deferring capital gains taxes, you have to start by knowing the extent of your taxes. Any one particular method of deferring taxes may seem like too much trouble for a $10,000 tax savings. However, it might be much more tolerable for a $50,000 tax savings, and for a $100,000 tax savings, it might seem the ideal solution. In fact, the extent of your tax liability will usually dictate how open-minded you are about exploring options. With that in mind, it makes sense to start with a discussion of how you can estimate your own taxes.

To estimate your tax liability on the sale of a property, you have to know what the gain will be. The gain on a property is the difference between the net sales price and the adjusted basis on the property. The adjusted basis of a property is:

> Original purchase price
> + Purchase expenses
> + Capital improvements
> − Depreciation taken
> = Adjusted basis

This information is usually calculated each year for filing your tax returns on a particular investment property; so most people just call their tax preparer and ask. You can also look at a previous tax return to see the amount of yearly depreciation and come up with a pretty good estimate.

Once you have your adjusted basis on the property, estimating the capital gain is fairly straightforward:

> Sales price
> − Selling expenses
> − Adjusted basis
> = Capital gain

Your capital gain on a property has two components: *actual gain* and *recapture of depreciation*. So before you can estimate the actual tax on the gain, you need to know how much of the gain will be considered recapture of depreciation. I've already covered the basic tax rate for capital gains, so if you have never taken any depreciation on the property, you can estimate your taxes now as simply 15 percent of your capital gain (plus state taxes). However, if you are like most people, you have taken the available depreciation on the property over the years and thereby reduced your adjusted basis (see Figure 3.1). As such, your tax estimate will have to take into account the higher tax rate on the recapture-of-depreciation portion of the gain.

FIGURE 3.1   Adjusted Basis Change Over Time

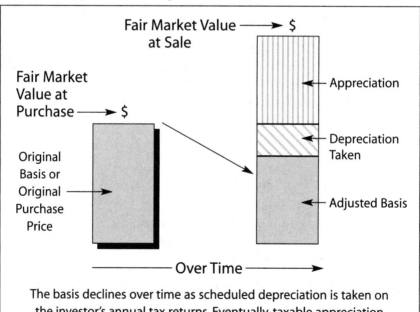

The basis declines over time as scheduled depreciation is taken on the investor's annual tax returns. Eventually, taxable appreciation (capital gain) and taxable recapture of depreciation represent the majority of the property's fair market value.

UNDERSTANDING RECAPTURE OF DEPRECIATION

Before 1997, capital gains and recapture of depreciation were taxed at the same rate. The 1997 tax changes reduced the tax on both capital gains and recapture of depreciation although not by the same amount. The capital gains rate was reduced from 28 percent to 20 percent (then subsequently reduced to 15 percent), but the recapture of depreciation was reduced to only 25 percent. Everyone initially celebrated the capital gains reduction, but a closer look showed that in almost all real estate situations a significant portion of the gain would be recapture of depreciation, and the gain would therefore be taxed at the 25 percent rate instead of the celebrated 15 percent rate.

The recapture of depreciation consideration is important because many property investors don't think in terms of adjusted basis. The average property investor owns one or two rental properties, usually rental houses, rental condominiums, or small multifamily buildings. Most of these investors have taken significant depreciation over the years and are appalled when they find out how that will impact their capital gains. Worse, in some cases market values have fluctuated so that perhaps the current value is approximately what an investor paid originally for the property, but because the adjusted basis is low, the tax liability is high.

Example: When Carl bought a triplex 15 years ago, the real estate market was strong and getting better. For a few years after he bought the property, the value of his purchase continued to increase, but then real estate values declined sharply. Carl was unable to sell the property for a number of years without taking an unacceptable loss, so he held it through the bad times and now values are rising. Having managed the property for 15 years, Carl no longer wants to be a landlord. Because real estate values are now back to where they were, Carl feels he can get his money out. Let's say he paid $300,000 for the triplex and can now sell it for $320,000. After selling expenses, Carl figures he will net the $300,000 he originally paid for it. However, Carl has taken the allowable depreciation each year on his taxes, and his adjusted basis currently stands at $190,000. Although Carl has no true gain because he is selling the property for approximately what he paid for it, he will still have to pay taxes on the recapture of depreciation. In this example, the recapture of depreciation is $110,000 that is taxed at 25 percent, a federal tax liability of approximately $27,500 (plus state taxes).

As you can imagine, anyone in a situation similar to Carl's is going to deeply resent having to pay any taxes at all. It's usually perceived as an insult added to the injury of bad investment timing. But is it really? Don't get me wrong; I don't usually take the IRS's side on anything, but in this instance a significant benefit was realized. In the previous example, if Carl is normally in the 30 percent tax bracket for income tax purposes, he was able to use that depreciation deduction over the years to shield himself from $33,000 in income taxes. So he actually would be $5,500 ahead. Okay, that doesn't really make it all better, but it is at least a silver lining in the dark cloud.

In any case, because recapture of depreciation is taxed at a higher rate, it is a crucial factor when estimating taxes.

ESTIMATING YOUR TAX LIABILITY

It doesn't take a CPA to estimate the potential tax liability on the sale of real estate. The math is fairly straightforward, but you have to know the three key factors previously described: the adjusted basis, the total depreciation taken, and the expected net sales price. From there you will be able to estimate what portion will represent capital gain and what portion will be taxed at the higher recapture-of-depreciation rate.

> **Example:** Tom has a rental property he has owned for 15 years. He originally paid $200,000 for the property, and it now has an *expected sales price* of $300,000. He has been depreciating the property for the full 15 years and *his total depreciation taken* to date is $100,000. His *adjusted basis* is now $100,000. If he sells the property, his taxable gain, setting aside selling expenses, would be $200,000 (sales price less adjusted basis: $300,000 - $100,000 = $200,000). One-half of the total gain on Tom's property is represented by recapture of depreciation and is therefore taxed at the 25 percent rate, and the remaining capital gain would be taxed at 15 percent, as shown in Figure 3.2. Thus, if the taxes were not deferred on the sale of this property, Tom would owe $40,000 in federal taxes.

In the previous example, it is easy to see that the tax consequences of selling Tom's property are significant. If this property were located in California or another state with similar state tax rates, the total state and federal taxes could be approximately $58,000 ($40,000 federal plus $18,000 state).

FIGURE 3.2   Appreciated Property Breakdown

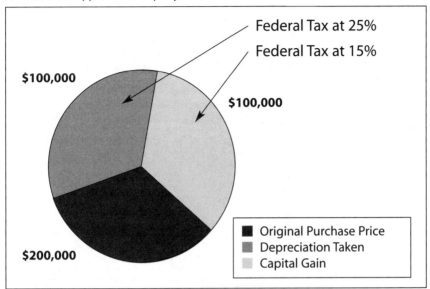

A side note: If you buy into all the political posturing about eliminating federal capital gains taxes, remember that recapture of depreciation is still going to incur a 25 percent tax rate and state capital gains taxes will still apply. So in the previous California example, even with full elimination of a federal capital gains tax, there would still be approximately $43,000 in tax liability because of the tax on recapture of depreciation and the state-level capital gains tax.

CHAPTER FOUR

The Benefits of Depreciation

One of the great advantages of real estate investment is the ability to take depreciation on a property. The benefit of depreciation is that it can shield you from taxes on paper, while providing a real dollar cash flow. Depreciation is a way of accounting for the costs associated with any tangible asset used in a business or for investment that has an expected useful life of more than one year. The one-year period is considered the line between assets you write off in a fiscal year and capital assets that must be depreciated. Capital assets have an initial cost and are expected to eventually wear out. Conceptually, depreciation is an expense that represents the yearly depletion or use of the life or cost of purchasing the asset. The IRS assigns the depreciation schedule that must be followed for different types of assets.

For example, let's look at a business that purchases a vehicle. Over time, the wear and tear of using the vehicle necessitates its replacement. So, if the IRS says that this particular asset, the vehicle, has a useful life of five years, then the business will depreciate or expense the vehicle on paper over that five-year period of time. The theory is that the business gets to write off that portion of the vehicle actually used or "consumed" in each of the five years.

The concept works the same with real estate. There are two basic recovery periods for real estate assets: residential real estate, which the IRS has determined has a useful life of 27.5 years, and commercial real estate with a useful life of 39 years.

Depreciation in the case of real estate is a fiction. In most cases, real estate appreciates in value instead of declining. However, that's not always true. A warehouse or industrial structure may actually have to be replaced because of wear, tear, and/or obsolescence. In that case, the 39-year useful life assigned to commercial property by the IRS might well be too long a period. However, residential real estate such as apartment buildings or rental houses rarely has to be replaced or rebuilt after 27.5 years of use.

For most real estate investment scenarios, depreciation is a planned for and relied upon tax advantage. However, there are occasional situations where an investor might not want to take the depreciation on an investment property. Unfortunately, in those unique situations, the investor is simply not given a choice. The IRS says you will take the allowable depreciation on residential and commercial real estate investments. Yes, depreciation is mandatory. If an investment property is sold and the investor did not take the allowable yearly depreciation, the IRS will tax the profits on the sale as if the depreciation had been taken and was being recaptured. Why? Maybe it's because recapture of depreciation is taxed at the higher rate (25 percent). Here's how IRS Publication 527 puts it:

> Claiming the correct amount of depreciation. You should claim the correct amount of depreciation each tax year. Even if you did not claim depreciation that you were entitled to deduct, you must still reduce your basis in the property by the full amount of depreciation that you could have deducted.

Again, in most real estate investment situations, depreciation is a big advantage and is part of the planned cash flow. But how much depreciation is given on any particular investment? That will depend on two things: your basis (or adjusted basis) in the property and the land-to-improvements ratio on the property. The land-to-improvements ratio is how much the land is worth in relation to the total price of the property. You can't take depreciation on land, so it must be subtracted from the total purchase price of the investment to establish the value of the improvements that will be depreciated. Why can't you depreciate land? Unlike buildings or other improvements, land never wears out. So, we have to subtract the value of the land as a nondepreciable portion of the investment. With the land value subtracted, we now know what amount to depreciate. From there, it will depend on the type of real estate investment—residential or commercial.

DEPRECIATION METHODS

There are three ways to figure depreciation. The depreciation method you use depends on the type of property and when it was placed in service. For property used in rental activities, you use one of the following:

1. Modified accelerated cost recovery system (MACRS) for property placed in service after 1986

2. Accelerated cost recovery system (ACRS) for property placed in service after 1980 but before 1987

3. Useful lives and either straight-line or an accelerated method of depreciation, such as the declining balance method, for property placed in service before 1981

(Source: IRS Publication 597)

At one time, there were also different types of depreciation methods to be considered. Prior to 1986, under the ACRS, the cost of an investment in real property could be written off over 19 years, using the 175 percent declining balance method of depreciation. This accelerated method allowed a larger proportion of the investment cost to be written off in the earlier years of the depreciation. That's long gone. Now all real estate depreciation is done on the MACRS and straight-line method. Meaning that, for the most part, real estate depreciation schedules evenly allocate the expense over either the 27.5-year depreciation schedule for residential property or 39-year depreciation schedule for commercial property.

UNDERSTANDING HOW DEPRECIATION SHIELDS YOU FROM TAXES

To help show how depreciation works in a real estate investment, we need to create a basic example property for discussion.

Example: James buys a four-unit apartment building (a fourplex). The purchase price is $400,000. Let's say James's basis in this case is the cost or purchase price of the property. James estimates the fair market value of the land and improvements at $125,000 for land and $275,000 for depreciable improvements.

Using the previous example, the available depreciation for James would be $275,000. Each year James would be able to deduct $10,000 of depreciation on Schedule E of his tax returns. James would be able to do this for 27.5 years. The net effect of having this depreciation is to offset profits otherwise made on the property. So, for example, if James's four-plex nets $15,000 a year after repairs, maintenance, and other expenses, the first $10,000 of that net income would be tax-free because the scheduled $10,000 of depreciation would offset that amount. Now this is a very simple example. Ordinarily, there are lots of factors that go into the income and expenses of a rental property; however, for the purposes of understanding how simple depreciation works, this example is useful.

It is important to understand that depreciation is an expense on paper only. It's an accounting fiction, meaning that in the previous example, James did not actually have to pay out $10,000. Also, hopefully James's property did not actually decline in value by $10,000. So, the net effect of James's $10,000 yearly depreciation write-off is to shield him from taxes on the first $10,000 of profits made in rental income from his property.

If you use this simple example as a starting place and imagine that James doesn't own just one rental property but rather has five similar properties, you can see how depreciation can have a significant impact on your tax-free income. Unfortunately, in the real world, investors rarely have this type of a positive cash flow on a newly purchased building. In fact, most investment property, if properly leveraged, is going to show at least a paper loss for the first years. So, the question becomes, What can we do with this depreciation if it's not shielding a rental income from the property?

UNDERSTANDING THE PASSIVE LOSS RULES

Prior to 1986, real estate investment had an additional advantage—sheltering other income. The pre-1986 rules allowed an investor to use the on-paper (depreciation) losses to shelter real dollar income from other unrelated sources. Prior to 1986, high-income earners, doctors, lawyers, business owners, and the like, invested heavily in real estate as a way to generate losses which could then be used to shield or offset portions of their non–real estate income from taxes. Those same pre-1986 rules also allowed a real estate investor to take accelerated depreciation on properties, which just added to the yearly write-offs and, thus, the desirability of real estate investment for those high-income earners.

In an attempt to end what the IRS saw as abusive tax sheltering of income, the Tax Reform Act of 1986 was enacted and had a major impact on real estate investment. The Tax Reform Act of 1986 added Internal Revenue Code Section 469, which limits a taxpayer's ability to deduct or write off losses from any business in which the taxpayer does not materially participate. The act specifically targeted real estate by including the language "any rental activities" in the definition of passive activity.

Okay, so what does that mean? It means, as a general rule, a taxpayer now cannot deduct losses from real estate investments in which he or she does not materially participate unless there is reported passive income on the tax return against which to offset the losses. In addition, losses from passive activities cannot offset nonpassive income such as wages, salaries, or other nonpassive income from sole proprietorships, partnerships, or entities in which the taxpayer materially participates.

Like most general rules in taxation, however, there are usually exceptions. In this case, there are two exceptions (actually three, but only two worth talking about). The first exception, the active participation exception, is for persons with adjusted gross incomes of less than $150,000; the second is an exception made for real estate professionals. The requirements for both of these exceptions are often misquoted in news articles and on the Internet. Fortunately, this is one topic about which the IRS's own publication provides good (and understandable) information. The following two explanations summarize the points from IRS Publication 527.

THE EXCEPTION FOR ACTIVE PARTICIPATION

If you or your spouse actively participated in a passive rental real estate activity, you can deduct up to $25,000 of loss from the activity from your nonpassive income. This special allowance is an exception to the general rule disallowing losses in excess of income from passive activities. Similarly, you can offset credits from the activity against the tax on up to $25,000 of nonpassive income after taking into account any losses allowed under this exception.

If you are married, filing a separate return, and lived apart from your spouse for the entire tax year, your special allowance cannot be more than $12,500. If you lived with your spouse at any time during the year and are filing a separate return, you cannot use the special allowance to reduce your nonpassive income or tax on nonpassive income.

The maximum amount of the special allowance is reduced if your modified adjusted gross income is more than $100,000 ($50,000 if married filing separately).

> **Example:** Jane is single and has $40,000 in wages, $2,000 in passive income from a limited partnership, and a $3,500 passive loss from a rental real estate activity in which she actively participated. $2,000 of Jane's $3,500 loss offsets her passive income. The remaining $1,500 loss can be deducted from her $40,000 wages.

Active Participation

You actively participated in a rental real estate activity if you (and your spouse) owned at least 10 percent of a rental property and you made management decisions in a significant and bona fide sense. Management decisions include approving new tenants, deciding on rental terms, approving expenditures, and similar decisions.

Example: Mike is single and had the following income and losses during the tax year:

Salary	$42,300
Dividends	$ 300
Interest	$ 1,400
Rental loss	($ 4,000)

The rental loss resulted from the rental of a house Mike owned. Mike had advertised and rented the house to the current tenant himself. He also collected the rent payments, which usually came by mail. All repairs were either done or contracted out by Mike. Even though the rental loss is a loss from a passive activity, because Mike actively participated in the rental property management, he can use the entire $4,000 loss to offset his other income.

Maximum Special Allowance

If your modified adjusted gross income is $100,000 or less ($50,000 or less if married filing separately), you can deduct your loss up to $25,000 ($12,500 if married filing separately). If your modified adjusted gross income is more than $100,000 (more than $50,000 if married filing separately), this special allowance is limited to 50 percent of the difference between $150,000 ($75,000 if married filing separately) and your modified adjusted gross income.

Generally, there is no relief from the passive activity loss limits if your modified adjusted gross income is $150,000 or more ($75,000 or more if married filing separately).

Modified adjusted gross income. This is your adjusted gross income from IRS Form 1040, figured without taking into account:

- Taxable Social Security or equivalent tier 1 railroad retirement benefits

- Deductible contributions to an IRA or certain other qualified retirement plans

- The exclusion allowed for qualified U.S. savings bond interest used to pay higher educational expenses

- The exclusion allowed for employer-provided adoption benefits

- Any passive activity income or loss included on Form 8582

- Any passive income or loss or any loss allowable by reason of the exception for real estate professionals discussed later

- Any overall loss from a publicly traded partnership (see Publicly Traded Partnerships, PTPs, in the instructions for Form 8582)

- The deduction for one-half of self-employment tax

- The deduction allowed for interest on student loans

- The deduction for qualified tuition and related expenses

FIGURE 4.1 Phaseout of $25,000 Passive Activity Loss Deduction

Adjusted Gross Income	Maximum Allowable Passive Loss
$100,000 or less	$25,000
$110,000	$20,000
$120,000	$15,000
$130,000	$10,000
$140,000	$ 5,000
$150,000 or more	$ 0

In summarizing the IRS info, it is most important to understand that if you have more passive losses from real estate than you have passive income and you can show active participation, you can get up to $25,000 to offset other income. However, your available deduction of $25,000 will phase out as your income rises. You'll lose $1 of the deduction for every $2 that your adjusted gross income rises above $100,000. Once your adjusted gross income hits $150,000 or more, the write-off is completely phased out. (See Figure 4.1.)

THE EXCEPTION FOR REAL ESTATE PROFESSIONALS

Rental activities in which you materially participated during the year are not passive activities if for that year you were a real estate professional. Losses from these activities are not limited by the passive activity rules. For this purpose, each interest you have in a rental real estate activity is a separate activity, unless you choose to treat all interests in rental real estate activities as one activity.

Real Estate Professional

You qualify as a real estate professional for the tax year if you meet both of the following requirements:

1. More than half of the personal services you performed in all trades or businesses during the tax year were performed in real property trades or businesses in which you materially participated.

2. You performed more than 750 hours of services during the tax year in real property trades or businesses in which you materially participated.

Do not count personal services you performed as an employee in real property trades or businesses unless you are a 5 percent owner of your employer. You are a 5 percent owner if you owned (or are considered to have owned) more than 5 percent of your employer's outstanding stock, or capital or profits interest.

If you file a joint return, do not count your spouse's personal services to determine whether you met the preceding requirements. However, you can count your spouse's participation in an activity in determining if you materially participated.

Real property trades or businesses. A real property trade or business is a trade or business that does any of the following with real property:

- Develops or redevelops it

- Constructs or reconstructs it

- Acquires it

- Converts it

- Rents or leases it

- Operates or manages it

- Brokers it

Material Participation

Generally, you materially participated in an activity for the tax year if you were involved in its operations on a regular, continuous, and substantial basis during the year. (We will look at this requirement in more detail in a moment.)

Participating spouse. If you are married, determine whether you materially participated in an activity by also counting any participation in the activity by your spouse during the year. Do this even if your spouse owns no interest in the activity or files a separate return for the year.

Choice to Treat All Interests as One Activity

If you were a real estate professional and had more than one rental real estate interest during the year, you can choose to treat all the interests as one activity. You can make this choice for any year that you qualify as a real estate professional. If you forgo making the choice for one year, you can still make it for a later year.

UNDERSTANDING THE MATERIAL PARTICIPATION REQUIREMENT

In the previous two IRS considerations, there were two participation standards: active participation and material participation. The two are not the same. You can meet the active participation standard by simply doing things like approving new tenants, deciding on rental terms, and approving expenditures. The requirements for material participation, on the other hand, are much more demanding. IRS Publication 925 sets out the material participation requirements as follows:

> For purposes of the passive activity rules, you materially participated in the operation of this trade or business activity during 2006 if you met any of the following seven tests:

1. You participated in the activity for more than 500 hours during the tax year.

2. Your participation in the activity for the tax year was substantially all of the participation in the activity of all individuals (including individuals who did not own any interest in the activity) for the tax year.

3. You participated in the activity for more than 100 hours during the tax year, and you participated at least as much as any other person for the tax year. This includes individuals who did not own any interest in the activity.

4. The activity is a significant participation activity for the tax year, and you participated in all significant participation activities for more than 500 hours during the year. An activity is a "significant participation activity" if it involves the conduct of a trade or business, you participated in the activity for more than 100 hours during the tax year, and you did not materially participate under any of the material participation tests (other than this test).

5. You materially participated in the activity for any five of the prior ten tax years.

6. The activity is a personal service activity in which you materially participated for any three prior tax years. A personal service activity is an activity that involves performing personal services in the fields of health, law, engineering, architecture, accounting, actuarial science, performing arts, consulting, or any other trade or business in which capital is not a material income-producing factor.

7. Based on all the facts and circumstances, you participated in the activity on a regular, continuous, and substantial basis during the tax year. However, you do not meet this test if you participated in the activity for 100 hours or less during the tax year. Your par-

ticipation in managing the activity does not count in determining if you meet this test if any person (except you) (a) received compensation for performing management services in connection with the activity or (b) spent more hours during the tax year than you spent performing management services in connection with the activity (regardless of whether the person was compensated for the services).

Participation by Your Spouse Counts

IRS Publication 925 allows your spouse's participation during the tax year to be counted as your participation. This applies even if your spouse did not own an interest in the property and whether or not you and your spouse file a joint return.

Participation as an Investor Does Not Count

Work you do as an investor in an activity is not treated as participation unless you are also directly involved in the day-to-day management or operations of the activity. IRS Publication 925 says work done as an investor includes:

- Studying and reviewing financial statements or reports on the activity

- Preparing or compiling summaries or analyses of the finances or operations of the activity for your own use

- Monitoring the finances or operations of the activity in a non-managerial capacity

CARRYING FORWARD UNUSED LOSSES

So what do you do if you have passive losses and don't qualify for either the active participation exception or the real estate professional exception to the passive loss rules? Well, unused passive losses can be carried forward to offset passive income generated in future years. These losses that are not deductible because there was insufficient passive income to offset are often referred to as "suspended losses." You can carry suspended losses forward indefinitely and can use them as deductions against passive income in later years when the property shows a greater income.

DISPOSING OF AN ENTIRE PASSIVE PROPERTY INTEREST

Suspended losses can also be used when the passive investment property is sold in a fully taxable disposition. A fully taxable disposition is one that is an arm's-length sale of the interest to an unrelated third party. However, if you dispose of a passive activity to a related party, you will not be able to deduct any suspended losses until that person disposes of the interest to an unrelated person.

There are three primary rules that apply when disposing of entire passive investment property interest:

1. Losses on an entire disposition of a passive property activity and its suspended losses can offset active income from all sources.

2. Gains on an entire disposition of a passive property can be used to offset suspended losses from other passive activities.

3. The disposition must be to an unrelated party. Family, lineal descendants, ancestral descendants, siblings, spouses, and half-blood relatives are all considered "related parties."

The 1986 tax revisions made it much more difficult to use losses from real estate investments to offset other sources of income. Under the rules today, the best-case scenario is to qualify as a real estate professional with material participation in your investment activities. If you can qualify, the passive loss rules will not limit your ability to use losses to offset income from other sources. The next best position to be in is to qualify for the $25,000 in passive loss write-offs by actively participating in your real estate investments.

Finally, even if you can't qualify for either exception to the passive loss rules, you will still get the benefit of your write-offs; however, this is not true until the property becomes profitable beyond its depreciation, or until you dispose of the property in a fully taxable sale.

CHAPTER FIVE

Benefiting from a Stepped-Up Basis

In Chapter 3, we looked at how capital gains taxes are assessed on the difference between the adjusted basis of a property and the net sales price. As such, it makes sense that anything that increases or "steps up" the basis will reduce the overall tax liability. Getting a partial stepped-up basis will reduce taxes and getting a full stepped-up basis may eliminate any taxes by eliminating the gain on the sale of the property. Remember, the taxable "gain" is the difference between the adjusted basis and net sale price, so if the basis is equal to or higher than the net sales price there is no gain to tax.

WHAT IS A STEPPED-UP BASIS?

The term *stepped-up basis* refers to an adjustment or reallocation made to the basis of an inherited property. The concept of a stepped-up basis is fairly important because it directly impacts the amount of taxes you will face on the sale of inherited property and indirectly impacts the taxes your heirs will face if you pass an appreciated property to them as part of your estate.

Let's start with the official definition; IRS Publication 551, *Basis of Assets*, states that your basis in property you inherit from a decedent is generally one of the following:

1. The fair market value of the property at the date of the individual's death

2. The fair market value on the alternative valuation date, if the personal representative for the estate chooses to use alternative valuation

3. The value under the special-use valuation method for real property used in farming or other closely held business, if chosen for estate tax purposes

4. The decedent's adjusted basis in land to the extent of the value that is excluded from the decedent's taxable estate as a qualified conservation easement

For most people who inherit property, either the first or second rule will apply. Basically, if you inherit property, any gain made by the decedent is simply forgotten. You get the property with a new basis equal to its current fair market value and can sell it immediately without any taxes. If you think this sounds too good to be true, you might be right; there are estate taxes that have to be taken into consideration.

Before estate property passes to the heirs, it is going to be taxed at the estate level. Generally speaking, estate taxes are very high, topping out at around 50 percent. So it makes sense that an asset taxed at the estate level should not be taxed again if the heir immediately sells it. To avoid double taxation, the regulations allow a full stepped-up basis for the heirs.

Example: Ralph owns an apartment building with a current market value of $500,000. His adjusted basis on the property is $100,000. If he sells the property today outright he will have to pay capital gains taxes on a $400,000 gain. If instead, Ralph had passed away and his son, Carl, who inherited it, was immediately selling the property, there would be no taxes because Carl would have received the property with a full stepped-up basis.

The potential problem is that if Ralph's estate was in excess of the estate tax exemption amount for that year, this asset might have been taxed as much as $250,000 (50 percent) at the estate tax level before Carl ever got it. However, the vast majority of people inheriting property receive it from estates valued at less than the estate tax exemption. At the time of this writing, the estate tax exemption is $2,000,000 per person and the exemption is scheduled to increase as shown in Figure 5.1.

FIGURE 5.1 Federal Estate Tax Exemption

Year	Exempt Amount
2007	$2 million
2008	$2 million
2009	$3.5 million
2010	Unlimited
2011	$1 million (reverts)

Basically, the estate tax exemption means that there are no federal estate taxes on estates valued at less than the exemption. So, in the previous example, if Ralph passed away in 2007 and his total estate was less than $2,000,000 there would be no estate taxes and his son would not face capital gains taxes because he received the apartment building with a full stepped-up basis. This is one of the few situations or "loopholes" where deferred tax liability actually disappears. The IRS is, however, moving to limit the amount of stepped-up basis that can be taken; but for the time being, the advantage is with the taxpayers.

STEPPED-UP BASIS ON JOINTLY OWNED PROPERTY

As previously discussed, a full stepped-up basis is available on inherited property. However, the rules vary a little when the property is jointly owned and the heir already owns a portion of the property. There are different ways or "vestings" possible in joint property ownership. Each vesting has it own survivorship characteristics and tax implications. Perhaps the best known are *tenants in common, joint tenancy,* and *community property.*

Tenants in Common

The vesting tenants in common is the easiest to understand because each of the owners is considered to own a fractional portion of the property and has the right to leave his or her fractional portion of the property to anyone through his or her estate. The tax and stepped-up basis calculations are also very straightforward because the inheriting person gets a full step-up in basis as to that portion of the property.

Example: Assume the same facts as the last example, but this time Ralph and his son Carl co-own the property, 50 percent each, as tenants in common. If Ralph passed away and left his portion to Carl, Carl would receive a step-up in basis for that portion he inherited, but still have his original basis on that portion of the property he already owned. Carl's combined basis on the property after his father's passing would be $300,000 (stepped-up basis of $250,000 on his father's 50 percent plus his own existing $50,000 basis on his 50 percent).

The tenants in common vesting is most often used on partnership or combined ventures where the individual owners want to have the ability to leave their share to someone other than the other co-owner(s).

Joint Tenancy

The concept of joint tenancy is a little hard for some to understand. Joint tenancy is commonly defined as a vesting where each joint tenant owns an equal and undivided interest in the whole property. Joint tenancy is most commonly used in family situations, usually between husband and wife or parents and children. The step-up in basis is very similar to the tenants in common example you just read, but there may be a need to allocate and deduct some depreciation from the portion getting the step-up in basis. The primary difference between joint tenancy and tenants in common is that in joint tenancy when one joint tenant dies, his or her ownership interest *automatically and instantly* vests to the surviving joint tenant or joint tenants. This means that individual joint tenants do not have the ability to pass their ownership by last will and testament to heirs or whomever they choose. Instead, their portion of the property goes directly to the other surviving joint tenant or joint tenants.

People often mistakenly use a joint tenancy vesting as an estate planning shortcut in an attempt to pass property to heirs and avoid the expenses associated with probating an estate. Unfortunately, this seemingly quick and easy probate avoidance tool usually results in undesirable tax consequences. When joint tenancy heirs do eventually sell the property, they pay significantly more taxes because they only received a partial stepped-up basis. Proper estate planning can avoid the probate expenses and provide the full stepped-up basis.

Community Property

If you live in a community property state (Arizona, California, Idaho, Louisiana, Nevada, New Mexico, Texas, Washington, or Wisconsin) and are married, you have the ability to hold property with your spouse as community property. There are some distinct tax advantages in doing so. Unlike the other forms of joint ownership, the community property vesting allows the surviving spouse to receive a full stepped-up basis on both the deceased spouse's share *and* on the surviving spouse's own share.

> **Example:** David and Mona lived in California for most of their lives and were married for over 30 years. They owned two investment properties: an apartment building with a basis of $100,000 and a fair market value of $500,000, and a large parcel of vacant land with a basis of $10,000 and a fair market value of $610,000. Both properties had been in the family for many years. David recently passed away leaving everything to his wife. Mona will receive a full stepped-up basis on both properties to the current fair market value. She can sell both properties and she will pay no capital gains tax.

This is a tremendous advantage over other forms of ownership vesting. In this example, if David and Mona had held the properties in joint tenancy, Mona would have received only a partial stepped-up basis and the capital gains taxes due would have been approximately $140,000 between federal and state taxes. This is a devastating result when compared to the zero tax due if stepped up as community property. This type of vesting mistake is usually pointed out and corrected in any basic estate planning. Unfortunately, most people don't even do basic estate planning. There is a simple rule here: community property avoids taxes, joint tenancy avoids probate, but only proper estate planning (usually a living trust) avoids both.

FILING FOR A STEP-UP IN BASIS

A step-up in basis does not have to happen immediately. If you inherited property in the past as a joint owner, you may still file for the step-up. You will need to establish the value of the property at the time you inherited it, but the effort and expense is usually well worthwhile. All property appraisers have the ability to give you an appraisal of the property at any particular point in time. You may even be able to get a local real estate agent to provide sufficient information to establish a fair market value on the date of death. However, if you have any reason to believe the valuation may be scrutinized, use an appraiser, not a real estate agent. Once you have your supporting documentation for a date-of-death value, it is a simple matter of having your tax preparer file for the step-up in basis.

USING FAIR MARKET VALUE TO YOUR ADVANTAGE

As you can see, getting a stepped-up basis on a property can greatly affect the tax consequences when the property is eventually sold. Just as important as getting a stepped-up basis is making sure you get the *most favorable* stepped-up basis. From the previous sections, it should be clear that a stepped-up basis is always tied to, and based on, the fair market value of the asset at a specific point in time. But what exactly is the fair market value of an asset? Whether you inherited a property ten years ago or if you are inheriting one now, *how* you establish the fair market value may determine your future tax liability.

To understand the variables here, we need to start by defining fair market value. According to the IRS, fair market value is "the price the property would sell for on the open market. It is the price that would be agreed on between a willing buyer and a willing seller, with neither being required to act, and both having reasonable knowledge of the relevant facts." By this definition it is going to be necessary to determine what price a willing buyer and seller would agree upon.

If you have just inherited a property and are selling it on the open market immediately, the actual sales price in an arm's-length transaction will almost always be considered the fair market value. However, if you intend to keep an inherited property for some time before selling, or if you are going back now to file for a stepped-up basis on property you inherited some time ago, you will want to establish a favorable fair market value. The IRS has published rules for determining the value of property. The following is the IRS's appraisal guidelines for determining the value of real estate:

> Because each piece of real estate is unique and its valuation
> is complicated, a detailed appraisal by a professional appraiser
> is necessary. The appraiser must be thoroughly trained in the

application of appraisal principles and theory. In some instances the opinions of equally qualified appraisers may carry unequal weight, such as when one appraiser has a better knowledge of local conditions. The appraisal report must contain a complete description of the property, such as street address, legal description, and lot and block number, as well as physical features, condition, and dimensions. The use to which the property is put, zoning and permitted uses, and its potential use for other higher and better uses are also relevant. In general, there are three main approaches to the valuation of real estate. An appraisal may require the combined use of two or three methods rather than one method only.

1. *Comparable sales.* The comparable sales method compares the property with several similar properties that have been sold. The selling prices, after adjustments for differences in date of sale, size, condition, and location, would then indicate the estimated fair market value of the property. If the comparable sales method is used to determine the value of *unimproved real property* (land without significant buildings, structures, or any other improvements that add to its value), the appraiser should consider all of the following factors when comparing the potential comparable property and the property:

   ■ Location, size, and zoning or use restrictions

   ■ Accessibility and road frontage, and available utilities and water rights

   ■ Riparian rights (right of access to and use of the water by owners of land on the bank of a river) and existing easements, rights-of-way, leases, etc.

   ■ Soil characteristics, vegetative cover, and status of mineral rights

   ■ Other factors affecting value

   For each comparable sale, the appraisal must include the names of the buyer and seller, the deed book and page number, the date of sale and selling price, a property description, the amount and terms of mortgages, property surveys, the assessed value, the tax rate, and the assessor's appraised fair market value. The comparable selling prices must be adjusted to account for differences between the sale property and the subject property.

Because differences of opinion may arise between appraisers as to the degree of comparability and the amount of the adjustment considered necessary for comparison purposes, an appraiser should document each item of adjustment. Only comparable sales having the least adjustments in terms of items and/or total dollar adjustments should be considered as comparable to the property.

2. *Capitalization of income.* This method capitalizes the net income from the property at a rate that represents a fair return on the particular investment at the particular time, considering the risks involved. The key elements are the determination of the income to be capitalized and the rate of capitalization.

3. *Replacement cost new or reproduction cost minus observed depreciation.* This method, used alone, usually does not result in a determination of fair market value. Instead, it generally tends to set the upper limit of value, particularly in periods of rising costs, because it is reasonable to assume that an informed buyer will not pay more for the real estate than it would cost to reproduce a similar property. Of course, this reasoning does not apply if a similar property cannot be created because of location, unusual construction, or some other reason. Generally, this method serves to support the value determined from other methods. When the replacement cost method is applied to *improved realty,* the land and improvements are valued separately. The replacement cost of a building is figured by considering the materials, the quality of workmanship, and the number of square feet or cubic feet in the building. This cost represents the total cost of labor and material, overhead, and profit. After the replacement cost has been figured, consideration must be given to the following factors:

- Physical deterioration—the wear and tear on the building itself

- Functional obsolescence—usually in older buildings with, for example, inadequate lighting, plumbing, or heating, small rooms, or a poor floor plan

- Economic obsolescence—outside forces causing the whole area to become less desirable

With this definition in mind, the IRS has told you exactly what it considers a valid appraisal. You may want to make sure your appraisal will conform. While these IRS valuation requirements may sound ex-

tensive and burdensome, they really are not. Almost all of the requirements are traditionally included in a standard professional property appraisal. In most cases, that is all you will need to support your requested
stepped-up basis value. However, all appraisers are not alike. Anyone in
the real estate industry will tell you there can be a significant difference
in "appraised" values on a given piece of real estate. Even in stable market conditions, it is not unusual to get appraisals differing as much as
20 to 25 percent. That variable can make a huge difference in how
much you will pay in taxes.

Example: Betty and Hal had been married for 30 years before Hal
passed away. Hal left everything to Betty including their California
home and a sizable piece of vacant land. Hal passed away ten years
ago. At the time of Hal's passing, the real estate market was booming,
but the year after he died the market slowed down and prices declined about 30 percent on average. Betty really wasn't aware of the
downturn in the real estate market because she had no interest in selling. Recently, however, she has decided to move out of state to be near
her daughter and grandchildren. Luckily, Betty's timing is good because the real estate cycle has come full circle and market values in
her area have climbed back to the previous highs of ten years ago.
Betty's home has a current market value of approximately $450,000
and she has recently been offered $400,000 for the vacant land. Both
properties were bought almost 40 years ago at $30,000 for the home
and $20,000 for the land. She has decided to sell both properties.

If Betty's advisors fail to tell her about filing for the stepped-up basis
on these properties, she will face taxes on the approximate $170,000
gain on her home ($450,000 sales price less the $250,000 primary home
exemption less the $30,000 original cost basis) and another $380,000
gain on the sale of the land ($400,000 sales price less the $20,000 basis).
Combined, Betty's gain would be $550,000 and her tax liability would
be approximately $133,650 (15 percent federal and 9.3 percent to California).

However, presuming Betty has good advisors and files for the available step-up in basis, her tax situation will depend on how the properties were vested and how she inherited them. If both properties were
held in either community property or in a revocable living trust as community or marital property, Betty will be able to file for a full stepped-

up basis on each. Because the properties were inherited ten years ago and the example states that the current values have climbed back to the highs of ten years ago, an appraisal of each property as of Hal's date of death (also ten years ago) should qualify Betty for a full basis step-up to today's values. Presuming valid appraisals did support a step-up to the current values, she could sell both properties and have no taxable gain at all. Even if the properties were both held in Hal and Betty's names as husband and wife as joint tenants, Betty would still be entitled to a stepped-up basis, but only on one half (Hal's half) of each property. If held as joint tenants, her basis on the home would be approximately $240,000 (Hal's half stepped-up to $225,000 plus Betty's half at her original $15,000). After the step-up there would be no tax liability on the sale of the home because the $250,000 primary residence exemption would shield Betty's $210,000 gain.

On the land however, there will be some taxes. Betty's new basis would be $210,000 (Hal's half stepped up to $200,000 plus Betty's half at her original $10,000) and the gain on the sale would be $190,000 with a tax liability of approximately $46,170 (15 percent federal and 9.3 percent to California).

All of the previous calculations presume one crucial factor—a supporting appraisal that shows the property values on Hal's date of death are approximately equal to today's market values. The example also presumes a real estate market down cycle occurred between the date of death and the sale of the properties. Even if there was no down cycle, a favorable appraisal to support a higher stepped-up basis will save a lot on taxes. Considering the 20 to 25 percent variations commonly seen between appraisers, which one you pick can save you or cost you a lot. In this example, both of Betty's properties had a combined $950,000 estimated date-of-death value. If an overly conservative appraiser's valuation came in at 25 percent lower, it might cost Betty tens of thousands in additional capital gains taxes.

Some appraisers are naturally more conservative than others. In addition, an appraiser's level of conservativeness may vary dramatically depending on the purpose and use of the appraisal requested. Although it is not discussed often, it is a common practice to look for the most favorable appraiser or "shop" appraisers. Real estate agents do it, mortgage brokers do it, attorneys do it, and it should be no surprise that the IRS will use their "favored" appraisers in a dispute.

If you are going to file for a stepped-up basis either because it is time to sell or to gain a basis advantage on a property you intend to keep a while, you might try to tap into any professional real estate resources you may have. Real estate agents, mortgage brokers, and real estate attorneys may have established relationships with appraisers. If you can use their existing relationships, do so.

Generally speaking, it will usually be to your advantage to establish the highest possible value for stepped-up basis purposes. However, there are times when a high date-of-death valuation is not to your advantage. Case in point, an optimistic or exaggerated value will hurt you if the property is subject to estate taxes.

> **Example:** Carl's father passed away a few months ago and left Carl and his sister an estate consisting of the father's home and two small apartment buildings. The father had owned all three properties for many years and Carl and his sister plan to keep all three for a few years before selling them. The approximate value of all three properties is $2,500,000. Carl knows he and his sister are entitled to a stepped-up basis on the properties and he is trying to arrange for the appraisals now. Carl knows there can be some variability in appraisals and wants to make the right decisions to minimize taxes. At the time of the father's death, the federal estate exemption was $2,000,000.

Estate taxes at the time of this writing, start at 37 percent and go up to 50 percent very quickly. In this example, Carl is going to face some estate tax on his father's estate, but how much? If he hires an appraiser that leans toward a higher valuation, Carl and his sister will receive a higher stepped-up basis, but will have to pay more in estate taxes now. In this situation, it is better to get as conservative a valuation as reasonably possible to minimize the estate taxes (37 percent or higher) at the expense of paying future capital gains tax (15 percent) later.

A second situation where an overly optimistic valuation may backfire is where there are multiple heirs or partners and one heir or partner will be buying out the interests of the others. Obviously, in this situation, a balancing of the respective interests will be necessary.

I am always surprised at how often people overlook or simply don't know about the tax benefits of getting a stepped-up basis on a property. This is one of the last remaining true tax loopholes. If you qualify for a step-up in basis, be sure you take advantage of it.

CHAPTER SIX

Understanding All the Advantages of the Primary Residence Exclusion

WHAT IS THE PRIMARY RESIDENCE EXCLUSION?

There is a significant difference between the tax liability on the sale of investment property and the tax liability on the sale of a primary residence. The main reason for this difference is a capital gains exclusion/exemption created by the Taxpayer Relief Act of 1997. Before the 1997 act, the tax laws provided a primary residence rollover provision that allowed a homeseller 18 months in which to reinvest the gains in another primary residence without triggering taxes. There was also a one-time $125,000 exemption for people over 55 years of age designed to let aging Americans buy down to a smaller home without being taxed on the first $125,000 of profit. Both of these provisions became history when the Taxpayer Relief Act took effect on May 6, 1997.

The new primary residence or "main home" exclusion is basically a $250,000 exemption for individuals and $500,000 exemption for married couples when selling a primary residence. As long as the property qualifies, there are no more rollover or reinvestment requirements and no minimum age requirements; further, the new exemption can be used as many times as one likes but not more frequently than once in a two-year period. The actual rule in IRS Publication 523 states that you can exclude the entire gain on the sale of your main home up to

1. $250,000 or

2. $500,000 if all of the following are true:

- You are married and file a joint return for the year

- Either you or your spouse meets the ownership test

- Both you and your spouse meet the use test

- During the two-year period ending on the date of sale, neither you nor your spouse excluded gain from the sale of another home

PROPERTY THAT QUALIFIES AS A PRIMARY RESIDENCE

There are two tests to determine whether a property qualifies for the $250,000/$500,000 primary residence exemption. To be entitled to the exclusion you must have (1) owned the home for at least two of the last five years and (2) lived in the home as your primary residence for at least two of the last five years.

These two requirements are referred to as the "ownership test" and the "use test." There are certain exceptions to the two-year ownership and use requirements (discussed later), but as a general rule both these conditions must be met for a property to qualify for the primary residence exemption. In addition, even if the property qualifies, you may be disqualified if you or your spouse has taken the exemption on another property within the last two years.

IRS publications refer to a primary residence as a "main home" (this book uses the terms *primary residence* and *main home* interchangeably throughout). A main home is not necessarily a traditional house; it can be a mobile or motor home, a boat that qualifies as a residence, a co-op apartment, or a condominium. Likewise, a fractional percentage of an investment property that is used as a primary residence may also qualify.

HOW THE REQUIRED TWO-YEAR PERIOD IS CALCULATED

One of the commonly misunderstood areas of the primary home exemption is how the periods are calculated to meet the ownership and use tests. For the average person who has owned and lived in his or her home for the past two or more consecutive years, there is usually no question of qualifying for the exemption. However, calculating the period becomes a little more difficult in situations where the use has not been continuous, the exemption has been previously claimed, or one of the spouses does not meet one of the tests. The general rule is that a taxpayer must have owned and lived in the home for two of the last five years. It does not matter *which* two of the last five years or that the two years are contiguous.

Example: When Bob moved to Denver three years ago from Los Angeles, he decided to rent his Los Angeles home for a while instead of selling it. He had owned and lived in the Los Angeles home for many years, including the two immediately prior to moving to Denver. Bob recently completed the sale on the Los Angeles home and would qualify for the primary home exemption on the sale of that home.

Example: Sally has had a beach house in New Jersey for 3½ years. Two years ago she moved to New York City after having lived in the beach house as her main home for 18 months. She has continued to use the beach house on weekends and holidays while living in the city. Currently, she is planning to rent her city home and move back to the beach house for six months and then relocate to the West Coast. After the six months back at the beach house, each of Sally's homes will qualify for the exemption but not if both are sold within a 24-month period. Before Sally relocates, she intends to sell the beach house and use her primary home exemption to avoid taxes on the profit. She also plans to sell the city home two years later and use the primary home exemption again to avoid taxes on the profit from that sale. Sally will qualify for both exemptions because she will be able to show that she meets the criteria for both homes and did not try to use the exemption more that once in a two-year period.

Example: Before Don and Julie got married about a year ago, both owned their own home. When they got married, they decided to live in Julie's home so Don sold his, using the primary residence exemption to shield him from taxes on the gain. Currently, Don and Julie have decided they need a bigger home and want to sell Julie's house and relocate. The estimated gain on Julie's house is $400,000; they plan to use the married couple primary residence exemption of $500,000 to shield them from taxes on the gain. Unfortunately, they do not qualify for the full married couple exemption because Don doesn't meet either the ownership or the use tests. Julie does meet both tests and could file a separate tax return and claim her exemption, but that would only shield $250,000 of the $400,000 anticipated gain. Don and Julie's two main alternatives are:

1. Wait one more year so they both qualify to use the married couple $500,000 exemption
2. Sell now using only Julie's $250,000 exemption (filing separate tax returns) and pay the taxes on the other $150,000 of gain

Don and Julie's situation in this example would not normally pose much of a problem because it usually takes a few months to sell a home and locate a replacement. This means that Don and Julie can start the selling process in about nine months and time the closing of the property for a day or two after the two-year mark.

In most cases, figuring whether a property (and taxpayer) qualify for the exemption is not difficult. If there are questions, be sure to discuss them with your tax advisor. Sometimes, however, a taxpayer simply does not meet the two-year tests but has no choice but to move now. In those situations, which will be discussed later, the regulations may allow a partial or fractional portion of the exemption to be taken.

EXCEPTIONS TO THE TWO-YEAR REQUIREMENTS

Because the general rule requiring a taxpayer to have owned and lived in a home for two of the last five years is firm but not set in stone, exceptions to the rule do exist. Likewise, there are exceptions to the rule that you not take the primary residence exemption more than once in any two-year period. The regulations provide an exception if you did not meet the ownership and use tests or your exclusion would have been disallowed because you sold more than one home in a two-year period if you are selling your home as a result of one of the following:

1. A change in your place of employment

2. Your health

3. Unforeseen circumstances "to the extent provided in the regulations"

Example: Ted and Tish bought their current home about one year ago. They sold their previous home one year ago and used their primary home exemption on that sale. Ted works for a large international corporation and has just been notified that he is being transferred to another state. Ted and Tish's current home will not qualify for a primary residence exemption because they have not met the two-year ownership or use test. In addition, even if they could otherwise meet the ownership and use tests, they would be disqualified from taking the exemption because they have used their exemption on the sale of another property less than two years ago. However, by applying the change-in-the-place-of-employment exception, Ted and Tish will be able to take a reduced exemption.

The first of these three exceptions—a change in your place of employment—is the most commonly used, and its meaning seems clear.

The employment change does not have to be an involuntary transfer or even one with the same company. In the previous example, if Ted had simply decided to take a better job in a different area of the country, the exemption would still apply. If the change in place of employment involves a considerable distance, there is usually no question that the exception can be used. The more difficult question arises when the change is close geographically. At the time of this writing, the IRS offers little guidance, so check with your tax advisor for any recent clarifications.

The health exception is more ambiguous. The regulations don't specify which health conditions qualify, so the exception may be a matter of opinion, and the IRS's opinion controls. Obviously, if an illness is well documented in your medical records and your physician writes a supporting letter stating that the change is necessary, your chances of being disallowed on an audit are lessened. However, if you are trying to use this exception because you *feel* the change will do you good, you are likely to get resistance from the IRS. The best approach is to have good documentation supporting the move as the result of a verifiable medical condition.

THE NEW "UNFORESEEN CIRCUMSTANCES" RULES

The last exception—unforeseen circumstances—sounds like a catch-all loophole. After all, just about anything that makes a person want to move twice in less than two years is arguably an unforeseen circumstance. In practice, however, this exception used to be useless because it only applied to unforeseen changes "to the extent provided in regulations," and originally there were *no* unforeseen circumstances provided in the regulations. Recently, however, a new set of rules regarding this issue went into effect. Accordingly, a sale will be considered as occurring primarily because of unforeseen circumstances if any of the following events occur that "involve" the taxpayer, his or her spouse, a co-owner of the residence, or a member of the taxpayer's household during the taxpayer's period of use and ownership of the residence:

- Death

- Divorce or legal separation

- Becoming eligible for unemployment compensation

- A change in employment that leaves the taxpayer unable to pay the mortgage or reasonable basic living expenses

- Multiple births resulting from the same pregnancy

- Damage to the residence resulting from a natural or manmade disaster, or an act of war or terrorism

- Condemnation, seizure, or other involuntary conversion of the property

Furthermore, the new regulations left open the possibility of additional qualifying situations by giving the IRS commissioner the discretion to determine other circumstances as unforeseen.

HOW TO CALCULATE A PARTIAL EXCLUSION

Okay, presuming you do qualify for an exception to the two-year requirement, how do you figure the exclusion to which you are entitled? Here's the official version:

Under Reg. Sec. 1.121 3(g)(1), the maximum exclusion is prorated by multiplying it (either $250,000 or $500,000) by a fraction. The numerator of the fraction is the shortest of the following three time periods (expressed in days or months): (1) the ownership period for the "early sale" residence, (2) the use period for the early sale residence, or (3) the time between the sale dates of the two residences. The denominator of the fraction is 730 days (24 months).

Don't you just love the way lawyers and accountants explain things? In plain English, you get a partial exclusion based on how long you were in the home; half the required time would equal half the exclusion and so on.

FRACTIONAL EXEMPTION USE
FOR INVESTMENT PROPERTY

Although the primary residence exclusion is normally associated with single-family homes, it does apply to other types of living arrangements. Resident-owners of apartment buildings can qualify on a percentage basis. If the resident-owners meet both the ownership and use tests for the property and have not claimed the exclusion on another property in the past two years, they are able to shield a percentage of the gain on the sale of their apartment building by claiming the primary residence exemption for that portion of the property used as their primary residence. The remaining portion will, of course, be taxed as investment property on the sale.

Even if an unfavorable allocation had been made on prior tax returns, it is possible to refile past tax returns to change the allocation. Alternatively, you can change the allocation for the current year and wait until the newly allocated portion meets the ownership and use tests as a primary residence. If you are going to change a past allocation, be sure to discuss it with your tax advisor first.

Example: Paul owns a four-unit property that consists of a large three-bedroom unit in the front and three smaller units in the rear. Paul lives in the front unit and meets all the other criteria for a main home exclusion. When Paul sells the property, he will be able to allocate a portion of the total gain to his primary residence and take the primary residence exclusion. The question: How much? That depends on how the property taxes for the property have been filed in the past. Presuming Paul has taken all the available depreciation on the investment property portion of the property, he or his accountant has probably already allocated the portion of the property that represents primary residence and the part that is investment property. If the allocation has not already been made in prior tax returns, Paul will be able to use just about any reasonable allocation method. On a four-unit property the taxpayer could simply allocate 25 percent (one of the four units) of the property as his main home and the remainder as investment property. On the other hand, if the owner's unit is 1,800 square feet and the other three units combined equal 1,800 square feet, Paul could allocate 50 percent of the property as his primary residence. The IRS allows any reasonable allocation; how Paul allocates is crucial in understanding future tax consequences. Herein lies a paradox: On one hand, investors usually want to maximize depreciation while the property is operational, so they tend to allocate a higher percentage as investment property; on the other hand, when owner-residents sell the property, they want to claim a higher percentage as primary residence. Remember, the primary residence portion of the gain up to the $250,000/$500,000 limit is tax-free. The remaining portion allocated as investment property gain is fully taxable.

INVESTMENT PROPERTY CONVERTED TO A PRIMARY RESIDENCE

One question that always comes up is whether a taxpayer can "convert" or "recharacterize" an investment property to a primary residence and thereby qualify for the primary residence exemption. The answer is clearly yes. But in 2006 new IRS rules make it harder to qualify. Prior to 2006, the owner and the property had to meet all of the primary residence exclusion tests; meaning the taxpayer actually had to use the property as his or her primary residence for the two-year use period.

The new rules state that you cannot claim the $250,000/$500,000 gain exclusion on the sale of your principal residence if you acquired the home in a like-kind exchange within the last five years. This would occur if you previously had an investment property, did a like-kind exchange, and then converted it to your principal residence.

Even if the investment property was not acquired in an exchange, the two-year period still applies. Sometimes that is simply too high a price to pay to qualify the property for the exemption. On the other hand, sometimes it is a smart move.

The downside to converting or recharacterizing investment property to primary residence or partial primary residence is that the depreciation taken on the property, as discussed further in the next section, will have to be recaptured on the sale.

Example: Jack and Barbara, who are both retired, live in a suburb of San Francisco but are planning a move to Palm Springs. They own a triplex within the San Francisco city limits that was left to them many years ago by Barbara's mother and has been fully depreciated since 1995. The triplex was originally built as a single-family house but had been converted over the years to three one-bedroom apartments. The property is very valuable already, but lately there has been a tremendous demand for restored San Francisco–style homes, and the neighborhood has become very upscale. Single-family homes in the immediate area have been selling for $700,000 to $800,000. Jack and Barbara both like to keep busy and think restoring their property would be a great project and a way to spend extra time in San Francisco before moving to Palm Springs.

This is a perfect situation for converting an investment property to a primary residence. Jack and Barbara will have to move tenants out to start the restoration project. But if they are willing to move in while working on the restoration, they can convert the property so that the entire triplex is restored to a residence and will qualify for the married couple's $500,000 gain exclusion. In California, that will save them approximately $121,500 in combined state and federal capital gains tax. In addition, the process of living in and restoring the property will probably enhance the property's fair market value. All in all, it seems like a smart move on Jack and Barbara's part.

RECAPTURE OF DEPRECIATION

As we saw in the previous example, it is possible to convert investment property to a primary residence. That example was, however, uncharacteristically perfect because the facts left no doubt that the taxpayers could increase the fair market value while at the same time decreasing the tax liability. The facts also stated that the property had been fully depreciated since 1995. In the real world, there is seldom such a large upside potential, and the property is usually still being depreciated. This complicates the issue because even though the primary residence exemption may apply, it will not shield that portion of the gain equal to the depreciation taken on the property after May 6, 1997 (the effective date of the Taxpayer Relief Act).

If Joe is like most people, he is going to forgo trying to convert the property to a primary residence and instead will look for other alternatives. For most people, moving to a property for two years just to save on taxes is simply too disruptive of their lifestyle to actually consider the option. However, it is nice to know that if the tax savings are high enough or the right situation presents itself, the option is available.

Example: In 1996 Joe bought a rental condominium in California for $200,000. He is considering selling the property and is looking at the tax issue. The current market value of the property is $300,000, and the current adjusted basis is approximately $35,235. Joe knows the capital gains tax on the sale is going to be approximately $44,200 if he sells it outright. The idea of writing a check to the IRS for that amount does not sit well with Joe, so he is trying to decide if it would be worthwhile to move into the property for two years to obtain the primary residence exemption. After doing the math, Joe realizes that he has taken approximately $45,000 in depreciation since May 6, 1997; and he knows none of that depreciation will be shielded by the primary residence exclusion. That means that even if he does move into the property for two years to qualify for the exclusion, he will still have to write a tax check for approximately $15,300.

CHAPTER SEVEN

Investment Property Taxation—Investor versus Dealer Status

One truly ambiguous tax topic in real estate investments is the dealer versus investor distinction and how to steer clear of being labeled a dealer. The amount of tax you pay and the tax advantages available to you in a given real estate investment may change drastically depending on whether the IRS labels you an investor or a dealer.

Investor versus dealer status is one of those areas of real estate tax law that can be very difficult to figure out. If you sell multiple properties in any single tax year or a few properties over the course of two or three years, you may find yourself at risk of being labeled a dealer. Unfortunately, there is no real distinction test or recognized "number of properties sold" criterion that determines whether a person has crossed a line into dealer status. You may come across real estate agents or accountants who will tell you that if you sell less than three or five (or whatever number) properties per year that you will not be considered a dealer. Unfortunately, this rumor is not based on fact. There is nothing in the tax code or in case law that sets any definitive number of properties as a dividing line between dealer and investor status. This ambiguity, compounded with possible severe tax consequences, has caused more than a few sleepless nights for real estate investors in the past. With this in mind, this chapter will try to shed some light on dealer versus investor status issues and offer some possible ways to avoid potential problems.

WHAT IS A PROPERTY DEALER?

A real estate dealer is a person who is involved on a regular basis in the development, improvement, and advertisement of property for sale. Subdividers and developers are almost always labeled dealers. However, even if you are not a subdivider or developer, you may be labeled a dealer if your real estate activities rise to the level of a trade or business in which your property investments appear more like inventory to be sold rather than long-term investments.

WHAT IS A PROPERTY INVESTOR?

Unlike a dealer, a property investor is a person who generally holds real estate for appreciation and/or cash flow from rental activities. But doesn't everyone invest in real estate with the hope that it will appreciate? Yes, but the IRS says there are two categories of real estate investment and for the sake of clarity let's call them "buy-to-sell" (dealer) properties and "buy-to-hold" (investor) properties.

WHY DOES IT MATTER IF YOU ARE A DEALER OR AN INVESTOR?

Our tax rules favor the investor over the dealer. An investor files a Schedule E for investment properties and a Schedule D for reporting profits from the sale of an investment property. These Schedule D profits qualify for capital gains tax rates, currently at 15 percent for federal taxes, and are not considered income from employment. A dealer, however, is forced to report operations and profits from the sale of his or her buy-to-sell real estate on a Schedule C as ordinary income and expenses. That's a bad thing because, generally speaking, ordinary income tax rates are higher than capital gains tax rates. Let's take a look at an example of the difference.

Example: Carl and Clint each buy similar investment/rental properties. Both are single-family homes and both have a purchase price of $300,000. Both Carl and Clint make $20,000 in improvements to their properties and the market value of each of the properties grows to $420,000 in 18 months (hot market). At that time, both properties are sold. Both Carl and Clint collected rent and depreciated their respective properties on their tax returns. This is Carl's first investment property, but Clint has bought and sold four or five other similar houses in the last few years.

The tax situation for Carl looks fairly straightforward. He has made the investment a capital asset by keeping it for more than 12 months and his intention was to buy to hold. He will have some amount of recapture of depreciation tax to deal with, but the gain on the property will be federally taxed at the long-term capital gains rate (currently 15 percent). As such, Carl's federal taxes on the gain will be approximately $15,000.

Clint, on the other hand, may have very different results. If the IRS decides to label Clint as a real estate dealer, a couple of things happen. First, any depreciation Clint has taken on the property will be disallowed. Second, all of the profit on the sale of the property will be taxed at federal ordinary income rates (currently as high as 35 percent). Third, the profit from the sale, now relabeled ordinary income, will trigger self-employment taxes that can be as high as 14.5 percent. As such, Clint would owe as much as $39,000 on the gain, plus whatever self-employment taxes may be triggered.

Obviously, there's a huge difference in the tax consequences between Carl and Clint. To make matters even worse, we really need to expand the example to consider the way these things can quickly get out of control in the real world.

Example: Instead of cashing out their investments on the properties mentioned above, Carl and Clint decided to do 1031 exchanges into other properties. Moreover, Clint has been doing exchanges all along selling one fixed-up property and exchanging into the next fixer-upper.

In Carl's case there's no problem. As a property *investor*, Carl can do a tax-deferred exchange into another property as long as he conforms to ordinary 1031 exchange requirements.

Clint, on the other hand, has a big problem. If the IRS labels Clint a property *dealer* things can get really ugly. Keep in mind that Clint won't be reporting the fact that he has done his most recent exchange until it is completed and he is doing his taxes for that calendar year. Also, keep in mind that IRS audits don't happen instantly. It might be a year or two after he files his taxes before the IRS gets around to auditing Clint. If the audit does result in Clint being labeled a real estate dealer, the IRS will disallow his exchange triggering immediate taxes, self-employment taxes, plus interest and possible penalties in cases of willful neglect or fraud.

To make matters worse, if Clint is labeled a dealer, the IRS will surely be basing their dealer determination partially on the number of properties Clint has sold in recent years. In the facts of our example, Clint had bought and sold four or five other similar houses in the few years preceding and had done exchanges with those as well. The IRS will likely disallow each of Clint's previous exchanges triggering, in each case, more immediate taxes, interest, and any self-employment taxes not paid in those previous years.

Hopefully, you are starting to see the potentially dire consequences of being labeled a real estate dealer. So you may still be wondering how many properties can you sell before being labeled a dealer? Although there are rumors of a rule stating that an investor may sell up to six properties a year, this is not true. The fact is that there is no written rule that states a set number of property sales in either the tax rules/regulations or the tax court case decisions.

Then how long do you have to hold a property to be sure you won't be labeled a dealer when you sell it—one year, two, five? No one knows. None of those time periods are a barrier to being labeled a dealer. There are no set rules.

Now you may be wondering, if there is no set number of sales and no set holding period in the regulations, how does the IRS label a person a dealer? Everything hinges on your intent at the time you buy the property. If you purchased the property with the intent of holding it for income and appreciation benefits, you are an investor. If, instead, you purchased the property with the intent of reselling it, you are a dealer. But doesn't everyone buy a property with the intent of eventually reselling it for a profit? Yes. Nevertheless, this is the distinction the IRS and the courts use to differentiate between an investor and a dealer.

Okay, so how does the IRS know what your intent was at the time you bought the property? How are they going to know what you were thinking when you bought the property? Well, the fact is they don't have to know. In law, there is this concept called "burden of proof." Usually, the burden of proof rests on the asserter, meaning that the person that makes an assertion has the responsibility of proving it. For example, if you are charged with a crime, it's the prosecutor's burden to prove it. If someone sues you, they have the burden of proving you did something wrong. In both of these examples, if the person with the burden of proof fails to "prove it" he or she loses their case or lawsuit. With the IRS, however, many times the burden of proof is shifted to the taxpayer. This means that all the IRS has to do is assert that your intent was to resell the property and *you* have the burden of "proving" it's not true. If you fail to prove that you actually intended to hold the property for income and appreciation, you lose.

As you can imagine, this dealer versus investor issue leads to a lot of tax court litigation and appeals. So, what do the courts use as criteria to determine if a person is a dealer or an investor? Unfortunately, the court decisions are almost as ambiguous as the IRS's definition. Courts usually look to other court decisions to see how a determination has been made in the past. However, in one case, one court actually reviewing the other courts' decisions stated that the dealer versus investor issue was "engulfed in a fog of decisions with gossamer-like distinctions, and a quagmire of unworkable, unreliable, and often irrelevant tests." [*United States v. Winthrop*, 417 F.2d 905, 906 (5th Cir. 1969).] Yes, that colorful language pretty much sums it up.

Fortunately, over time a list of criteria has emerged that the tax courts will apply on a case-by-case basis. The courts have consistently held that no single factor is controlling in any given case and that each case must stand on its own set of circumstances. With that said, here are some of the factors the courts use in determining dealer status:

- How long the property was held. Properties held for less than two years appear more like dealer property.

- The number of sales by the taxpayer in that year. Although this is very important, there is no definitive number. Even one sale can be considered dealer property if the intent was to resell rather than to invest.

- The types of improvements made to the property. The more extensive the improvements, the more likely the property was intended for resale.

- The purpose of acquiring the property

- The amount of income from the property sales compared to taxpayer's other income

- Extent and nature of efforts to sell the property. Constant advertising and control agents are seen more like the characteristics of a dealer.

- The subdivision and development of the property

- The use of a business office to sell the property

You may think some of these factors would be present whether a property was bought to sell or bought to hold. I would agree. Nevertheless, these are the factors the tax court uses in trying to determine if a person's actions add up to a pattern of regular, frequent, and continuous sales. If so, being labeled a dealer is almost a certainty.

Because the courts have stated that a determination must be made on a property-by-property basis, it is possible a taxpayer can be considered a dealer with respect to some properties and an investor with respect to others. This is a very important concept because many people with mostly buy-to-hold properties run across good fixer-uppers occasionally that they buy simply to fix up and sell. The danger is, if a person does too many of these buy-to-sell properties, the IRS may decide to label that person a dealer. If so labeled, there is a significant chance that the IRS will lump all of that person's buy-to-hold properties into the dealer category as well.

You may be able to cure the taint on your buy-to-hold property by meeting the burden of proof on a property-by-property basis, but this is definitely not a predicament in which you want to find yourself. Remember, a real estate dealer is not entitled to depreciation, so if the IRS says you are a dealer, you may face losing any depreciation write-offs you have taken not just on your buy-to-sell properties but also on your buy-to-hold properties. Obviously, if the IRS disallows your previously taken depreciation, you will probably be facing potentially considerable back taxes and interest.

POSSIBLE WAYS TO AVOID BEING LABELED A DEALER

There is no foolproof way to avoid being labeled a dealer if you look and act like a dealer when buying and selling a lot of properties. However, if you are the person who does the occasional fix-and-flip or subdivision, *and also* has buy-to-hold properties, there are ways to protect yourself from having the IRS label *all* your properties as dealer properties. The secret is to understand and use separate entities.

Most sophisticated investors would immediately agree that it is wise to use differing entity types to separate your real estate dealer-like activities from other real estate investments. Besides holding property in your own name, there are three basic entity types commonly used for real estate: corporations (usually S corporations), limited liability companies (LLCs), and limited partnerships (or family limited partnerships). Setting aside any discussion of the asset protection characteristics of these entity choices, let's just focus on their suitability for separating real estate investments.

1. *S corporation.* An S corporation is generally considered the best entity for buy-to-sell (dealer) type of properties. Because of the way dealer properties are taxed, a corporation offers the benefit of the profits being passed through to the investor as profits of the corporation rather than self-employment earnings. That's an important consideration when you remember that the profits from the sale of dealer-type property in an individual's name are considered ordinary income and may trigger self-employment tax. Those same profits to an S corporation are ordinary income to the corporation, but S corporations pay no income taxes directly. Instead, the design of the S corporation is that all profits pass through to the shareholders as profits from the corporation—not self-employment earnings. With no self-employment earnings, there are no self-employment taxes.

2. *Limited liability company.* An LLC is generally considered the best entity choice for buy-to-hold (investor) type properties. The structure of an LLC is not all that different than an S corporation. An LLC does not pay taxes directly; rather, profits from the LLC pass through to the owners. However, the profits from an LLC may create self-employment tax issues. As such, the LLC is preferred for the buy-to-hold properties where profits are considered and taxed as capital gains.

3. *Limited partnership.* Limited partnerships and family limited partnerships are considered best for buy-to-hold properties for the same reasons stated for LLCs. The main difference between an LLC and a limited partnership is the well-established protection offered to the limited partners. Generally speaking, an LLC would be more appropriate for an individual or husband and wife who own a couple of investment properties. A limited partnership would be more appropriate for a larger group of owners with passive investors.

Although the use of S corporations, LLCs, and limited partnerships in real estate investment is becoming common, the vast majority of investment properties are still held in the names of the individual owners. However, if you are one of those people doing fix-up-and-sell-type investments or subdividing and you also own long-term investment properties, you would be wise to separate your real estate activities by use of separate entities.

Incorporating an S corporation or forming an LLC or limited partnership is no longer difficult. If you are already fairly well versed on business entities, there are services right on the Internet that can do the job for you quickly and inexpensively. One Internet-based company my clients have used in the past is MyCorporation.com (*www.mycorporation.com*). If instead, you think you might need or want a little more guidance, most small business or real estate attorneys will set up your entity for you and point you in the right direction for less than $1,200. That fee will be money well spent if you need to segregate your buy-to-sell ventures from your buy-to-hold investments.

In summary, the dealer versus investor issue is one that causes a lot of anxiety for people who find themselves selling properties that might fit into the dealer property category. The bottom line is that real estate *dealers* get stuck with the highest tax rates and self-employment tax, they can't take depreciation, and they can't use any of the tax advantages normally associated with tax deferral on real estate investments. Real estate *investors*, on the other hand, get one of the lowest tax rates, have no self-employment tax, can write off depreciation, and get to use 1031 exchanges and installment sales.

STATUTES AND CASE LAW

Because of the importance and relative ambiguity of this topic, this will be one of the few chapters that will include case citations. If you find yourself in a position where you think you may be seriously at risk of being labeled a real estate dealer, you will want to do further research by taking a look at these case decisions and comparing your own situation to the set of facts in a given case. The full text of these cases is available on the Internet or at your local law library. As you'll see from the quick summary of these reviews, there is no clearly defined line of when a person becomes a dealer. Each case cited below has a specific set of facts associated with the taxpayer's situation. The facts in your situation may seem close, but remember, this is an area of law where even identical sets of facts may result in completely different court decisions.

These are by no means the only cases on this issue, but the ones here will be sufficient to get you started.

- The courts are pretty much in agreement that a pattern of regular, frequent, and continuous sales coupled with substantial development activity will almost certainly be characterized by the IRS and the courts as dealer activity. See *Biedenharn Realty Co., Inc. v. U.S.*, 526 F.2d 409 (5th Cir. 1976), cert. denied, 429 U.S. 819 (1976); *Achong v. Comr.*, 246 F.2d 445 (9th Cir. 1957); and *Gault v. Comr.*, 332 F.2d 94 (2d Cir. 1964).

- No single factor is controlling in any given case. *Biedenharn Realty Co., Inc. v. U.S.*, 526 F.2d 409 (5th Cir. 1976).

- The fact that one court case reached one conclusion on a given set of facts is not necessarily indicative of a similar result by the same or another court on essentially the same facts. *Scheuber v. Commissioner*, 371 F.2d 996 (7th Cir. 1967).

- The Fifth Circuit has indicated that frequency of sales is the most important determining factor. *Biedenharn Realty Co., Inc. v. U.S.*, 526 F.2d 409 (5th Cir. 1976), cert. denied, 429 U.S. 819 (1976).

- Taking the previous case note one step further, the court in the following case found the property in question to be dealer property *solely* based on the factor of sales frequency. *Suburban Realty Co. v. U.S.*, 615 F.2d 171 (5th Cir. 1980), cert. denied, 449 U.S. 920 (1980).

- Property primarily held for sale is dealer property. The term *primarily* means "of first importance" or "principally." *Malat v. Riddell* (1966) 383 US 569, 16 L Ed 2d 102, 86 S Ct 1030.

- Property is not dealer property if it is held for investment because it has income-producing potential, is offered by the taxpayer for lease but not actively for sale, is held for a significant period of time, and is exchanged for another income-producing property that was later leased out rather than sold. *Margolis v. Commissioner*, (9th Cir. 1964) 337 F.2d 1001, 1005.

CHAPTER EIGHT

Starker 1031 Tax-Deferred Exchanges

Like-kind or 1031 exchanges are perhaps the best known and most commonly used tax-deferral tool for real estate. Almost every experienced real estate agent has been involved in such an exchange at some time. Exchanges go by a lot of different names, such as 1031 exchange, Starker exchange, tax-free exchange, tax-deferred exchange, trading properties, delayed exchange, like-kind exchange, and more. All of these names describe the same thing—an exchange of property and tax deferral under the provisions of Internal Revenue Code section 1031.

A 1031 exchange allows the complete and indefinite deferral of capital gains taxes and recapture of depreciation, allowing taxpayers to do the following:

- Trade up to larger investment properties

- Relocate real estate investments

- Change the type or character of real estate investments

- Diversify or consolidate real estate investments to or from multiple properties

- Trade nonproductive property for real estate investments that produce income

DEVELOPMENT OF EXCHANGES

The original exchanges were true exchanges in that the owner of a property actually traded one property for another. As you might imagine, it was difficult to find two property owners who wanted each other's properties and agreed on the fair market value of each, so in the early days the property exchange concept saw sparse usage. Then in 1979, one of a series of court decisions, referred to as the *Starker* cases, created the legal authority for a delayed exchange. Following this 1979 Starker decision, property owners could now sell one property and wait up to six months before purchasing another without losing the right to consider the transaction an exchange for tax-deferral purposes.

The IRS initially had a difficult time with the concept of a delayed exchange because of its position that if sellers of a property were allowed an extended period during which they received proceeds from the sale, then it was not truly an exchange but rather a sale (triggering taxes) and a subsequent purchase. The IRS's main concern was not over the time allowed but rather over the receipt of funds. To make everyone happy, the *Starker* court allowed sellers the extended time to find and purchase a replacement property but agreed with the IRS's position that any actual or constructive receipt of funds by sellers would trigger taxes. From these cases a new segment of the real estate industry sprang to life: the qualified intermediary or accommodator. The job of a qualified intermediary or accommodator is to facilitate and document 1031 exchanges by receiving the proceeds of a sale under the terms of an exchange agreement and then applying those funds at the direction of the exchanger for the acquisition of the replacement property.

HOW 1031 EXCHANGES WORK TODAY

Today, 1031 exchanges are accomplished with little effort on the part of buyers and sellers. Most of the paperwork is handled quickly and smoothly in the background by qualified intermediaries or accommodators and then channeled through escrow/title companies or closing agents to the buyer and seller of each property for signatures, as shown in Figure 8.1.

If you are the seller-exchanger, the process of selling the relinquished property goes like this:

FIGURE 8.1 How a 1031 Exchange Works

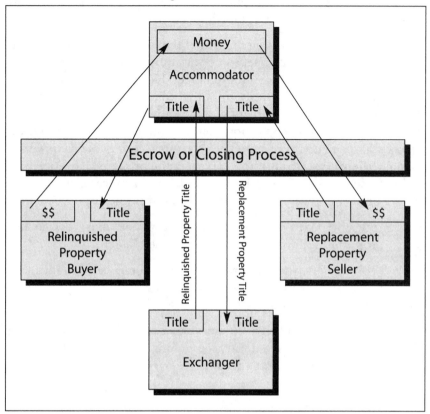

1. List your property for sale with your chosen real estate agent, making sure the agent understands you intend a 1031 exchange for another property.

2. When you get an offer, your agent will include a counteroffer provision that states the "buyer agrees to cooperate with seller's 1031 exchange."

3. Open escrow, and then choose your accommodator (your real estate agent or escrow/title agent can give you names of companies in your area).

4. You will sign an exchange agreement with your accommodator through escrow along with the other customary escrow paperwork.

5. At the close of escrow, your proceeds will be transferred to your accommodator's trust fund on your behalf and held there until you begin the process of buying your replacement property.

As you can see, the selling portion of the exchange is fairly straightforward. There are, of course, some variations to this simple example and there are also simultaneous exchanges. However, for the most part, the sequence of events indicates how the relinquished property side of the exchange goes in 95 percent of all traditional exchanges today.

Once the sale on the relinquished property is completed and the proceeds are in the accommodator's trust account, the taxpayer-exchanger then must acquire the replacement property. The timelines and requirements that must be followed I cover more in depth later, but generally the purchase of the replacement property goes like this:

1. You, the taxpayer-exchanger, identify potential replacement properties following IRS rules (discussed later).

2. You negotiate the purchase agreement, being sure to include a provision that the seller of the replacement property will cooperate with the 1031 exchange.

3. Open escrow and have the purchase contract earnest money deposit transferred from the accommodator's trust fund to the escrow or closing agent's account.

4. You, the taxpayer-exchanger, then continue the purchase process normally, doing inspections, arranging financing, and so forth.

5. When all is ready to close, the accommodator transfers the balance of the exchange funds to the escrow or closing agent, who then closes the transaction.

Once again, this is a simple example, but it does show how most replacement property transactions occur today. Keep in mind that the requirements and formalities that must be followed to ensure your 1031 exchange conforms to IRS requirements have been left out of both of these examples. I discuss these requirements and formalities fully later in the chapter, but right now let's take a look at the advantages of doing an exchange.

ADVANTAGES OF 1031 EXCHANGES

Full, Indefinite Capital Gains Tax Deferral

The most important advantage of 1031 exchanges is the fact that you can defer all capital gains *indefinitely*. The other deferral tools available (installment sales and private annuity trusts) allow a deferral period that begins when the property is sold or traded for the private annuity and ends when the note or annuity payments are made. Although installment sales and private annuity trusts can postpone the payment of taxes for an extended period, they are still only a scheduled deferral of a capital gain. On the other hand, 1031 exchanges do not create deferral periods but instead allow you to continue to roll your real estate profits into other properties as many times as you want without recognizing any taxable gain. No limit is placed on the number of times you can do a 1031 exchange in your lifetime. Thus, a person could (and many people do) start out with a small rental property early in life, "exchange" the property into successively larger rental properties every five to ten years, and end up with a substantial amount of income property at retirement.

Most important is that if you never sell an investment property without exchanging it into another, you will never have to pay taxes on your real estate capital gains during your lifetime. And when you die, your heirs may be entitled to receive a stepped-up basis on the investment property you leave them and will escape paying taxes on the capital gains you deferred throughout your life.

Building Wealth

One of the more common reasons for executing 1031 exchanges is to build wealth. As mentioned in the previous section, it is fairly common to find people parlaying real estate investments into successively larger investments over their lifetime. It isn't hard to understand a plan whereby an investor makes an exchange every so many years so as to double the size of an investment.

Example: A 30-year-old couple buys a small four-unit apartment building with the idea of gradually increasing their real estate investment. Their plan is to hold the property for ten years and gain equity through appreciation and mortgage reduction. They plan to sell the property at the ten-year mark and use their increased equity as the down payment for two four-unit apartment buildings. They intend to do the same thing every ten years until they retire at age 70. According to their plan, at age 40 they will own two four-units buildings, at 50 they will own four four-unit buildings, and at age 60 they will own eight four-unit buildings. At age 70 they could double the number of rental units again, but instead they intend to travel abroad during their retirement years. They are therefore planning to sell the properties at that time to create a lifetime stream of income from whatever equity they have created from the property investments.

This kind of planning is not hard to understand. What is hard is following through on the plan. If you can follow through with this type of plan, your ability to indefinitely defer capital gains through 1031 exchanges enables you to continue to build wealth tax free throughout your life.

Trading Up

Trading up is another common reason for executing a 1031 exchange. The two types of trading up are (1) buying a bigger property or increasing the overall amount of your real estate investment (described in the preceding section) and (2) buying a higher-quality property.

Example: Bob owns an eight-unit apartment building in the downtown neighborhood of a medium-sized city. As the property grows a little older, the rental market in the area has become increasingly competitive. With the high turnover of tenants and the increasing cost of maintenance, Bob finds himself spending more time on a property whose bottom line is shrinking. Bob has found another property, a six-unit building, in an outlying area that is newer and in a better rental area. Both properties have approximately the same market value. Bob does a 1031 exchange, selling the downtown property and trading up to the smaller (but better) building.

Lots of exchanges occur for a similar reason. It's not so much trading up for quantity or cash flow but rather for quality and the perceived soundness and suitability of the investment. Even if the projected cash flow on the replacement property is not as good, Bob may be much happier not having to drive into town twice a week to meet repairpeople or prospective tenants. Whatever the reason, Bob sees the exchange as a trade-up, and assuming all the other requirements of a 1031 exchange are met, the IRS lets him do it tax free.

Leveraging

Leverage is king—well, at least to an aggressive investor. It is also another of the more common reasons motivating 1031 exchanges. Leveraging is simply the concept of putting down as little of your own money as possible on a property and maximizing the amount of financing. The strategy looks brilliant in an up market but can result in a lot of foreclosures in down times.

> **Example:** John and Tom each have $150,000 to invest. Tom finds what he considers a suitable property investment priced at $300,000. With his $150,000 as a down payment and another $150,000 in financing, he buys the property. John is more aggressive in his investing than Tom and is trying to maximize his leverage. The customary loan-to-value lending ratio in his region is 70 percent, which means he can invest up to $500,000 on a property with $150,000 down. He finds a property he considers suitable, puts down his $150,000, and gets a $350,000 mortgage to buy it.

According to John's investment philosophy, all other things being equal, it is better to have a 30 percent equity in a $500,000 property than to have a 50 percent equity in a $300,000 property. After all, *if* the real estate market is expected to increase in value at a steady 6 percent for the next few years, isn't it better to get a $30,000 ($500,000 × 6 percent) equity growth rather than an $18,000 ($300,000 × 6 percent) one? Another way to look at this is that with a 6 percent increase in property values, John can boast a 20 percent return on his initial investment ($30,000 ÷ $150,000), whereas Tom realized a return of only 12 percent ($18,000 ÷ $150,000). Sounds like John's got the better approach, but there is, of course, a downside. If the property is too highly leveraged, the rental income alone will usually not support the debt in a down cycle, so suddenly Tom's approach may start looking like the wiser of the two. Whatever your personal perspective, leveraging is an important part of real estate investing.

In the previous example, a 1031 exchange is the perfect tool for John. If the $500,000 property he bought increased a total of 50 percent in market value over a ten-year period, its market value would be

$750,000 and he would owe just under $350,000. This means he could sell the property and use the $400,000 equity as a down payment to leverage into a $1,300,000 property without paying any taxes.

Additional Depreciation

Depreciation in real estate is a wonderful accounting fiction. It allows a certain amount of the income from operating rental property to pass to the owner without taxes. The concept is that buildings and improvements on a property have a life expectancy and will eventually have to be replaced. As such, depreciation is a way to allocate and account for the diminution in value for those buildings and improvements in each successive year. That allocation of depreciation is an "on-paper" expense that offsets an equal amount of *real* dollars coming from rental income. For example, if an investment property generates a predepreciation net cash flow of $10,000 and the scheduled depreciation for the year happens to also be $10,000, no taxes would have to be paid. The on-paper expense would offset the real dollars of income.

Obviously, people view the depreciation write-off as highly desirable. Unfortunately, anyone who has owned a particular investment property 25 years or more has either used up all the available depreciation or soon will. As such, some people use 1031 exchanges to move to a larger or more valuable property for the additional depreciation. Note, however, that the adjusted basis of the relinquished property will transfer to the replacement property. That means that the replacement property can provide additional depreciation only for the amount of value beyond the market value of the relinquished property.

Example: Don has owned a rental property for 25 years and over the years has taken all of the scheduled depreciation available on the property. The property has a fair market value of $250,000. Don sells it and exchanges into another property with a fair market value of $400,000. His adjusted basis on the relinquished property was $50,000. That adjusted basis would transfer and represent the basis allocated to the first $250,000 of the replacement property. As such, the beginning basis on the replacement property after the exchange will be $200,000 (the $50,000 from the relinquished property and the $150,000 additional paid to get to the $400,000 purchase price).

There would be no depreciation benefit in exchanging properties of equal value, because the adjusted basis from the relinquished property would simply transfer to the replacement property. The only exception would be a trade of vacant land for a property of equal value with buildings and improvements. The basis would transfer, but there would be a reallocation between land and improvements that would allow scheduled depreciation.

Reducing Your Workload

One big difference between investing in real estate and other types of investments is that real estate requires time and effort to maintain. You may have a management company handle the property for you, but a good management company is hard to find and is sometimes simply too expensive. For this reason, many investors take a hands-on management approach and eventually get to a point where they are able to run the properties efficiently themselves.

Real estate investments run the spectrum from high-maintenance and time-consuming properties to relatively maintenance-free ones. For example, at the high-workload end of the spectrum would be a 60-year-old residential apartment building with all singles or one-bedroom apartments. This type of property, although it can be profitable, is considered less desirable because it usually means a high tenant turnover along with constant repair and maintenance. At the low-workload end of the spectrum are commercial properties with reliable tenants on long-term triple-net leases. Setting aside the workload considerations, both these examples have their own advantages and disadvantages depending on your investment philosophy. And, of course, many types of properties fall somewhere between the two examples given.

With this in mind, many 1031 exchanges are done simply to lighten an investor's workload.

Example: Hal owns a small high-maintenance four-unit apartment building that has been having a lot of tenant problems and turnover lately. He feels the property is taking up too much of his time and is afraid it will only get worse. He is tired of being a landlord and is considering selling the property to free up his time for other interests. Hal has a son who is getting married in a few months, and even though the newlyweds will not be ready to buy their first house for some time, they will be looking for a home to rent. Homes in their desired neighborhood are selling for approximately the same amount as the fair market value of Hal's apartment building. Moreover, the fair rental value of those homes is approximately the same as the net rental income from the apartment building after taking into consideration the vacancy rate and higher cost of maintenance.

The obvious solution for Hal in this example is to make an arrangement with the soon-to-be newlyweds to rent them a house. Using a 1031 exchange, he would sell the apartment building and buy a house in the young couple's desired neighborhood for them to rent. In that way, Hal has accomplished his goal of reducing his workload without incurring any immediate tax on the capital gain or having to recapture any of the depreciation taken on the apartment building over the years.

Hal's situation is actually very common, but even if he didn't have a family looking to rent a house, he could have still accomplished his goal by trading into a rental house. Likewise, investors might be able to lighten their workload by trading from eight units to four or from residential property to commercial.

Whatever the change in the size or type of property may be, a 1031 exchange is the perfect tool when a person wants to lighten the workload but still wants to retain certain real estate investments.

Relocating Investments

One of the best features of investing in real estate is an investor's ability to supervise directly or indirectly the performance of the property. If you own a property near your own neighborhood, you can drive by it on a regular basis to keep abreast of its condition. This is a significant advantage of real estate investments over other types of investing such as stocks or mutual funds. With the burst of the dot-com stock market bubble, corporate accounting improprieties, and major corporate bankruptcies, many property investors find it comforting to be able to drive to their real estate investments and actually touch and see where their money is invested.

With this in mind, many people use 1031 exchanges as a way of keeping their property investments geographically nearby. Wanting to relocate or being relocated by your employer to another region of the country can be a problem, especially if you are a hands-on type of property owner. As mentioned before, good property management companies are hard to find and usually expensive. In some cases, having a management company handle the property while you are out of the area might be a good interim solution, but if your move is to be permanent, using a 1031 exchange to move the investment closer to your new home is probably a better plan.

Assuming you meet all of the other 1031 exchange requirements, you can relinquish an investment property in Maine and replace it with one in Arizona, Florida, Hawaii, or anywhere else in the United States for that matter. Any investment property in the United States is considered like-kind and is allowed under the 1031 exchange provisions. However, you *cannot* exchange into a foreign replacement property. So if you are moving to a foreign country, sorry, but your investments have to stay here or you have to settle your tax bill before taking your profits out of the country.

Exchanging to a Different Property Type

A 1031 exchange is also referred to as a like-kind exchange because the regulations allow only for exchanges of like-kind property—that is, a property of the same nature or character. Keep in mind that the provision of section 1031 of the tax code provides for tax-deferred exchanges of much more than just real property. You can exchange many business and investment capital assets for like-kind property. You can do a 1031 exchange of aircraft, boats, trucks, and even cattle, but they have to be exchanged for like-kind property. For example, qualifying exchanges would include aircraft for aircraft, trucks for trucks, or cattle for cattle (but strangely enough, not male cattle for female cattle or vice versa).

One of the most common questions asked by real property investors concerns the like-kind requirement. Thankfully, the answer is fairly straightforward. Just about any domestic real estate that you use in business or have held for investment qualifies for a 1031 exchange to any other domestic real estate that you intend to use in business or hold for investment. Arguably, all real estate is held for investment, so the category definition is very broad. However, the rules specifically exclude a primary residence, a vacation home, or a second home.

Under the like-kind rule covering property used in business or held for investment, all of the following exchange examples would qualify for a tax deferral under a 1031 exchange:

- A rental house or condominium to an apartment building

- Residential income property to commercial property

- Vacant land to a rental house or apartment building

- Industrial warehouse to vacant land

- Desert or mountain land to urban income property

As you can see, just about any real estate you intend to trade to any other real estate qualifies as long as the properties have been, and will be, used in business or held for investment.

RECHARACTERIZING PROPERTY FOR AN EXCHANGE

The way the IRS determines whether a property has been used in business or held for investment usually hinges on your treatment of the property. One of the best indicators is how you have characterized the property on your tax returns. If you have historically taken depreciation and shown rental income, there usually isn't any question that the property will qualify. However, what about a vacation home that you occasionally rent to others but usually leave vacant for your own or your family's use? The answer depends on how you have characterized the property. If you have previously declared the home a second home and have been taking a second-home mortgage deduction on your taxes, the property will not *immediately* qualify.

You can always *recharacterize* a property, however, by simply using it differently. In the case of a vacation property, if you were to change its use to a rental property instead of the family vacation home, it would qualify under the 1031 exchange rules. For example, you could list your vacation home with the local vacation home rental agents and rent it for a couple of years. You would show rental income and expenses (including depreciation) from the property on your tax returns. If you did so, the property would qualify under the rules for a 1031 exchange. The question always becomes, for how long do you have to rent it? Conventional wisdom says that two years is a safe number, but many people wait only one year.

Some people even amend previous tax returns to recharacterize a property. The amendments would show income and expenses attributable to the property and take any depreciation available. Of course, if any tax deficit exists because of the changes made, the back tax would be immediately due along with any applicable interest, but sometimes it is well worth the back taxes if the property will qualify sooner. Still, the question is, how long should you wait? The answer is not entirely clear, so if you are thinking about recharacterizing a property to qualify for an exchange, see your accountant or a tax attorney for advice and guidance.

SPLITTING UP PARTNERSHIPS AND JOINT VENTURES

Another common use for 1031 exchanges is to split up partnerships, joint ventures, and other types of co-ownership of property without triggering unwanted taxes. Properties frequently have more than one owner, usually as the result of a loosely formed partnership of several people who joined together for the sole purpose of investing in a specific property. Also prevalent are situations in which a property was inherited from parents years before and the names of all the children were placed on the title. However the joint ownership came to exist, a time will come when at least one of the joint owners wants his or her money out. When this happens, a number of options are available to the departing owner; the remaining owner(s) can buy out the interest of the person wanting out, the departing owner can sometimes attempt to sell his or her share, or, if everyone agrees, the property can be sold. If the property is sold and a capital gain is involved, the remaining owners are usually not happy about their taxes being triggered because one owner wants out. Luckily, each person has the ability to execute an exchange of his or her portion of the investment property.

Example: John and Jane are married to each other, as are Bob and Betty. In 1980, the two couples decided to pool funds and invest in an apartment building. They owned the property in equal shares of 50 percent to each couple. They jointly managed the apartment building for six years and everything went smoothly. In 1986, Bob and Betty moved out of state when Bob was temporarily transferred by his big aerospace employer. The apartment building was fairly trouble free, so John and Jane agreed to continue managing it until Bob and Betty returned. In 1992, John and Jane divorced with an agreed marital settlement that called for an equal split of their ownership in the apartment building. At the time, the real estate market was very bad, so everyone agreed to hang on to the investment until the market recovered. Jane continued to manage the property. In 2000, the fair market value of the apartment building was $1 million; the adjusted basis on the property stood at $200,000. The ownership of the property had evolved into Bob and Betty's owning 50 percent as joint tenants with each other and as tenants in common with both John and Jane, who separately own 25 percent each.

What usually happens in a case like this is that the person who still lives near the property is continuing to manage it but will want out. After all, Bob and Betty in the example have been living out of state for 14 years, and the management of the property fell to John and Jane for a number of years and to Jane alone for a number of years thereafter. At some time (usually much sooner than the time in the example), the inequity of the situation forces the sale of the property.

In the previous situation, each person has the ability to use a 1031 exchange for his or her portion of the property and will be able to go his or her own way; in most cases, however, married couples exchange jointly. So Betty and Bob will be exchanging jointly out of their one-half ownership, or the equivalent of a $500,000 property investment with an adjusted basis of $100,000. Both John and Jane will be exchanging out of their respective one-quarter ownership, or the equivalent of a $250,000 property investment with an adjusted basis of $50,000 each. Although all the parties can make a 1031 exchange, any of them could individually also choose *not* to make an exchange and would simply receive the appropriate portion of the sale proceeds and be responsible for his or her own taxes attributable to the appropriate ownership share.

The division and sale of property in this way is fairly common and uncomplicated. Had the two couples created instead a formal general partnership, limited partnership, LLC, or corporation to own the property, the complexity would have increased significantly. The tax consequences of the dissolution of any of the more formal business entities are beyond the scope of this book, and you will need expert tax advice. It's not smart to begin the process of buying out a partner or making a 1031 exchange on the dissolution of a business entity without knowing the specific tax consequences of your actions. Get expert advice before you act.

1031 EXCHANGE REQUIREMENTS

Many requirements, rules, exceptions to rules, time restrictions, and formalities are involved in and govern 1031 exchanges. In fact, the authoritative law books on 1031 exchanges contain from 800 to well over 1,000 pages, so it is not possible to cover all the possible variables here. What I do cover are the everyday basics and certain danger areas that let you know how complex this area of law can be, depending on your specific situation. Do not rely solely on the information in this book or the comments of real estate agents without verifying the information with your own legal and/or tax professional.

The basic requirements for making a fully tax-deferred 1031 exchange fall into five general categories:

1. Properties exchanged must be for business use or held for investment.

2. The price of the replacement property must be equal to or higher than that of the relinquished property.

3. The taxpayer must not get actual or constructive receipt of the proceeds.

4. Qualified intermediaries or accommodators must be used.

5. Identification and closing-time requirements must be met.

In the next sections, I examine each of these categories and discuss some of the ways people have run afoul of the rules by misinterpreting the requirements.

Business Use or Held for Investment

The first basic requirement of a valid exchange is that the property being exchanged and the property being acquired both be for business use or held for investment. Section 1031 of the Internal Revenue Code (IRC) reads in part:

> No gain or loss shall be recognized on the exchange of property held for productive use in a trade or business or for investment if such property is exchanged solely for property of like kind which is to be held either for productive use in a trade or business or for investment.

As discussed previously, for real estate, the category of "for investment" is quite broad, but remember that primary residences, vacation homes, and second homes are excluded by implication. In addition, a foreign replacement property is not considered like-kind property even if it meets all of the other requirements.

Equal or Higher Price

To completely defer all capital gains taxes on the sale of a property through a 1031 exchange, the replacement property must have a price equal to or higher than the relinquished property. It doesn't matter if you sold one larger property and bought multiple smaller properties, sold multiple smaller properties and bought one larger property, or sold multiple properties and bought multiple properties as long as the replacement property or properties have an equal or higher aggregate value. For example, if your relinquished property is sold for $100,000, the value of the replacement property or the combination of replacement properties must be priced at $100,000 or more. That doesn't mean you can't make a 1031 exchange into a lesser-valued property; it simply means you would have to pay taxes on the difference. For example, if your relinquished property had a value of $100,000 and the replacement property a value of only $90,000, you could still do the 1031 exchange, but you would have to pay a capital gains tax on the $10,000 difference.

The minor exception to the equal-or-higher-price rule is that acquisition expenses are counted toward the total value of the replacement property. Acquisition expenses would include escrow fees, inspection fees, loan fees, points, commissions, and all other fees incidental to the purchase itself.

The equal-or-higher-price requirement is clear-cut, but many people, including a few real estate agents, mistakenly think that only the capital gain portion of the investment has to be exchanged and reinvested. After all, you are only deferring the taxes on the gain itself, right? *Wrong.* To qualify under the provision of a 1031 exchange, the entire property value must be exchanged or taxes paid on the portion that isn't exchanged.

Another common misconception: If the replacement property is priced lower than the relinquished property, then the taxes due on the portion not reinvested are figured on a capital gain percentage similar to the payments received in an installment sale. For example, if the relinquished property is sold for $100,000 (with an adjusted basis of $80,000) and the replacement property is $90,000, the misconception is that the taxes on the $10,000 received will be based on the ratio of gain to total value, meaning that $8,000 of the $10,000 received would be return of invested money and $2,000 would be capital gain. Wrong. The IRS takes the position that the first dollars taken out of an exchange represent capital gain or recapture of depreciation and are fully taxed accordingly. So in the previous example, if the replacement property had been only $90,000 and $10,000 in cash had been received by the taxpayer-exchanger, the full $10,000 would be considered taxable capital gain. If the replacement property had been only $80,000 with $20,000 in cash received, no taxable benefit at all would have resulted from the exchange.

If the desire is to buy down, there are ways to structure an exchange in combination with other tax-deferral devices and thereby defer the whole gain. However, most people are buying up in exchange situations, so the equal-or-higher-price requirement is usually not a concern but rather just a rule that must be followed.

Remember, you do not *have* to buy a higher-priced property, but if you don't, you will have to pay the taxes on the difference.

No Receipt of Funds

The basic concept of an exchange is that one property is traded for another. That we can now make exchanges with a time delay between the relinquishing of one property and the purchasing of the replacement property doesn't mean, however, that we can have control of the cash during the time delay. Originally, the exchanges had to be simultaneous, meaning that you had to close escrow on the relinquished property and the replacement at the same time. As you can imagine, all kinds of problems arise when trying to do simultaneous exchanges, and the end result was a lot of failed exchange attempts.

The commonsense solution was to allow flexibility, or delay, between the relinquishing of one property and the separate process of acquiring a replacement property. In the court battles over this issue, the IRS fought hard to disallow any delay period to avoid giving the exchanger use of the proceeds during the delay period. The courts agreed that some flexibility in time was needed to facilitate the exchange process but also agreed with the IRS that the exchanger should not have use of, or even access to, the proceeds from the sale of the relinquished property during the delay period. From this decision grew delayed exchanges with built-in time allowances to facilitate the exchange but also the strict requirement that the exchanger not get actual or constructive receipt of funds at any time during the delayed exchange process. The rule is pretty much set in stone; if at any time during the exchange process you get an actual or constructive receipt of funds, your exchange will not withstand an audit.

Amazingly, many exchange attempts fail today because an exchanger runs afoul of this no-receipt-of-funds rule. It is a typically regular occurrence for an accommodator or real estate attorney to get a phone call from a person who wants to make a 1031 exchange after the property is already sold and closed and the person has already received the proceeds from the sale. The proper time to arrange the exchange is before the sale closes on the relinquished property. A paperwork process and an exchange agreement must be in place before closing so that funds go to your exchange accommodator's trust fund account rather than to you. Many times these failed exchange attempts occur because people were so focused on the time requirements that they paid no attention to the other required formalities. Being given poor information and simply misunderstanding the exchange process are other factors also often at fault. Whatever the reason, by the time that phone call is made, it's too late. If the sale has already closed, there has been either actual or constructive receipt of funds, and there is no recovery from that. It is a failed exchange attempt, and the capital gains tax liability has already been triggered.

Using Qualified Intermediaries

Today, the typical 1031 exchange involves the use of an IRS-defined qualified intermediary or accommodator to hold the proceeds of the sale while the exchanger locates and arranges the purchase of the replacement property. The terms *qualified intermediary* and *accommodator* both refer to the same thing: a business entity or person who acts as a facilitator for the exchange process; and the terms are used interchangeably here. Generally, a qualified intermediary's function is to document the exchange through what is usually called an "exchange agreement" and to hold the proceeds from the sale of the relinquished property until the purchase of the replacement property is ready to close.

Ways are available to accomplish a valid exchange without using an intermediary or accommodator, but none are worth discussing because today's accommodators are low cost and easy to use. In addition, by using a qualified intermediary, you create a "safe harbor"—that is, a legal presumption that there was no actual or constructive receipt of funds. Even in a simultaneous closing exchange, in which an accommodator is not required, the cost of having one is still worthwhile to ensure the safe harbor presumption and as a safety measure in case anything goes wrong.

There is no government supervision or licensing requirements for exchange accommodators. That tends to make attorneys nervous, especially when you consider the large amounts of money entrusted to accommodators on a regular basis. There have been a few cases of accommodators running off with the money or filing for bankruptcy and tying up an exchanger's funds, but such cases are very rare. The best way to protect your funds is to use a bonded and well-known intermediary or exchange attorney; large title companies sometimes offer this service as well.

Although no set rules establish who can act as your accommodator, the IRS has set out who cannot be your accommodator by describing "disqualified persons." Disqualified persons include your real estate brokers, accountants, spouses, other family-related parties, and any companies or businesses owned or controlled by otherwise disqualified persons. Family attorneys or attorneys with whom you have other attorney-client dealings are also disqualified, but attorneys are not disqualified if they are retained specifically as an exchange accommodator or to advise you on exchange matters.

The process of using an accommodator has been streamlined over the past 10 to 15 years so that basically, once you have selected an accommodator, it's a matter of paperwork. Your escrow or closing agent supplies the necessary property and closing information to the accommodator. The accommodator in turn drafts an exchange agreement that documents your intent to conform to the requirements of IRC section 1031 for the tax-deferred exchange (an example of a commonly used form of exchange agreement has been provided in the appendix). The exchange agreement probably comes to you through your escrow or closing agent for your signature. At the same time, a copy of the agreement goes to the buyer of your property, because the buyer's signature is also necessary. In essence, the agreement states that both parties are instructing the accommodator to act as intermediary by accepting title to the property on behalf of the seller and then deeding it to the buyer under the terms of the purchase contract. The accommodator is then authorized to accept and hold the proceeds from the sale in trust for the seller while the seller is looking for a replacement property.

Originally, on the sale of the relinquished property, the seller-exchanger would deed the property to the accommodator and the accommodator would deed the property to the buyer in exchange for the contract price. Likewise, on the purchase of the replacement property, the seller of the replacement property would agree to deed the property to the accommodator in exchange for the purchase price, and then the accommodator would deed the property to the exchanger, thereby completing the exchange process. However, with the rise of liability for property conditions (toxics), most accommodators are less willing to have any ownership (vesting) in the exchanged properties at all. Most now do what is called direct deeding, which means that buyer and seller in both stages of the exchange deed directly to each other. This approach is common now, and the IRS will not audit or disallow your exchange for that reason alone. Whichever deeding method your accommodator chooses to use should make no difference to you. What is important is that the proper qualified intermediary paper trail is created.

Time Requirements

Before the landmark *Starker v. United States* decision in 1979, 1031 exchange provisions were thought to require a simultaneous exchange, meaning that both the relinquished property and the replacement property had to close at the same time. That requirement limited the use of like-kind exchanges because it was overly cumbersome trying to sell one property, locate a suitable replacement, and negotiate the simultaneous closing of both. And, as noted earlier, the alternative of finding two property owners who actually wanted each other's property and would make a true property-for-property exchange was simply not practical. The 1979 *Starker* case challenged and defeated the IRS's position that 1031 exchanges had to be simultaneous, giving rise to the terms *Starker exchange* or *delayed exchange*. Five years after *Starker*, Congress enacted changes to IRC section 1031 that specifically allowed delayed exchanges and set the time requirements that remain in effect today.

The 45-day and 180-day requirements. According to Congress's revision of IRC section 1031, in order for a delayed exchange to be valid, it must meet two requirements (as illustrated in Figure 8.2):

1. The replacement property must be identified within 45 days of the closing and transfer of the relinquished property.

2. The replacement property must be received (title acquired) within 180 days of the closing and transfer of the relinquished property (or the due date with extensions) for the transferor's tax returns for the taxable year in which the transfer of the relinquished property occurs.

FIGURE 8.2 1031 Exchange Time Requirements

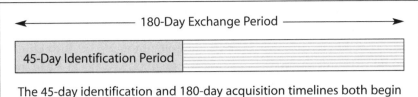

The 45-day identification and 180-day acquisition timelines both begin at the closing on the sale of the relinquished property.

The IRS takes both of these requirements very seriously. If you are a day late, your exchange will be disallowed. Count on it. With this in mind, let's look more closely at what both of these time requirements mean in practice.

The 45-day identification period seems more like a requirement designed to annoy than to actually accomplish any useful purpose. Nevertheless, the rule as enacted is strictly followed today. Many people are hesitant to engage in 1031 exchanges knowing they have only 45 days to locate and identify replacement property. However, in practice, it usually takes time to sell the relinquished property and more time still to complete the escrow process. Presuming you are diligent in trying to locate your replacement property, in practice there is usually much more time than just the 45 days available. For example, if it takes 30 days to sell your relinquished property and another 45 days to close the escrow, you really have 120 days to identify the replacement property (30 days to sell plus 45 days of escrow plus 45 days allowed by code). Of course, that presumes you are out there trying to find the replacement property as soon as you decide to sell and make an exchange.

It is also common to negotiate a longer escrow period (60, 90, or 120 days) to allow you extra time to locate your replacement property. It is even possible to negotiate a contingency in the sale agreement that makes the closing contingent on your ability to locate a suitable replacement property. Even though these types of contingencies are possible, they will not be warmly received by real estate agents and buyers because they introduce a sometimes unacceptable degree of uncertainty into the transaction.

The best way to increase your available time to locate and identify a replacement property is to start looking for it as soon as you have made the decision to sell and make the exchange. Unfortunately, many people don't even consider what they will be buying or start looking for a replacement property before they actually close on the sale of their relinquished property.

How to identify your replacement property. The 45-day identification period is an area ripe for abuse for two reasons: the severe consequences of being late and the considerable ambiguity in the required method of notification and the person or persons who must be notified. The official rule is [Treasury Regulation 1.1031(k)-1(c)(2)]:

> A replacement property is properly identified only if it is designated as replacement property in a written document signed by the taxpayer and hand delivered, mailed, telecopied, or otherwise sent to either:
>
> 1. The person obligated to transfer the replacement property to the taxpayer, even if that person is a disqualified person, or
>
> 2. To any other person involved in the exchange other than the taxpayer or a disqualified person before the end of the 45-day identification period.

Crystal clear, right? It seems fairly straightforward if the identification is made to the person who is obligated to transfer the replacement property to the exchanger, that person being usually your intermediary or accommodator. But there is also the alternative category of providing the identification to "any other person *involved* in the exchange" except a disqualified person (italics mine). Examples of disqualified persons would include your real estate agent, family members, and your accountant. Examples of involved persons not disqualified would include your escrow company, title company, or an attorney hired specifically to oversee or advise you on the exchange.

Properties actually acquired prior to the 45-day identification are considered as satisfying the code requirements, so you will not have to notify anyone if the escrow on the replacement property actually closes within the identification period. Otherwise, identification of the replacement property must be sent or delivered before the end of the 45-day identification period, *without* extensions for Saturdays, Sundays, or holidays.

Identifying alternative and multiple properties. Generally, the rules allow you to identify three potential replacement properties. This is important because if something happens to make your first choice of a replacement property undesirable or unavailable after the expiration of your 45-day identification period, you are out of luck. If you identified only one property and this situation arises, your exchange will be disallowed and your capital gains taxes will be triggered. So make sure you allow yourself a backup position by identifying at least three potential replacement properties.

There are also some obscure exceptions to the three-property-identification rule that allow you to identify as many properties as you want as long as the aggregate value does not exceed 200 percent of the value of the relinquished property (the 200 percent rule) or if the exchanger actually acquires 95 percent of the aggregate value of all the properties identified (the 95 percent rule). If you find yourself wanting or needing to use either the 200 percent rule or the 95 percent rule, get an attorney experienced in 1031 exchanges to actively oversee your exchange.

The properties you identify must be unambiguously described in the notification. For real estate, an adequate description is the street address, legal description, or a tax assessor's parcel number. A sample of a 45-day identification has been included in the appendix.

AVOIDING POTENTIAL PROBLEMS

Exchanges are fairly commonplace today and in most cases go smoothly with little risk of problems. When there *are* problems, however, the consequences can be harsh. The IRS typically doesn't audit exchanges, but when it does, it is usually a few years after the exchange was completed; and its recognition of a problem or unmet requirement at that point can be devastating. For example, if you deferred a capital gain of $200,000 and your exchange was disallowed three years later in an IRS audit, you would immediately owe the original tax due on the gain plus interest and, in cases of willful neglect, a 25 percent penalty. So even though it is not common for the IRS to disallow an exchange, the severity of the sanctions imposed when it does justifies due care.

Getting Professional Advice and Guidance

You'll find a tremendous number of exchange accommodators and qualified intermediaries in the industry today. Just typing "1031 exchange" into a search engine on the Internet yields hundreds of accommodators, qualified intermediaries, exchange advisors, real estate agents, attorneys, accountants, and so on.

Given the availability of e-mail, faxes, and overnight express mailing, there is probably no compelling reason for a qualified intermediary in Oregon not to handle the exchange agreement paperwork for an exchange of property in Florida. On the other hand, if there are qualified advisors and accommodators in your area, why not pick someone local?

Real estate agents are usually the first place people turn for advice on exchanges. Some agents know enough about exchanges to advise you but some don't. Advice is only as good as the experience and qualifications of the advisor, so it is in your own best interest to make sure you are comfortable with the level of your advisor's expertise.

The two best sources of information about exchanges are real estate attorneys and experienced accommodators. The problem is, of course, that attorneys' services are never free, whereas the "words of wisdom" from local real estate agents are; as a result, many people tend to settle for the advice that's free, good or bad. There is, however, a way to get a good advisor without the attorney's fees. If you are contemplating an exchange, you *will* want to use a qualified intermediary, and most qualified intermediaries have attorneys either on staff or on retainer; and some real estate attorneys are also qualified intermediaries. Handling exchanges is such a competitive business that most qualified intermediaries are known for excellent customer service. If you call one with questions, you'll probably get a return call from someone who can actually answer your questions. Your real estate agent knows the names of a few qualified intermediaries in your area or can find names for you— a good resource that's usually free, so take advantage of it.

If you find your situation is more complicated than a garden-variety exchange, make sure you are clear on the legal process and tax outcome before you commit yourself. In the more complicated exchanges, having your own real estate attorney to at least oversee the process is probably well worth the cost.

Follow the Timing Rules and Don't Cut Your Time Short

As noted earlier in this chapter, for an exchange to be valid, the IRS requires you to meet two time requirements:

1. The replacement property must be identified within 45 days of the closing and transfer of the relinquished property.

2. The replacement property must be received within 180 days of the closing and transfer of the relinquished property or the due date (with extensions) for the transferor's tax returns for the taxable year in which the transfer of the relinquished property occurs.

The IRS takes the 45-day identification and 180-day acquisition time requirements very seriously. If you are a day late and your exchange is audited, the exchange will be disallowed; as far as the IRS is concerned, these time requirements are firmly enforced. In addition to the 45-day and 180-day timelines, two lesser-known rules also tend to trip people up.

The first potential problem arises if the 45th day of the identification period or the 180th day of the acquisition period falls on a holiday or a weekend, in which case the time requirements are not extended to the following business day. In other words, if the 45th day of your identification period falls on a Sunday, you must identify your replacement property by the Friday before.

The reason the second lesser-known rule tends to cause problems stems from the way the 180-day replacement property time requirement is written. The rule states that the property must be received within 180 days but then goes on to add "or [by] the due date (with extensions) for the transferor's tax returns for the taxable year in which the transfer of the relinquished property occurs." The problem is that everyone focuses on the 180-day requirement and fails to pays attention to the secondary language.

Example: Hal is making a 1031 exchange. His relinquished property was a rental house, which has already been sold. The escrow for the relinquished property closed a little more than three months (approximately 105 days) ago on December 31. It is now the second week of April and Hal has properly identified three potential replacement properties. He has decided on one of the three properties and is on schedule to close at the end of April, well within the 180-day requirement. Hal has always been diligent about filing his taxes on time and, true to form, files them on April 15. At the end of April, on the 115th day of the exchange period, Hal closes on his replacement property. Two years later, Hal receives a letter from the IRS disallowing his exchange for not receiving the replacement property within the statutory exchange period.

In the example above, Hal was his own worst enemy. He focused on the "within 180 days" language of the requirement but failed to follow the secondary language: "or [by] the due date (with extensions) for the transferor's tax returns. . . ." Hal cut his own exchange period short by filing his income tax return on time.

What Hal did is a potential problem faced by every exchanger who closes the sale of a relinquished property during the late months of the calendar year. If Hal had been aware of the situation, he could have sidestepped the problem by simply filing an extension for his income tax returns and waited to file until after the replacement property had been received. The tax code specifically allows you to file an extension of your tax return so the 180-day requirement won't be cut short, but once again you have to be aware of the potential problem to know to fix it. Almost all qualified intermediaries have you sign a form that is intended to alert you to this situation. Unfortunately, it is sometimes buried in the stack of paperwork that comes to you in the sale and exchange process and may go unnoticed.

Partnership Capital Gain Allocation Problems

Certain special and fairly complex issues have to be taken into consideration when a dissolving partnership is engaged in a 1031 exchange or is buying out one of the partners. If you are the exiting partner and intend to make an exchange on your ownership percentage of the partnership property into a solely owned replacement property, you need expert advice. Whole-day seminars for lawyers and accountants are given on this subject alone. What may seem like a straightforward, commonsense approach could have unintended and undesirable accounting results. If you are in this situation, get expert advice before taking any action.

EXCHANGES BETWEEN RELATED PARTIES

Special rules apply and special issues arise when a 1031 exchange is made between related parties. This is how the IRS defines related parties:

> you and a member of your family (spouse, brother, sister, parent, child, etc.), you and a corporation in which you have more than 50 percent ownership, you and a partnership in which you directly or indirectly own more than a 50 percent interest of the capital or profits, and two partnerships in which you directly or indirectly own more than 50 percent of the capital interests or profits.

Basically, the rule is that if either person resells or otherwise disposes of the exchanged property within two years, the exchange will be disallowed and the tax on the original exchange must be recognized as of the date of the *later* disposition.

If you are contemplating an exchange with a related party, be sure to consult your tax advisor and keep in mind the general rule requiring a two-year *after-exchange* holding period.

REVERSE EXCHANGES

In a typical deferred exchange, the taxpayer, conforming to the requirements of the code, sells and transfers the relinquished property first and then goes about the process of identifying and acquiring the replacement property. In a reverse exchange, the replacement property is acquired *before* the relinquished property is sold. At first, this sounds simple enough, but in practice reverse exchanges are considerably more sophisticated and complex. Nevertheless, in the right situation a reverse exchange is a viable exchange method and offers unique opportunities.

> **Example:** Carl, in the process of selling an apartment building, has accepted an offer that calls for a 90-day escrow closing period. His intention for making the exchange is to buy a significantly larger apartment building, and he has had his eye on one property in particular. Carl just received a phone call from his real estate agent informing him that the price on the property he wants to buy is about to be reduced significantly. It seems the seller of that property has to sell it quickly and close in the next 60 days (by year-end) to take advantage of some offsetting capital losses in that calendar year. Carl knows that if the price on the property he wants is reduced, the property will sell. Carl wants to buy it so he approaches the buyer of his property in an attempt to get the closing on his property moved up. Unfortunately, the buyer of Carl's property is not able to close sooner than the 90 days.

This situation is perfect for a reverse exchange. Presuming Carl can arrange the financing and be able to close on the replacement property, he can structure the purchase of the new property and have it qualify as the replacement property in his exchange even though he will have to close on it prior to the closing on the relinquished property.

Reverse Exchange Opportunities

Although the preceding section had only one example of an appropriate situation for a reverse exchange, many others exist. Some of the other common reasons for a reverse exchange include:

- *Concern about finding the right property.* Many times a property owner is interested in an exchange but is not confident a desirable property can be found within the 45-day and 180-day time requirements. A reverse exchange allows that person to find the "perfect" property and arrange for its purchase before placing the relinquished property on the market.

- *Picking up a "great deal" on distressed property.* Sometimes taxpayers have no intention of selling a property they already have, but an irresistible opportunity presents itself. Maybe it's a great price on a foreclosure property, a divorce situation, or a bankruptcy liquidation. Good deals never last long, and a successful buyer usually has to close very quickly. The reverse exchange can be the perfect tool when trading into an unforeseeable opportunity.

- *The sale on the relinquished property falls apart.* Any real estate agent can tell you that not all property sales close. So if you have already found your perfect replacement property and the escrow on your relinquished property falls apart, you can use a reverse exchange to complete your acquisition while seeking another buyer for your relinquished property.

- *The desire for construction of a customized, or build-to-suit, property.* In some cases, reverse exchanges can be the best approach when a taxpayer wants to exchange into a different property, but the proposed replacement property has not yet been built. Build-to-suit exchanges, whether normal or reverse, can be risky because of the potential for construction delays. If a reverse exchange is used in a build-to-suit situation and the project exceeds the time requirements, the reverse exchange may no longer work, but the yet unsold "relinquished property" can be retained and the capital gain tax liability never triggered. Build-to-suit exchanges are tricky; see your tax attorney or accountant.

Legal Status and Costs Involved

Historically, reverse exchanges met significant resistance from the IRS and, in fact, have never been authorized under 1031 regulations. Before

2000, the most common way to make a reverse exchange was to arrange for a friendly party to buy and hold (warehouse) the desired replacement property. A taxpayer would then sell the relinquished property and complete the exchange by acquiring the replacement property from the friendly party. This type of arrangement was called "parking" the property and caused a great deal of anxiety for accountants and attorneys.

No real authority supported the concept of reverse exchanges prior to 2000, and most attorneys and qualified intermediaries avoided them. Without clear authority, advisors feared that the IRS would audit and attack the parking arrangements by disputing the acquired property as a valid replacement property, by disputing the relinquished property as qualified, or by attacking the friendly party titleholder as a sham or straw man owner having no true beneficial ownership of the property. The reverse exchange itself was thought to be a red flag that could potentially draw an audit or at least some extra scrutiny of the taxpayer's tax returns. And if any of the three attacks above succeeded in an actual audit, the exchange would be disallowed, triggering harsh tax consequences.

In September 2000, Revenue Procedure 2000-37 was published to address these parking arrangements and to specifically allow reverse exchanges under certain circumstances. It laid out a set of conditions that, if followed, created a safe harbor allowing taxpayers to arrange the acquisition of a replacement property prior to selling the relinquished property. Specifically, Revenue Procedure 2000-37 contained this stated purpose:

> This revenue procedure provides a safe harbor under which the Internal Revenue Service will not challenge (a) the qualification of property as either "replacement property" or "relinquished property" (as defined in section 1.1031(k)-1(a) of the Income Tax Regulations) for purposes of section 1031 of the Internal Revenue Code and the regulations thereunder or (b) the treatment of the "exchange accommodation titleholder" as the beneficial owner of such property for federal income tax purposes, if the property is held in a "qualified exchange accommodation arrangement."

Revenue Procedure 2000-37 put most reverse exchange advisors at ease and created the new terminology "exchange accommodation titleholder" (also referred to as an EAT or an AT) and "qualified exchange accommodation arrangement" (QEAA). Both these terms and their acronyms are in common use today. An exchange accommodation titleholder is usually just the qualified intermediary you select, and a qualified exchange accommodation arrangement is simply the written agreement between the taxpayer and the EAT setting out the requirements specified in Revenue Procedure 2000-37 (a copy of the relevant sections of the revenue ruling has been provided in the appendix). In summary, a QEAA must be in writing and must specify that the accommodation titleholder is holding the parked property for the benefit of the taxpayer in order to facilitate an exchange and that the AT will be the "beneficial owner" of the parked property for income tax purposes.

Interestingly, the revenue ruling allows the taxpayer five business days to enter into a QEAA *after* the accommodation titleholder acquires "qualified indicia of ownership" (which usually just means legal title) of the parked property. The QEAA relationship is allowed to exist for up to 180 days. Arguably, this extends the total time an AT can park a property from the 180 days of the QEAA to the 180 days plus the five business days provided for in the revenue ruling. It is unclear if the IRS actually intended this result.

Revenue Procedure 2000-37 also attempted to clear up some of the other issues that can arise in a QEAA by specifically listing "permissible agreements" between the accommodation titleholder and the taxpayer. The revenue ruling allows a QEAA to include provisions that allow the following:

- An accommodation titleholder to act concurrently as the qualified intermediary in the 1031 exchange

- The taxpayer to guarantee the obligations of the accommodation titleholder

- The taxpayer to loan or advance funds to the accommodation titleholder

- The taxpayer to rent or lease the property from the accommodation titleholder

- The taxpayer to manage the property or otherwise provide services on or related to the property

With the guidance and relative certainty of Revenue Procedure 2000-37, reverse exchanges, previously shunned by most professional qualified intermediaries, are now being embraced. The expenses associated with a reverse exchange are still much higher than with a traditional exchange, but the growing competition among professional intermediaries performing the services has significantly reduced the fees. At the time of this writing, in the Los Angeles area, where the cost of doing a traditional exchange is $500 to $700, the cost of a reverse exchange with a professional qualified intermediary costs about $5,000. That cost may seem high, but in the right situation it can be well worthwhile.

PRIMARY RESIDENCE ISSUES IN EXCHANGES

There are two 1031 exchange issues that seem to arise constantly. The first is whether an existing investment property can be converted to, or recharacterized as, a primary residence to qualify under the primary residence tax exemption. The second issue is whether a taxpayer can make an exchange from an investment property and purchase a replacement property that will be used immediately or in the future as a primary residence.

The two issues are closely related because they both require a recharacterization of investments. In the first case, the taxpayer is *directly* attempting to qualify investment profits for exempt treatment. In the second case, the taxpayer is *indirectly* attempting to exempt investment profits by using a 1031 exchange of an investment property to purchase a replacement primary residence. In either case, the taxpayer is looking for a tax loophole and in some situations may find one.

New Rules on Converting an Investment Property to a Primary Residence

The Taxpayer Relief Act of 1997 changed the way we are taxed on our primary residences. Before 1997, the tax code provided an 18-month capital gain rollover on a primary residence and a one-time $125,000 exemption for persons over 55 years of age. Both of those provisions were basically discarded in 1997 and a new exemption created. The new exemption allows everyone, regardless of age, a capital gains tax exemption up to $250,000 for an individual and $500,000 for a married couple on the sale of their primary residence. For the property to quality for the exemption, the taxpayer has to show that the property was used as the taxpayer's primary residence for two of the last five years. If the property qualifies, the first $250,000 of a capital gain for individuals or $500,000 for couples is absolutely tax free.

Understandably, this primary residence exemption is looked at longingly by real estate investors because it eliminates, not just defers, taxes on the sale of the asset up to the $250,000/$500,000 exclusion. As such, many investors owning rental homes or condominiums look for any possible way to convert, or recharacterize, rental property so that it qualifies for primary residence tax treatment.

Example: Sally and Bob own two single-family homes in the same neighborhood. They live in one of the homes, their primary residence, and rent the other. Both their rental house and their primary residence have been in their family for a long time. The rental house has been rented for over 20 years and has been fully depreciated. The adjusted basis on both properties is very low—about $20,000—and their current market values are about $350,000 for the rental house and $400,000 for their primary residence. Sally and Bob want to move out of state but are in no hurry and have decided to sell both properties, because they don't want to be long-distance landlords. After looking at the tax situation, Sally and Bob realize that if they sell the rental property outright, they will have to pay capital gains taxes on approximately $330,000 ($350,000 sales price less a $20,000 adjusted basis). Their tax person has estimated the capital gains and recapture of depreciation taxes due on the sale of the rental property at about $81,000. Bob and Sally decide to sell their primary residence first and move into their rental property for two years. By doing this, Sally and Bob intend to use their primary home exemption to shield them from taxes on the sale of their first home and then again two years later when they sell their newly qualified primary residence.

Presuming Bob and Sally have no objection to actually moving into, and residing at, the rental house for two years, they will be able to use the primary home exemption twice to shield themselves from all capital gains taxes. However, is the hold period two years or five years? It depends on how Bob and Sally acquired the property. Recent IRS rules say that if the investment property being converted to a primary residence was acquired in a 1031 exchange, then Bob and Sally would have to meet the ownership and use tests for a full five years before they would qualify for the exemption. This new rule has both a good and a bad side to it. First, the bad side is obviously the extended waiting period. However, the good side is that the rule actually validates a taxpayer's right to convert investment property into a primary residence.

The ability to convert a rental house into a primary residence can be well worth the two-year or five-year relocation, but another potential downside must be considered. Although a rental home converted to a primary residence will escape capital gains taxes to the extent of the primary residence exemption, it will not escape taxes due as a result of recapturing any depreciation taken on the property. This is one of those situations that presents an interesting dilemma. If the property is sold after waiting the necessary period, and the primary residence exemption applies, the Federal Paperwork Reduction Act passed by Congress says that the taxpayer is not to file any tax documents reporting the sale. If taxpayers are not allowed to report the sale under these circumstances, how are they going to tell the IRS there is a taxable recapture of depreciation?

Exchanging into a Future Primary Residence

Another common question that arises in 1031 exchange discussions is whether a taxpayer may exchange an investment property into a replacement property he or she intends to occupy as a primary residence in the future. If the question is stated exactly as it is here, the answer is clearly no. Remember, the Internal Revenue Code provides that for like-kind exchanges:

> No gain or loss shall be recognized on the exchange of property held for *productive use in a trade or business or for investment* if such property is exchanged solely for property of like kind which is to be held either for *productive use in a trade or business or for investment.*

Obviously, if the replacement property is intended as a primary residence, it will not fit the "productive use in a trade or business or for investment" requirement. Seemingly at odds with this is what was discussed in the previous section—that you are allowed to convert a property from investment property to primary residence and vice versa. So a rental house or condominium you owned would fit the "productive use in a trade or business or for investment." If you decided to move into that rental house or condominium as your primary residence, you could and no capital gains taxes would be triggered. So logically it follows that you should be able to make a 1031 exchange into a house or a condominium, rent it for a period, and then move in and make it your primary residence. Right? The answer is maybe. Whether the 1031 exchange is disallowed in an audit will depend on your *intention* at the time of the exchange.

Example: Pete has a triplex he has owned and managed for about 20 years. He has been showing the income and expenses as well as taking the depreciation each year on his taxes. Pete also has a home he has lived in for about 20 years. Both properties have appreciated significantly since he originally purchased them. Pete is planning to retire in about a year and wants to move to the small beach community of Seaside, where he has friends and family. Both Pete's house and his triplex have a fair market value of approximately $300,000. The adjusted basis on the triplex is approximately $50,000 and there is a mortgage on the property. Pete has calculated his taxes and knows that if he sells the triplex outright, he faces about $70,000 (state and federal) in capital gains taxes and recapture of depreciation. Prices of homes in Seaside are selling for about $320,000. Pete plans to avoid taxes by selling his triplex immediately and transacting a 1031 exchange for a home in Seaside that he intends to rent for the one-year period until his retirement. At retirement, Pete plans on selling his current home (avoiding taxes on that sale by using his $250,000 primary residence exemption) and then moving into the Seaside house.

Pete's exchange will be disallowed if audited and the IRS feels that Pete's "intent" at the time of the exchange was to use the replacement property as a future primary residence. Even though the replacement property was rented for one year, Pete's "intent" at the time of the exchange is the deciding factor in whether the exchange will be disallowed. How would the IRS know what Pete was intending? After all, it is unlikely that Pete is going to volunteer any information about his plans or intentions. In Pete's case, however, his intention was fairly easy to see. The biggest red flag was the relatively short time during which the Seaside property was rented and the timing of the exchange in relation to Pete's scheduled retirement. If the Seaside house were rented for a few years instead of just one, the exchange would probably never be scrutinized at all. But once an audit is started, the IRS will probably look at all of Pete's actions and conduct. Pete will have the burden of proving his intent was to use the house for business or hold it as an investment.

On the other hand, Pete could have made the 1031 exchange with the primary intention of simply moving the investment closer to the area where he planned to retire. As such, there would be no question that the exchange would be valid. And if, after the exchange was completed, an unforeseeable change in Pete's circumstances occurred and Pete *then* decided to move into the rental house and recharacterize it as his primary residence, he could legally do so.

THE FUTURE OF 1031 EXCHANGES

A considerable amount of political rhetoric about eliminating capital gains taxes has been floating around. That possibility seems remote when you consider the IRS's appointed task of taxing increases in wealth. A capital gain is, of course, an increase in wealth, but, nevertheless, the entire qualified intermediary industry would probably collapse if capital gains taxes were abolished. Arguably, 1031 exchanges might still be used even if capital gains taxes were abolished because recapture of depreciation on the sale of a property would still be taxed. Realistically, though, capital gains taxes are probably going to exist in one form or another into the foreseeable future and for that reason so are 1031 exchanges.

FREQUENTLY ASKED QUESTIONS

Q. *Can I transact a 1031 exchange on only the capital gain portion of the sale price and take out my original investment money?*

A. *No. The concept of a 1031 exchange is based on trading one property for another like-kind property. Any money taken out during the exchange is the equivalent of receiving non–like-kind property (boot) and would be taxable. However, see Chapter 11 for information about combining an exchange with an installment sale as a possible alternative.*

Q. *I have been told that one of the requirements of doing a tax-free exchange is that I must buy a higher-priced replacement property. Does that mean I cannot exchange into a smaller or less expensive property?*

A. *No. You are able to use a 1031 exchange to defer the gain on a portion of your sale price. So if you buy a less expensive property, you will have to pay taxes on the net difference (boot) or else structure the sale as part 1031 exchange and part installment sale (see Chapter 11). You also have the ability to buy more than one smaller property as long as the total replacement property value is equal to or higher than the relinquished property value.*

Q. *I just sold an investment property and my accountant has told me how much I am going to have to pay in taxes. Can I still do a 1031 exchange and buy another property instead of paying the taxes?*

A. *Only if the transaction has not closed. Once the transfer deed is recorded and you have either actual or constructive receipt of the proceeds from the sale, it is technically too late to do a 1031 exchange. If the property is still in escrow, however, you are not too late. It is possible to find a qualified intermediary to handle the exchange agreement very quickly.*

Q. *One of my children wants to buy my investment property. Can I sell it to her and make an exchange into another investment property?*

A. *Yes, but special rules apply when exchanging with related parties. The most important of these rules is a required two-year holding period. If the property is resold before that time, the exchange will be disallowed.*

Q. *What is the difference between 1031 exchanges, Starker exchanges, tax-free exchanges, and deferred exchanges?*

A. *Usually no difference. Although these terms actually had different meanings at one time (and still do to lawyers), the real estate industry and most property investors typically use them interchangeably. Technically speaking, 1031 refers to the tax code section allowing exchanges; Starker was the name of a court case that reshaped the way exchanges could be executed; tax-free refers to the fact that no taxes are triggered in the exchange process; and deferred refers to nonsimultaneous closings or deferred taxes depending on whom you ask.*

Q. *Can I exchange a single-family house for an apartment or office building?*

A. *Yes. As long as you meet all the other requirements, all real estate is considered like-kind for exchange purposes. Any domestic property used for business or held for investment purposes meets the requirements. So land to rental house, apartment building to land, or industrial to residential would all be okay.*

Q. *I have a triplex and live in one of the units; can I still do an exchange?*

A. *Yes. For tax purposes, you divide up the property with a certain percentage allocated as your residence and the remainder as rental property. You will be able to do an exchange of the portion that was used as rental property as long as you meet the other 1031 exchange requirements. You will also be able to shield yourself from taxes on the residence portion by claiming your primary residence exclusion up to $250,000 or $500,000 for married couples.*

Q. *Can my accountant or my real estate agent act as my accommodator?*

A. *No. Although the tax code does not specify any requirements for who can be a qualified intermediary, it does specify who cannot by listing "disqualified persons." Your accommodator must be a nonrelated party who normally cannot be an agent, your CPA, or a business associate. Attorneys you retain specifically to advise you on exchange matters can be your accommodator, but attorneys with whom you have other nonexchange dealings cannot.*

9

Tenant-in-Common Exchanges

INTRODUCTION TO TENENT-IN-COMMON OR TRIPLE-NET OFFERINGS

Since the beginning of property exchanges, investors have looked for a way to exchange into properties that involve little or no management activity on their part. The perfect solution was to buy a replacement property that was occupied by a long-term "triple-net" tenant. The term *triple net* basically means that the tenants are responsible for all the expenses (including insurance and taxes), as well as doing all the repairs on the property. This may seem strange to you if you own residential property, but it is common in commercial landlord-tenant situations (large retail or restaurant tenants in a mall would be a good example). Obviously, whenever possible, triple-net leases would be the preferred landlord-tenant arrangement. Unfortunately, triple-net situations are generally only workable in fairly large properties that are usually too expensive for most individual investors. Enter the concept of fractional ownership.

At one time, there were a lot of promoters suggesting that a taxpayer could sell a relinquished property and exchange into an interest in a real estate investment trust (REIT) or a partnership specifically designed to own and operate real estate. At the time, these promoters argued that, regardless of the entity type, the taxpayer was exchanging from one real estate investment to another real estate investment and therefore it was an exchange of like-kind property. The IRS did not agree. At this time, it is clear that the IRS's position is that an exchange of real estate for an interest in a REIT or a real estate partnership does not qualify as an exchange of like-kind property. However, that is not the end of the line.

As alternatives to the REIT or real estate partnership structure, some promoters started packaging their triple-net properties into smaller "undivided fractional interests" and selling those interests as replacement property in 1031 exchanges. These undivided fractional interests are commonly marketed as tenant-in-common (TIC) or triple-net (NNN) interests. Generally, the tenant-in-common offerings are made on properties that are already occupied by long-term triple-net corporate or government tenants. Occasionally, however, there are offerings on newly built or planned developments.

> **Example:** Carla has owned an eight-unit apartment building for about 25 years. She has managed the property herself during that time and does not like the idea of having a management company manage it for her. She does however want to retire and spend more time traveling. The building has a small mortgage and is almost fully depreciated. Carla knows if she sells the building outright she will have to pay capital gains tax as well as tax on the recapture of the depreciation she has taken over the years. Carla's main goal is to have a dependable stream of income without any management headaches to keep her from traveling. Carla has done her homework and has decided to do a 1031 exchange into a fractional ownership of large tenant-in-common commercial property. By doing so, she is able to defer her taxes and create steady stream of income for her retirement.

As indicated in this example, the way these tenant-in-common offerings work is that the exchanger buys into a fractional portion of the property and becomes one of a group of owners. The appeal is that the real estate investor can achieve the desired workload reduction and eliminate management headaches by becoming a co-owner of a large property, which is then professionally operated by a management firm (usually owned by the promoter). By doing this type of exchange, the taxpayer ends up with a more equity-like stream of income based on the scheduled performance of the rental activities of the larger investment property.

Many landlords approaching retirement find this concept very appealing and there is no shortage of companies offering these arrangements. Traditionally, however, the problem has been that these offerings sound a lot like prohibited REIT or real estate partnership interests so they tend to make advisors leery. Adding to the problem, the IRS had resisted providing any supporting documentation or guidance as to whether these undivided fractional interests will qualify as like-kind property under the provisions of IRC §1031.

REVENUE PROCEDURE 2002-22

Some of the anxiety surrounding tenant-in-common offerings was relieved in October of 2002 when the IRS released Revenue Procedure 2002-22, which contained information related to tenant-in-common interests. This revenue procedure does not provide a simple yes or no answer on whether tenant-in-common arrangements qualify as like-kind property. Instead, it contains guidelines that must be met before the IRS will provide an advance ruling on particular tenant-in-common structure. Nevertheless, Revenue Procedure 2002-22 has been quietly celebrated as an implicit approval of the prepackaged tenant-in-common programs.

Here is a summary if the 15 conditions set out in Revenue Procedure 2002-22 that must be satisfied before the IRS will provide an advance ruling:

1.   *Tenancy-in-common ownership.* Each of the co-owners must hold title to the property (either directly or through a disregarded entity) as a tenant in common under local law.

2.   *Number of co-owners.* The number of co-owners must be limited to no more than 35 persons.

3.   *No treatment of co-ownership as an entity.* The co-ownership may not file a partnership or corporate tax return nor hold itself out as a form of business entity.

4.   *Co-ownership agreement.* The co-owners may enter into a limited co-ownership agreement that may run with the land.

5.   *Voting.* The co-owners must retain the right to approve the hiring of any manager, the sale or other disposition of the property, any leases of a portion or all of the property, or the creation or modification of a blanket lien.

6.   *Restrictions on alienation.* In general, each co-owner must have the rights to transfer, partition, and encumber the co-owner's

undivided interest in the property without the agreement or approval of any person.

7. *Sharing proceeds and liabilities upon sale of property.* If the property is sold, any debt secured by a blanket lien must be satisfied and the remaining sales proceeds must be distributed to the co-owners.

8. *Proportionate sharing of profits and losses.* Each co-owner must share in all revenues generated by the property and all costs associated with the property in proportion to the co-owner's undivided interest in the property.

9. *Proportionate sharing of debt.* The co-owners must share in any indebtedness secured by a blanket lien in proportion to their undivided interests.

10. *Options.* A co-owner may issue an option to purchase the co-owner's undivided interest.

11. *No business activities.* The co-owners' activities must be limited to those customarily performed in connection with the maintenance and repair of rental real property (customary activities).

12. *Management and brokerage agreements.* The co-owners may enter into management agreements.

13. *Leasing agreements.* All leasing arrangements must be bona fide leases for federal tax purposes. Rents paid by a lessee must reflect the fair market value for the use of the property.

14. *Loan agreements.* The lender on the property may not be a related person to any co-owner, the sponsor, the manager, or any lessee of the property.

15. *Payments to sponsor.* Payment to the sponsor for the acquisition costs must be those ordinary and customary for an acquired co-ownership interest.

The IRS has been very clear that meeting these 15 conditions does not approve the tenant-in-common structure, but rather qualifies it for an advance ruling on whether the structure will be approved. That said, the obvious *implication* is that structures meeting these guidelines will be okay.

This revenue procedure was expected and has given rise to a whole new approach to marketing tenant-in-common structures as having a "favorable advance ruling" or being "Revenue Procedure 2002-22 compliant." Although the new revenue procedure doesn't go as far as creating a true safe harbor, it does reduce the anxiety that existed from the complete lack of guidance that existed before it. The new guidelines are considered strong support that tenant-in-common arrangements are a valid approach for clients seeking to exchange their current property into a more management-free position that provides a steady stream of income.

HOW TIC PROPERTY INVESTMENTS ARE STRUCTURED

Conceptually, the way TIC property offerings work is fairly easy to understand. The sponsor acquires a large property, puts together the best possible long-term triple-net lease arrangement, divides the property into smaller fractional interests (undivided fractional interests or UFIs), and then sells the UFIs. The exact structure, risk, and return on each of the TIC offerings vary depending on how well the sponsor does his or her job. Ideally, the sponsor is able to put together a package that contains a long-term lease with built-in rate increases that will cover the expenses of operating the property, service the mortgage debt, and pay the investors a more predictable return. Most TIC offerings provide the investor an increasing stream of income based on projected or scheduled tenant lease payment increases.

HOW A 1031-TO-TIC EXCHANGE WORKS

The process is basically the same as the traditional 1031 exchange:

1. You list your property for sale with your chosen real estate agent making sure he or she understands that you intend to do a 1031 exchange for another property.

2. When you get an offer, your agent will include a counteroffer provision that states the "buyer agrees to cooperate with seller's 1031 exchange."

3. You open escrow, and then choose your accommodator (your real estate agent or escrow/title agent can give you names of companies in your area).

4. You sign an exchange agreement with your accommodator through escrow along with the other customary escrow paperwork.

5. On the close of escrow, your proceeds will be transferred to your accommodator's trust fund on your behalf and held there until you begin the process of buying your replacement property.

After selling your relinquished property and documenting the exchange process with your chosen accommodator, you would complete the following steps:

1. You identify three potential tenant-in-common replacement properties within the 45-day identification period. You choose three in case the first one you have in mind doesn't work out for whatever reason. (More on this in the next section.)

2. You execute the TIC intent to purchase agreement and do your due diligence investigation of the offering.

3. Once you are satisfied with your investigation of the sponsor and the offering, you instruct your accommodator to complete the transaction.

4. Your accommodator transfers your exchange funds to the sponsor in exchange for the deed to your TIC replacement property.

SELECTING THE RIGHT
TENANT-IN-COMMON PROPERTY

There is no shortage of sponsors or TIC offerings across the country. Remember, you won't be a managing owner any more, so as long as it is a solid property, it shouldn't matter where it is located. In fact, you will find that properties offered will be located all over the country. The standard operating procedure is that sponsors will have their own in-house sales representatives with whom they would prefer you work. That's both good and bad. The good part is that in-house sales representatives are usually (but not always) very knowledgeable about the properties being offered by that particular sponsor. The bad part is you will only have that one sponsor's packaged properties from which to choose. You do, however, have another choice.

In the TIC exchange industry, there are TIC sponsors and then there are TIC advisors/brokers. Sponsors put together properties and then must sell their offerings to the public. The advisors/brokers, on the other hand, make it their job to compare and know which sponsors are the most reputable and which property offerings represent the best investment choices. Obviously, common sense should tell you to work with an advisor/broker rather than being locked in with any one specific TIC sponsor. The best part is you pay nothing for the services of your advisor/broker. All the reputable TIC sponsors offer compensation to outside advisors/brokers, and it doesn't raise your cost of buying into the property. The cost of compensating outside advisor/brokers is built into the overall project at the planning stage. Now, with that said, you are going to hear arguments from sponsors or in-house salespeople about them not cooperating with outside advisors/ brokers because they want to "keep the costs down," or because it's a "private" offering, or some other nonsense. Presumably, the sponsor's salespeople get paid a commission, so it's not going to change the costs involved. Likewise, a reputable sponsor is always looking for more investors so why would they keep the offerings "private." Besides, how "private" can the offering be if they are trying to sell it to you or me? The bottom line usually is that sponsors who won't cooperate with outside advisors/brokers know that their offering won't measure up when compared to other offerings in the market. My suggestion is, if a particular TIC sponsor discourages you from having your own advisor, walk away from that sponsor.

You can find TIC advisors/brokers on the Internet by simply doing a search for "tenant-in-common advisor." However, the TIC advisor/broker I recommend to clients is Ed Dowd. You can find Ed Dowd's contact information in Chapter 15 under the heading "Recommended Advisors."

Installment Sales

An installment sale is one in which a seller of a property agrees to accept payments on the purchase of the property. Installment sales are sometimes the perfect way to sell real estate property when the seller's goal is to defer the capital gains taxes and create a stream of income. Installment sales on real estate are a well-recognized and commonly used tax-deferral technique. The IRS allows the seller of an appreciated property to provide financing for the buyer and defer the payment of the capital gain and recapture of depreciation until the future payments are actually received.

The IRS defines an installment sale very broadly as the "sale of property where the seller receives at least one payment after the tax year of the sale." The buyer's obligation to make future payments is usually documented in a separate financing agreement. These financing agreements are commonly (and sometimes incorrectly) referred to as a mortgage, a debt contract, or simply a note. There are different types of financing agreements and different legal requirements on debts secured by property, depending on where the property is located. For example, in California, mortgages are not commonly used; instead, property financing is done through a note and deed of trust. Nevertheless, the common terminology in California is to call property financing a "mortgage." Through the rest of the chapter, I use the terms *mortgage* and *note* interchangeably.

A taxpayer using an installment sale when selling a property may

- defer the capital gains taxes on the sale until the installment payments are received;

- defer the tax liability on the recapture of depreciation until the installment payments are received (in most cases);

- create a stream of income from the sale of the property; and

- convert unproductive property into an interest-earning investment.

TERMS—HOW TO "TALK THE TALK"

If you have ever listened to a mortgage broker describe the different loan products available, you have probably wondered what language the broker was speaking. The lending world is full of acronyms, abbreviations, and terms of art that can be completely confusing to someone outside the industry. Many commonly used mortgage terms can be found in this book's glossary, but for understanding this chapter, you need to at least understand the following terms:

- *Loan-to-value ratio (LTV).* A measure of the amount of total financing in relation to the fair market value or sales price of a property. A $160,000 loan on a $200,000 property has an 80 percent LTV.

- *Adjustable-rate mortgage (ARM).* A mortgage with an interest rate that changes based on changes in an indicator such as Treasury bills or the prime rate. An ARM is a good way to make sure that the amount you finance stays attractive to the buyer and still pays a reasonable return. For example, an "ARM at two points over prime" would mean an adjustable rate mortgage with interest at whatever the prime rate is plus two (if the prime rate is 5 percent, the interest on the note would be 7 percent). If you decide to do this, get help because the adjustments and calculations can be problematic.

- *Stepped-rate mortgage.* A mortgage that has an increasing (or decreasing) interest rate over time.

- *Interest-only note.* A note that provides for monthly payments consisting of only the interest on the principal. Usually this is done to lower the buyer's payments for a certain period to simplify the calculations for the seller on small notes. However, capital gains taxes are fully deferred on interest-only notes because the monthly payments contain no portion of principal.

- *Due-on-transfer clause.* A clause within a mortgage agreement or trust deed that requires the buyer to pay off a note if the property is resold or transferred. This is commonly referred to as a "due-on-sale" or "acceleration" clause.

- *Prepayment penalty.* A clause in a note that requires the borrower to pay a monetary penalty if the note is paid off before a certain amount of time. Each state has its own laws restricting the use of prepayment penalties. In California, for example, on certain residential property the prepayment penalty period cannot exceed five years and the monetary penalty cannot exceed an amount equal to six months of interest on the prepaid amount of principal. The legal rules affecting prepayment penalties may differ between residential and investment property.

- *Assumption clause.* A clause within a note that details the conditions under which another person may assume the note. In some cases, the lender may not want the note to be assumable at all, in which case the note must be paid in full if the property is sold (if there is a due-on-transfer clause). In other cases, the seller may want to continue the deferment of his or her capital gains taxes and the income stream provided by the note. The best approach may be to include a clause in the agreement that the note is assumable but only with the note holder's approval.

- *Tax service.* A fee usually paid by the buyer-borrower that provides a service notifying the seller-lender if the buyer falls behind in his or her payment of property taxes.

- *Loan service.* Refers to the service banks and other financial institutions, for a fee, provide a mortgage by, for example, collecting the payments, handling the accounting, and interacting with the buyer-borrower on the seller's behalf.

- *Balloon payment.* A payment larger than the regularly scheduled monthly payments and that can be included in a note either for reducing some portion of the principal or for a required early payoff of the whole note (see following).

- *30 due in 7.* Most mortgages are amortized over 30 years, which means the payments are calculated to pay the accumulated interest each month and gradually pay off the principal due over the amortization period. In many cases, however, the seller-lender doesn't want to carry the loan for the full 30 years, but simply shortening the period (and amortization) usually makes the payments undesirably high for the buyer-borrower. To solve that difficulty, most seller-lenders use the 30-year amortization schedule but require a balloon payment in the amount of the outstanding principal at some time sooner. For example, a "30 due in 10" would indicate that a note has monthly payments based on the 30-year amortization schedule, but a balloon payment is due in ten years and would fully pay off the loan. Likewise, a "20 due in 5" would be a note amortized over 20 years but due to be fully paid off in five years by a balloon payment. Any amortization schedule can be used, but the usual and customary method in seller financing is to amortize the note over 30 years and set the due date for 5, 7, or 10 years. These terms are completely negotiable between the buyer and seller.

HOW INSTALLMENT SALES WORK

The concept of an installment sale is fairly simple: the seller of a property offers to provide the financing for the buyer by agreeing to accept a series of scheduled payments. This is sometimes referred to as a "seller carryback," an "owner will carry" situation, or just plain "seller financing." In most cases, the market reacts favorably to seller financing because many traditional buyer costs involved in getting a commercial loan (appraisal fees, processing fees, points, etc.) are avoided. There is little difference in the sale process except in the negotiating. In addition to negotiating the ultimate sale price, the buyer and seller have to also agree to terms and conditions of the financing, but once they have agreed on the price and financing terms, the transaction proceeds like any other. Depending on your area of the country, you will have either an escrow company or closing agent facilitate the transaction and draft the note for you according to the purchase agreement. Some people prefer to have an experienced attorney draft the financing agreement (the note) to make sure it is drafted correctly and provides the seller any advantages available under lending laws. Even if the note is simple and is drafted by the escrow or closing agent, it is probably a good idea to have a real estate attorney review it before the transaction closes.

ADVANTAGES OF INSTALLMENT SALES

Like every other method of deferring capital gains, installment sales have their advantages and disadvantages. One of the big advantages of installment sales—and perhaps the main reason they are so widely used—is that they are easily understood. You don't have to be an attorney or an accountant to understand the pros and cons of an installment sale, although you should discuss with your tax advisor exactly how a proposed installment sale will impact you from an accounting standpoint. Let's first look at the main advantages of installment sales before exploring the disadvantages.

Tax Deferral

The main advantage, of course, is the ability to defer capital gains and recapture depreciation (straight line) for a certain period. How long you can defer capital gains taxes is basically up to your own creativity. Capital gains taxes are due only on that portion of the payments received that represent repayment of principal on the note. An interest-only note for ten years could effectively defer all capital gains taxes (on the note portion of the sale) for a full ten years. Taken to an extreme, a 30-year carryback that is set for interest-only payments would mean 30 years of tax deferral.

Stream of Income

Many times the monthly payments from a note on the sale of a property will actually be higher than the net profit of operating the property. Obviously, the less productive the property (vacant land, for example), the more attractive trading it for a stream of income from a mortgage note. Installment sales on real estate have become widely used as a hedge against the ups and downs of other investments like stocks and mutual funds. The ability to control the interest and, to some extent, the amount of risk is appealing to persons looking for a long-term stream of income.

Investment Leverage

The rate of return on an installment sale note is hard to beat when you consider the leverage provided by the capital gain portion of the note. In the simplest terms, a capital gain tax-deferred dollar earns approximately 20 to 30 percent more interest than the after-tax dollar. Why? On tax-deferred dollars you earn interest on both your dollars and the dollars that would have gone to the government for taxes. Figure 10.1 shows the difference in deferred proceeds invested at an 8 percent rate of return and an after-tax investment at the same rate.

FIGURE 10.1   Installment Sale Investment Advantage

	After-Tax Investment	Installment Sale
Sale amount	$120,000	$120,000
Adjusted basis	20,000	20,000
Capital gain	100,000	100,000
Net proceeds	120,000	120,000
Taxes (state & federal)	30,000	0
Amount invested	90,000	120,000
Yearly income at 8 percent	7,200	9,600
Net advantage	0	$2,400

This example is overly simple, excluding expenses and down payments and generalizing the tax impact. Nevertheless, it makes the point that installment sales that include a deferred capital gains component enhance the return on investment.

Marketability and Desirability of the Property

In the open real estate market, seller financing is almost always preferred by buyers. Lower costs and less administrative hassle are among the main reasons. Most commercial mortgages have a processing time of 45 to 90 days, and the costs involved include appraisal fees, processing fees, and, most important, discount points. A discount point is 1 percent of the loan amount. On a $200,000 loan, if the points are 1.5, the fee to the buyer for points alone is $3,000. When you add together all of the lender fees, loan-related title insurance fees, and processing fees, the cost of borrowing $200,000 can easily reach $4,000 to $8,000. In most cases, seller financing eliminates all of these buyer fees and expenses, so it's no wonder buyers prefer properties the seller will carry.

Another situation that favors seller financing is one in which properties have limited commercial financing available. For example, commercial financing is hard to find for mixed-use and nonconforming properties. Vacant land can also sometimes pose a problem because many banks won't make loans of more than 50 percent of the value of the land. In both of these cases, seller financing greatly enhances the marketability of the property and may offer the only realistic way of getting the property sold.

DISADVANTAGES AND RISKS OF INSTALLMENT SALES

Despite their advantages, however, installment sales are not for everyone. Likewise, some types of property and/or proposed property uses are not appropriate because the financing risks are simply too high. Taking the time to thoroughly think through the risks and how they would affect you in a worst-case scenario is always important.

Installment sales have one huge advantage over other types of investing: the note is secured by the underlying real estate. With that in mind, it is easy for some to shrug off the potential risks by thinking, "I'll just take the property back if they don't make the payments, right?" Yes . . . and no. The idea of being able to take the property back if the borrower defaults is correct, which is why the note is secured by the property. However, along with the risk of default, other concerns exist. In the following sections I explain some of the more common risk considerations associated with seller carryback and retaking property in case of a default.

Risk of Foreclosure

The mortgage lender on a property has the right to the underlying property in case of a default. Unfortunately, it's not as easy as it sounds because a host of laws specifically control lending practices and especially foreclosure practices. If a borrower stops making payments, the lender must follow the state-required legal formalities of filing notice, service of process, and publication. The rules themselves vary greatly by state and are beyond the scope of this book. Most banks and commercial lending institutions have entire departments to deal with the day-to-day issues of handling their foreclosures. Even smaller lending institutions have legal counsel on staff or on retainer to foreclose on properties if borrowers default.

Unfortunately, the concept of foreclosing on a property or even getting involved in this type of legal process intimidates many property sellers and prompts them to shy away from offering seller financing no matter how attractive the tax benefits. The reality, however, is that not only is the foreclosure process streamlined in most states but mortgage and trust deed service companies specialize in providing this service. Today, the process of foreclosing on a property is relatively quick and inexpensive. Of course, we hear of "nightmare" situations in which a borrower mounts an extensive legal battle, but such cases are rare. In the vast majority of cases, the property is back in the hands of the seller-lender in four to five months.

Risk of Early Payoff

Some people might consider a borrower paying off a debt early a benefit and not a risk. However, the motivation for a seller to offer seller financing is usually to defer taxes and establish a fixed return on the invested funds. So for the installment sale noteholder, early payoff is undesirable. There is virtually no legal way to stop people from paying off a mortgage early, but there are ways to strongly discourage them.

The most common way to discourage an early payoff is to include a *prepayment penalty* in the note itself. Prepayment penalties are discussed in more detail later, but it is important to note that certain types of residential properties have restrictions on the amount of a prepayment penalty that can be negotiated. On residential property, legally allowable prepayment penalties are controlled by state law and in most states cannot exceed five years for the prepayment period and cannot exceed six months of interest as the penalty (check with your state rules).

Even though a prepayment penalty may discourage an early payoff, it will not stop it in some situations. In certain cases, the profit opportunity for the new owner to resell the property simply outweighs the penalty. In the alternative, in other cases the need to refinance the property is more attractive than avoiding the penalty. In situations in which an equity line or second mortgage is needed on the property, there may be no alternative other than refinancing and paying off the seller's carryback. Commercial lending equity lines and/or second mortgages are generally not available in back of private mortgages. The term *in back of* refers to situations in which a private note would have a creditor priority over a commercial lender's note. In situations where a property improvement loan is desired, the borrower may be forced to refinance the whole property. The private mortgage noteholder usually has the option of subordinating to the (presumably) smaller equity line or property improvement loan, but the risk factor of holding the note changes and needs to be re-evaluated.

> **Example:** Mr. Jones sells a rental house to a young couple and carries back the whole mortgage to defer his capital gains taxes on the sale. One year later, the couple attempts to get a home equity loan. Although they qualify for the equity line, the bank won't grant the loan because the existing first mortgage is private-seller financing. The couple didn't want to refinance the whole property, and the seller didn't want the note paid off early. In this situation the seller-note-holder was comfortable with the couple's ability to repay both notes, so the note-holder agreed to subordinate to the equity loan. The money from the equity loan was specifically intended for improvements to the property, and when the improvements were completed, both loans combined were less than 80 percent of the new (improved) market value of the property.

In this example (an actual case) everyone emerged pleased—the couple was able to get the equity loan funds they wanted to remodel the house, and the private noteholder suffered no real loss of security because the funds were used to enhance the value of the noteholder's security. Had the private noteholder not agreed to subordinate to the equity loan, the couple would have had no choice but to refinance the property and pay off the private note. And by doing so, they would have triggered the capital gains tax for the noteholder.

The best way to discourage an early payoff of the note is to simply make sure the terms on the seller carryback note are more attractive than other available financing options. Common sense should tell you that if the private note has an 9 percent interest rate and the current market rate is 7.5 percent, the private noteholder should probably expect an early payoff. If you don't want to be paid off, stay flexible and competitive with your interest rate, and your willingness to subordinate when reasonable.

Risk of Property Deterioration

Perhaps the highest risk associated with an installment sale is the possibility that the new owner will let the property fall into serious disrepair. In such a case, the risk of having to foreclose on the property increases, *and* at the same time the value of the security itself declines.

The thought of foreclosing on a property that needs tens of thousands of dollars in repairs is not comforting. To avoid this situation, it may be smart to make sure the person buying the property is capable of managing it. Sometimes it is smart to find out if the proposed borrower has other similar property and, if so, drive by those other properties to see how well they are maintained. How a person maintains a property he or she already owns is probably a strong indication of how well the person will maintain your property.

Some of the more sophisticated commercial lenders go so far as to contractually give themselves the right to inspect the property. They inspect periodically and require repairs if there is any unreasonable deferred maintenance. If the borrower then fails to make the required repairs, the acceleration clause of the note is triggered and the entire principal is due immediately. If the borrower then fails to pay off the note, the note goes into default and the lender can foreclose immediately. In the alternative, the lender could bring legal action to compel the borrower to make repairs and hold the borrower responsible for the legal fees.

A Mortgage Higher Than the Adjusted Basis

When a potential installment sale seller has an existing mortgage on the property that is higher than his or her adjusted basis, a special IRS rule comes into play. The IRS generally treats the excess of the mortgage over the adjusted basis as 100 percent taxable when the seller is relieved of this debt in the year of sale. Under IRS rules, the seller is usually relieved of this debt when the debt is repaid, when the debt is assumed, or when the property is taken "subject to" that existing mortgage. As a result, you can actually have capital gains tax liability in the year of sale even though you may not have received any cash. For example, assume that a taxpayer's basis is $175,000 and there is a loan against the property of $200,000 that the buyer is going to assume. The difference of $25,000 is taxable to the seller in the year of sale.

Lack of Liquidity

Another consideration that is usually overlooked in agreeing to an installment sale is the lack of liquidity on the note, the flip side of the early payoff concern. In most situations, investors try to pin down the borrower to prevent an early payoff of the note that would in turn trigger liability for the deferred taxes. However, what if the seller-turned-noteholder encounters a situation in which he or she needs to cash out?

The note itself will, of course, lock the noteholder into the periods agreed to in the terms of the note. In a case in which the noteholder really does have to cash out, attractive options are few.

A resale market for mortgage notes does exist. The market itself has little or no formal structure; rather, it is simply private parties who purchase private notes. Mortgage brokers in your area would likely be able to point you in the right direction, but you probably won't like what you find. Buying private mortgage notes is typically considered a high-risk investment, so the people willing to take that risk want a significant discount from the face value of the note. Many variables are taken into consideration when valuing a note for resale, but a reasonably well-drafted and secured (second mortgage) note with a face value of $10,000 will usually have a resale value of only $5,000 to $8,000. Even a strong first mortgage with a good loan-to-value and an excellent borrower will have to be discounted if sold.

In most cases, however, the lack of liquidity is not a significant factor because the long-term, locked-in investment is exactly what the investor wants.

BALANCING THE RISK

You should consider three things when trying to balance the risks with the benefits of installment sales: (1) Decide on an acceptable loan-to-value ratio, (2) determine how long you are willing to carry the note, and (3) structure the terms and conditions of the note so that the foreseeable risks are addressed.

Deciding an Acceptable Loan-to-Value Ratio

As mentioned earlier, a loan-to-value ratio is the amount of financing in relation to the market value of the property; an $80,000 note on a $100,000 property is an 80 percent loan-to-value ratio; if you were going to carry back $10,000 and the buyer were going to get an $80,000 bank loan, the *total* loan-to-value ratio would be 90 percent. The loan-to-value ratio is important because it is traditionally the first risk criterion considered by commercial lending institutions. From a lender's perspective, all other things being equal, an 80 percent loan-to-value ratio mortgage is less risky than one with a 90 percent loan-to-value. Likewise, a 70 percent loan-to-value is better than an 80 percent, and so on. Lenders traditionally have what they consider a "preferred" loan-to-value ratio.

The next loan-to-value consideration is property type. Risks of mortgage default differ according to property type, so the customary practice in commercial lending is to assign varying loan-to-value requirements for each type of property. A commercial strip center would have a significantly different preferred loan-to-value than a residential duplex and a different one still from a 20-unit apartment building. Finding out what the preferred loan-to-value ratio is for your property type in your particular area is pretty simple; just ask your local lender, or perhaps your real estate agent may know.

The lending industry's preferred loan-to-value ratio on your property may be a good indicator of the acceptable risk to a commercial lender, but you aren't a commercial lender. Commercial lenders are traditionally much more conservative than sellers who offer financing. After all, banks really don't know much about a given property before they make a loan. Sure, they do an appraisal, but they're not in the property business; they're in the money business. The last thing a bank wants is to foreclose on a property. On the other hand, a seller who is offering financing on his or her property does know the property and whether it is a solid basis for security on the note. Sellers who carry the notes on their properties generally don't want to foreclose on the property either but are usually not as afraid of that risk as a bank.

The other main difference between a commercial lender and a seller offering financing is that a seller is motivated by tax deferral. The interest earned on the tax-deferred portion of the principal greatly enhances the overall return on the mortgage investment. Many banks do offer loans in higher-than-customary loan-to-value ratios if they are able to get a better-than-usual return on the investment.

How much down payment you should require depends on the level of your personal comfort with the security and the person buying the property. Simply put, a higher down payment (lower loan-to-value ratio) is better for security, but a lower down payment (higher loan-to-value ratio) is better for tax deferment and investment return.

Determining How Long to Carry the Note

How long to carry a note is also a matter of your comfort level. Many sellers who offer financing are older, so they realize they may not be around to continue collecting on a note 20 or 30 years into the future. Even if they aren't, the note would pass to their heirs just as any other asset would. Nevertheless, most seller financing is set for less than the commercial lending standard of 30 years. Common terms, previously defined in this chapter, are "30 due in 5," "30 due in 7," or "30 due in 10." The "30" represents the amortization schedule followed and the "due-in-X" represents the number of years until the loan becomes due and payable. The example previously given, a 30-due-in-5, means that the borrower's monthly payment amount is based on the 30-year amortization schedule, and a balloon payment is due to pay off the loan in five years.

Why use a 30-year amortization schedule? First, from the buyer's perspective, business and profit planning on income property is usually based on 30-year amortized monthly mortgage payments. Using a shorter amortization period usually makes a property less profitable from an operating perspective and therefore less appealing. Second, from the seller's perspective, a 30-year amortization schedule monthly payment (in the beginning years) is almost all interest. As such, the seller-noteholder is able to maximize the capital gains tax deferral and the interest earned on the deferred portion.

The real question is how long you want the note to run before you want it paid in full. I have seen seller notes as short as 90 days and notes set for a full 30-year payment period with interest-only payments. In the case of the interest-only note, no capital gains taxes are assessed until the principal is paid. The payment period is up to you, but remember that as long as you are comfortable with the property as security for your note, very few investments perform as well as a mortgage note made from tax-deferred capital gains.

Drafting the Note to Protect Yourself

How the mortgage agreement is drafted is important in the overall security and performance of the note. It is crucial for the seller to have control over the note drafting and to use that control to incorporate well-thought-through terms and provisions. In this area, it may be smart to hire an attorney specifically experienced in real estate note drafting. Real estate agents and escrow personnel can draft a note for you, but it will be a neutral third-party generic document with basic provisions only. If you are going to offer the financing, you are in the driver's seat; why not have your note drafted to afford yourself a favorable position if things become difficult in the future. The following are some of the less obvious drafting provisions that should be considered:

- *Late fees.* When is a payment late and what is the penalty?

- *Attorney fees.* If a dispute arises, the prevailing party should be entitled to reimbursement of attorney fees.

- *Due-on-sale clause.* A provision that the note becomes due if the property is resold should almost always be included.

- *Due-on-transfer clause.* Because some people have gotten around a due-on-sale clause in notes by simply not selling the property but transferring it instead, a due-on-transfer clause acts to prohibit potentially undesirable transfers.

- *Due-on (further)-encumbrance clause.* A provision that requires the repayment of your note should the borrower further encumber the property and thus lessen your security. An alternative that accomplishes a similar objective would be a maximum loan-to-value ratio clause.

- *Tax service.* A service paid for by a borrower to notify the lender that the borrower has failed to keep property taxes current.

- *Insurance requirements.* You should require a borrower to maintain a minimum amount of property insurance and name you as a payee under the policy.

- *Assignment-of-rent provision.* A provision for a rental property that allows the lender to collect rents if the note goes into default.

- *Inspection and maintenance provision.* A provision allowing you to require reasonable maintenance of the property and giving you the right to inspect.

- *Prepayment penalties.* Because most states set the maximum allowable prepayment penalties on certain types of properties by law, you need to make sure you conform to what is allowed if you want to include a prepayment penalty.

- *Assumption clause.* Are you willing to allow the note to be assumed by a subsequent buyer? If so, under what conditions and terms?

This list is by no means complete, but it does show the many provisions that should be considered beyond the basic interest rate and time period. Not all of the provisions listed here have to be included in every note, but the better you protect yourself up front, the more likely your seller-financing will go smoothly.

STRUCTURING THE DEAL

The transactional mechanics are fairly straightforward, so a more important focus should be deciding the rate and terms.

Higher Down Payment or Lower Taxes

Common sense says that a seller or any other lender offering financing would want the best possible security for the loan. From a commercial lender's perspective, the best possible security means obtaining the highest down payment possible and providing financing at a low loan-to-value ratio. In seller financing, as noted earlier, however, a competing goal is deferring taxes. A high down payment does provide a better security position, but the down payment is taxed immediately because it is a payment received. The other extreme would be for the seller to offer 100 percent financing and thereby defer 100 percent of the taxes until the payments are received. In most situations, however, there are the expenses of selling the property—real estate commissions, title insurance, repairs, property tax proration, escrow fees—that must be paid.

If you are more interested in security than you are in deferring the taxes, then you may want to require the same amount of down payments that banks find commercially acceptable: 10 to 20 percent down on one to four residential units where the buyer will be occupying the property; 25 to 30 percent down on residential apartment buildings; and 30 to 40 percent down on commercial property.

On the other hand, if you are more interested in deferring the taxes and are reasonably comfortable with the buyer and the property, then you would want to minimize the down payment. In a normal and customary sale of a property, you can expect the selling expenses to be approximately 7 to 7.5 percent (based on 6 percent sales commission, title, and escrow fees). You would therefore need to get at least that amount as a down payment just to cover the expenses of the sale. However, keep in mind that there will be taxes due on the payment received for the down payment just as there will be on all the other payments received over time. That means you need to require a down payment of sufficient size to cover the costs of selling the property as well as the taxes that will become due on the down payment itself.

Interest Rate Considerations

Obviously, people want to maximize their own investment returns, but this is one area where more (interest) may actually cost you money. If you are doing an installment sale to defer taxes and create a stream of income, then you want to create a situation that discourages the buyer from refinancing or prepaying the loan. This comes down to simple economics: if the interest rate you charge is higher than that available from commercial lenders, the buyer will eventually refinance. A direct relationship is apparent here; the higher your rate, the sooner the buyer will refinance. With this in mind, seller financing is usually offered at an interest rate slightly better than prevailing commercial rates. How much better? Generally speaking, it's smart to set the rate at one-quarter to three-quarters of 1 percent less than the prevailing rate for the same type of property. And remember that interest rates vary depending on the property type and occupancy status. Residential property having one to four units, houses, condos, duplexes, triplexes, and the like usually fall into standard, or conforming, mortgage rates—that is, those that most people think of as regular mortgage rates. But mortgage rates on residential income properties are almost always higher and those on commercial properties higher still.

Deciding what interest rate you should charge requires a little homework on your part. Probably the easiest way to find out what is reasonable is to simply call a lender in your area and ask what rates would be available to you if you were to refinance the property yourself. If you're willing to accept a reasonable financing rate, you'll create a win-win situation and probably won't have to worry about your taxes being triggered by the buyer's refinancing and paying off your loan early.

Assumption, Acceleration, and Due-on-Transfer Clauses

A seller considering an installment sale has to think, act, and protect himself just like a commercial bank or other lending institution. That means you must be comfortable with the property as an underlying security for the loan, be comfortable with the borrower's ability to repay the loan, and contractually protect yourself from potential future problems. How a mortgage note is drafted is very important; get professional help if you have never done it before. If you are selling your property through a real estate agent, you or your agent will probably have to provide an "arranger of financing" disclosure form to the buyer-borrower. The form discusses many of the issues that arise and provides valuable guidance for dealing with the types of issues that should be addressed in the mortgage note itself.

One consideration that must be addressed in negotiating the financing contract is what happens if the property is subsequently sold or transferred. The commercial bank approach is to include a provision in each mortgage note that accelerates the due date if the property is subsequently sold or transferred. These contractual clauses are called "due on sale," "due on transfer," or "acceleration provisions." Whatever the provision is called, the purpose is to provide a contractual requirement that the outstanding balance of the note be paid off if the property is sold or transferred, the reasoning being that lenders don't want the loans freely assumable by just anyone. When the loan was originally made, the lender checked out the buyer's credit history and ability to repay the loan. Presumably the lender made the loan, in part, because it was comfortable with that particular borrower's ability to repay. However, if mortgages were freely assumable, the person assuming the note at a later time might not be as creditworthy as the original buyer-borrower. In commercial lending, a due-on-sale or due-on-transfer contractual provision usually works well.

In seller financing, on the other hand, there is the additional consideration of wanting to continue capital gains tax deferral. If the mortgage note contains a due-on-transfer provision and the property is subsequently sold, the note will be paid off and the liability for paying all the deferred capital gains taxes triggered. A middle ground, however, exists between leaving the note fully assumable and requiring the due-on-transfer requirement.

Adding a *qualified assumption provision* to a seller-financed mortgage note is usually a good idea. After all, the goal for the seller-lender is to obtain a return from the investment, but also to continue the deferment of capital gains taxes. So if the original buyer-borrower decides to sell the property and the next buyer-borrower is equally creditworthy, why not continue the loan and tax deferral? A qualified assumption should allow the buyer-borrower to offer the property for sale with "assumable financing" but still allow the seller full and sole discretion as to the acceptability and creditworthiness of the next potential buyer.

Basically, the idea behind a qualified assumption clause is to indicate that the noteholder would be willing to entertain assumption proposals, but is not obligated to allow the assumption. If the potential buyer is not acceptable or the noteholder is not willing to allow the assumption, the new buyer would have to arrange other financing, and the note would have to be paid off on the sale or transfer, as otherwise required in the due-on-transfer clause.

PREPAYMENT PENALTIES

If a seller is trying to defer capital gains taxes by providing seller financing, then it stands to reason that the seller won't want the loan paid off early. Unfortunately, laws prohibit the ability to contractually agree that the loan cannot be prepaid. Why? The laws were developed to help curtail unconscionable lending practices and unreasonable restraints on alienation. That's legalese for saying you can't make a loan that's too one-sided, and you can't impose unreasonable restrictions that prevent a person from selling his or her property. The point is that laws do exist to control or limit allowable prepayment penalties. The extent of these laws and how they could affect you depends on whether your property is categorized as consumer residential property or investment property.

Prepayment Penalties on Consumer Residential Properties

In determining allowable prepayment penalties, the first important factor is whether your note will be secured by residential property. Over the years, consumer protection statutes emerged to help curtail abusive lending tactics. Most of these laws are really targeted at predatory lenders, who have a history of taking advantage of consumers. Nevertheless, these consumer protection statutes have an impact on anyone offering financing on a property. They are found in almost every state and directly restrict prepayment penalties on notes of residential property if all three of the following conditions are true:

1. The property is made up of one to four residential units, which would include all homes, condominiums, duplexes, triplexes, and quadruplexes.

2. The property is owner occupied, which means that the property is being used as the buyer-debtor's *primary residence.*

3. The note represents *purchase money,* a term that means the note represents a portion of the total price paid for the property when originally purchased.

Generally, if all three of the conditions listed here apply, it's likely that statutory legal restrictions limit prepayment penalties. Each state has different laws; for example, at the time of this writing, California law limits prepayment penalties on residential and owner-occupied property obtained with purchase money notes to periods of not more than five years and limits the monetary penalty to an amount not more than six months' interest on the amount of prepaid principal. California law also allows the borrower to prepay up to 20 percent of the outstanding balance of the note in any given year without any penalty.

Some mortgages have built-in prepayment penalties that exceed the penalty period or monetary penalties limited by state law. In some cases, excessive prepayment penalties were simply drafting errors, but at other times they seem intentional, perhaps as a bluff to discourage uninformed debtors. Whatever the reason, a prepayment penalty greater than the amount allowed by statute is unenforceable.

Prepayment Penalties on Investment and Commercial Properties

The consumer protection statutes previously described are designed to do exactly what their name implies—protect *consumers*. Investors are usually considered more knowledgeable and therefore less in need of the type of protection afforded unsophisticated consumers. As a result, lending on investment property doesn't have the same statutory prepayment restrictions as lending on residential and owner-occupied property obtained with purchase money loans. There are still going to be certain legal restrictions on prepayment penalties, but investors have a lot more freedom to make contractual agreements.

For our purposes here, the simplest definition of an investment property is any property that is not residential and owner occupied. For example, you may carry the note on a single-family home, but so long as the buyer is not going to occupy it as a primary residence, it is considered investment property. Likewise, a *five-unit* residential property sold to someone who intends to live in it as his or her primary residence is still considered investment property because it does not fit the *one-unit to four-unit* criterion.

As for prepayment penalties, seller financing of investment property enjoys a significant advantage. The amount and term of the prepayment penalty can be just about whatever you can negotiate. You may still face some legal restrictions, but what is legally acceptable is much more helpful in deterring an early payoff. In fact, one California court ruled that a 50 percent prepayment penalty was not unreasonable when the seller carrying the mortgage faced significant tax consequences if the note were paid off early. Again, each state has a different view as to what is reasonable, so you have to check with a local real estate attorney.

Amazingly, most real estate advisors mistakenly apply the consumer protection prepayment penalty rules to investment property situations.
Make sure your advisor knows the difference.

Being able to negotiate a 10 to 15 percent prepayment penalty in a
note can make a huge difference in the desirability of an installment
sale option. How huge a difference?

> **Example:** Paul sold a triplex to Mike, an investor who didn't intend to
> occupy the property. The terms were that Mike would put down 20
> percent and Paul would carry a note for the 80 percent balance for 20
> years at 8 percent with interest-only payments. The principal of the
> note was initially $200,000, and Paul had a 50 percent gross profit ratio
> (meaning 50 percent of the note's face value represented a capital
> gain). Paul was willing to sell the property only if he could defer the
> taxes long term. Paul and Mike agreed to a 10 percent prepayment
> penalty if Mike paid off the note within the first ten years.

In this example, if Mike pays off the note in the first ten years, it
would trigger Paul's capital gains taxes. With a 50 percent gross profit
ratio on the note, Paul would be responsible for paying capital gains
taxes on $100,000. If we assume a straight 15 percent capital gains rate,
the taxes would be $15,000. However, Paul and Mike agreed to a pre-
payment penalty of 10 percent, so if the note is paid early, Mike will
have a penalty of $20,000 ($200,000 $\times$ 10 percent). In this case, the
penalty exceeds the amount of the taxes triggered. If Mike does pay off
the note early, Paul will lose the income that would have come from the
deferred capital gain but is compensated by having the penalty amount
available to pay his prematurely triggered taxes. In some situations, this
may be a very agreeable win-win scenario for both seller and buyer. The
buyer is not going to want to pay off the loan early unless some situation arises that makes it financially worthwhile, and the seller may not
want to lose his projected stream of income, but, if so, he is compensated by the penalty.

Prepayment penalties may discourage prepayment but can never
guarantee it. Depending on the situation, the sting of a prepayment
penalty can easily be outweighed by the economic benefit of selling or
refinancing the property. Aside from prepayment penalties, the best
way to prevent a borrower from refinancing is to make sure the terms
of your financing are equal to or better than those available in the open
market. Obviously, if you are charging 8 percent on a mortgage and the

borrower can get 7 percent from a commercial bank or lending institution, the borrower is going to be enticed to refinance and pay off your note. Likewise, if the market value of the property increases dramatically, the borrower may sell in spite of a prepayment penalty, but again a prepayment may be avoidable if the noteholder is willing to be competitive with the market and allow an assumption of the note.

HOW AND WHEN TAXES ARE PAID

Each year that you receive payments, you report them on your tax returns. The payments are broken down into three components:

1. Interest income

2. Return of your adjusted basis on the property

3. Gain on the sale

The "interest income" is treated and reported as you would any other source of interest income. The "return of your adjusted basis on the property" is not taxed at all because it represents the return of your dollars invested in the property. And the "gain on the sale" component is taxed at the capital gains and/or recapture of depreciation tax rate.

Example: Chuck has a rental house he wants to sell. He originally paid $50,000 for it and has never taken any depreciation. Chuck sells the property for $200,000 with the buyer paying $75,000 down. Chuck carries back (finances) the remaining $125,000, amortized over 30 years with interest at 7 percent; monthly payments are $831.63. During the first year the buyer makes six payments at $831.63 in addition to the $75,000 down. Chuck is able to defer some of the capital gains taxes on the property but will owe taxes on the payments received that year (including the down payment). Chuck will report the sale of the property on his 1040 for that taxable year along with any payments received on IRS form 6252.

In this example, the payments that Chuck received will be broken down into the three components by first calculating gross profit percentage and then figuring the interest paid. In this simple example, the gross profit percentage is calculated as follows:

Sales price	$200,000
Cost	– 50,000
Gross profit	$150,000

The gross profit percentage here is: $150,000 ÷ $200,000 = 75 percent, which means that 75 percent of every dollar of *principal* is profit and will be taxed at the capital gains or recapture of depreciation tax rate. That does *not* mean that 75 percent of every dollar of payments received, but rather 75 percent of that portion of the payments received that represent principal. Remember, a large portion of the monthly payments will be interest, not principal. The other 25 percent of every dollar of principal will be tax free, as it represents your return of dollars invested (cost). We arrive at the interest component by consulting a standard amortization table.

Thus, in the first year, Chuck received $75,000 down plus $4,989.78 (six payments of $831.63); $4,365.96 is interest and $623.82 principal. In this case, the down payment plus 75 percent of the principal is taxed as a capital gain; 25 percent of the principal is a tax-free return of capital; and $4,365.96 is taxable interest income.

Now, let's complicate matters slightly with a more realistic situation: a 6 percent commission and $1,000 escrow fee. The gross profit ratio would look like this:

Contract price	$200,000
Cost	– 50,000
Expenses	– 13,000
Gross profit	$137,000

The gross profit ratio: $137,000 ÷ $200,000 = 68.5 percent (see Figure 10.2, line 19). The seller pays tax on 68.5 percent of every principal payment received, even though all of the costs of the sale are paid in the first year. As before, in the first year the seller reports $75,000 down plus $624. principal (Figure 10.2, line 22) with 68.5 percent of this total ($51,802) representing taxable installment sale income (Figure 10.2, line 26). Eventually, the seller will get the full $200,000 of principal (before payment of selling expenses of $13,000), $137,000 that is taxable just as if he had made an outright sale.

It is possible that the tax due is more than the payments actually received by the seller in the year of the sale (as all payments go first to cover expenses of the sale). If the same property as in the previous example had been mortgaged for $35,000 and had closing costs of $13,000 with the buyer paying $50,000 down, the seller would net $2,000 at the close of escrow.

FIGURE 10.2 Installment Sales Income

Form **6252**	**Installment Sale Income**	OMB No. 1545-0228
Department of the Treasury Internal Revenue Service	▶ Attach to your tax return. ▶ Use a separate form for each sale or other disposition of property on the installment method.	**200__** 79

Name(s) Shown on Return	Identifying Number
CHUCK	000-00-0000

1 Description of property ▶ INVESTMENT PROPERTY

2a Date acquired (month, day, year) ▶ 6/30/86   b Date sold (month, day, year) ▶ 6/30/0__

3 Was the property sold to a related party (see instructions) after May 14, 1980? If 'No,' skip line 4 .... ☐ Yes ☒ No

4 Was the property you sold to a related party a marketable security? If 'Yes,' complete Part III. If 'No,'
complete Part III for the year of sale and the 2 years after the year of sale .... ☐ Yes ☐ No

Part I Gross Profit and Contract Price. Complete this part for the year of sale only.

5 Selling price including mortgages and other debts. **Do not** include interest whether stated or unstated	5	200,000.
6 Mortgages, debts, and other liabilities the buyer assumed or took the property subject to (see instructions)	6	
7 Subtract line 6 from line 5	7	200,000.
8 Cost or other basis of property sold	8	50,000.
9 Depreciation allowed or allowable	9	
10 Adjusted basis. Subtract line 9 from line 8	10	50,000.
11 Commissions and other expenses of sale	11	13,000.
12 Income recapture from Form 4797, Part III (see instructions) ..	12	
13 Add lines 10, 11, and 12	13	63,000.
14 Subtract line 13 from line 5. If zero or less, **do not** complete the rest of this form (see instructions).........	14	137,000.
15 If the property described on line 1 above was your main home, enter the amount of your excluded gain (see instructions). Otherwise, enter -0-	15	0.
16 **Gross profit.** Subtract line 15 from line 14	16	137,000.
17 Subtract line 13 from line 6. If zero or less, enter -0-	17	0.
18 **Contract price.** Add line 7 and line 17	18	200,000.

Part II Installment Sale Income. Complete this part for the year of sale **and** any year you receive a payment or have certain debts you must treat as a payment on installment obligations.

19 Gross profit percentage. Divide line 16 by line 18. For years after the year of sale, see instructions	19	0.6850
20 If this is the year of sale, enter the amount from line 17. Otherwise, enter -0-	20	0.
21 Payments received during year (see instructions). **Do not** include interest, whether stated or unstated	21	75,624.
22 Add lines 20 and 21	22	75,624.
23 Payments received in prior years (see instructions). **Do not** include interest, whether stated or unstated	23	
24 **Installment sale income.** Multiply line 22 by line 19	24	51,802.
25 Enter the part of line 24 that is ordinary income under recapture rules (see instructions)	25	
26 Subtract line 25 from line 24. Enter here and on Schedule D or Form 4797 (see instructions)	26	51,802.

Part III Related Party Installment Sale Income. Do not complete if you received the final payment this tax year.

27 Name, address, and taxpayer identifying number of related party

28 Did the related party resell or dispose of the property ('second disposition') during this tax year? .... ☐ Yes ☐ No

29 If the answer to question 28 is 'Yes,' complete lines 30 through 37 below unless one of the following conditions is met. Check the box that applies.

   a ☐ The second disposition was more than 2 years after the first disposition (other than dispositions of marketable securities). If this box is checked, enter the date of disposition (month, day, year) .... ▶

   b ☐ The first disposition was a sale or exchange of stock to the issuing corporation.

   c ☐ The second disposition was an involuntary conversion and the threat of conversion occurred after the first disposition.

   d ☐ The second disposition occurred after the death of the original seller or buyer.

   e ☐ It can be established to the satisfaction of the Internal Revenue Service that tax avoidance was not a principal purpose for either of the dispositions. If this box is checked, attach an explanation (see instructions).

30 Selling price of property sold by related party	30	
31 Enter contract price from line 18 for year of first sale	31	
32 Enter the **smaller** of line 30 or line 31	32	
33 Total payments received by the end of your 2001 tax year (see instructions)	33	
34 Subtract line 33 from line 32. If zero or less, enter -0-	34	
35 Multiply line 34 by the gross profit percentage on line 19 for year of first sale	35	
36 Enter the part of line 35 that is ordinary income under recapture rules (see instructions)	36	
37 Subtract line 36 from line 35. Enter here and on Schedule D or Form 4797 (see instructions)	37	

Form **6252**

Source: Tax Form Courtesy of Matthew Crammer, Crammer Accountancy, Downey, CA, 562-923-9436

Down payment	$ 50,000
Mortgage payoff	− 35,000
Commissions, etc.	− 13,000
Net to seller	$ 2,000

Contract price	$200,000
Cost	− 50,000
Expenses	− 13,000
Gross profit	$137,000

In this scenario the gross profit ratio is $137,000 ÷ $200,000 = 68.5 percent. The seller must pay taxes on $34,250 on the $50,000 even though he or she netted only $2,000.

If the buyer assumes (or takes the property subject to) the seller's mortgage, the contract price is reduced. If the mortgage assumed by the buyer is $35,000, closing costs are $13,000, and the buyer pays $15,000 down, the seller nets $2,000. The seller's gross profit ratio is:

	Gross Profit	Contract Price
Sales Price	$200,000	$200,000
Mortgage		35,000
Contract price		$165,000
Cost	− 50,000	
Expenses	− 13,000	
Gross profit	$137,000	

The gross profit ratio would be 83 percent ($137,000 ÷ $165,000), which means that the seller pays taxes on 83 percent of every principal payment (Figure 10.3, line 19).

The seller's first-year profit is $12,455 (83 percent of $15,000), even though the seller nets only $2,000 (see Figure 10.3). Confused yet? Not to worry; this is run-of-the-mill stuff for your accountant. What is important is the concept that the payments received will actually be made up of components that will be taxed or not taxed according to what they represent.

Once again, the seller will eventually get the whole $200,000 of principal, a percentage of which is taxable just as it would have been in an outright sale. So why do it? The obvious advantage in doing the installment sale is the ability to spread the taxes due over a long period. But more important is what that tax money does for you while you are still "holding" it. It earns interest.

Let's look at a fairly typical economic situation. Generally speaking, there is about a three to four point spread between mortgage rates and stable investment rates like certificates of deposit (CDs). When mortgage rates are around 7 percent, CDs are paying about 3 to 4 percent. For that reason alone, investing money by carrying the mortgage on a property seems to make good financial sense. There are, of course, risks and lack of liquidity factors to be considered, but if you are comfortable with the risk and are looking for a long-term investment, financing the property would seem the better choice. How much better? The return on $100,000 at 7.5 percent is $7,500 per year, and the return on $100,000 in CDs or Treasury bills at 4 percent is $4,000 per year—a yearly difference of $3,500. Sounds fairly straightforward, but that's not really an apples-to-apples comparison.

Remember that if you are investing $100,000 of deferred gain, you are getting a return not only on your money but also on the portion represented by what you would have had to pay the IRS in an outright sale. So if you were in California, you would have a capital gains tax liability on $100,000 of approximately $30,000 between state and federal taxes. In an outright sale, the dollars available to you after paying the taxes would be only $70,000. The true comparison is really between $100,000 invested or $70,000 invested, so even if you were able to get the exact same rate of return on your investments, the return would be larger based on the larger principal drawing a return. The difference between these two over a ten-year period at 7.5 percent is approximately the $22,500 you would have earned had you deferred and $22,500 that you would not have earned had you made an outright sale and paid the taxes. Looking at it another way, the deferred investment provided a 42 percent greater return than the after-tax investment.

FIGURE 10.3   Installment Sales Income

Form **6252**	**Installment Sale Income**	OMB No. 1545-0228
Department of the Treasury Internal Revenue Service	► Attach to your tax return. ► Use a separate form for each sale or other disposition of property on the installment method.	**200**___ 79

Name(s) Shown on Return	Identifying Number
CHUCK	000-00-0000

1 Description of property ► INVESTMENT PROPERTY

2a Date acquired (month, day, year) ► 6/30/86   **b** Date sold (month, day, year) ► 6/30/0__

3 Was the property sold to a related party (see instructions) after May 14, 1980? If 'No,' skip line 4. .... ☐ Yes   ☒ No

4 Was the property you sold to a related party a marketable security? If 'Yes,' complete Part III. If 'No,'
complete Part III for the year of sale and the 2 years after the year of sale. .... ☐ Yes   ☐ No

Part I   **Gross Profit and Contract Price.** Complete this part for the year of sale only.

5 Selling price including mortgages and other debts. **Do not** include interest whether stated or unstated		**5**	200,000.
6 Mortgages, debts, and other liabilities the buyer assumed or took the property subject to (see instructions).	**6** 35,000.		
7 Subtract line 6 from line 5	**7** 165,000.		
8 Cost or other basis of property sold.	**8** 50,000.		
9 Depreciation allowed or allowable.	**9**		
10 Adjusted basis. Subtract line 9 from line 8.	**10** 50,000.		
11 Commissions and other expenses of sale.	**11** 13,000.		
12 Income recapture from Form 4797, Part III (see instructions)	**12**		
13 Add lines 10, 11, and 12.		**13**	63,000.
14 Subtract line 13 from line 5. If zero or less, **do not** complete the rest of this form (see instructions).		**14**	137,000.
15 If the property described on line 1 above was your main home, enter the amount of your excluded gain (see instructions). Otherwise, enter -0-.		**15**	0.
16 **Gross profit.** Subtract line 15 from line 14.		**16**	137,000.
17 Subtract line 13 from line 6. If zero or less, enter -0-		**17**	0.
18 **Contract price.** Add line 7 and line 17.		**18**	165,000.

Part II   **Installment Sale Income.** Complete this part for the year of sale **and** any year you receive a payment or have certain debts you must treat as a payment on installment obligations.

19 Gross profit percentage. Divide line 16 by line 18. For years after the year of sale, see instructions.	**19**	0.8303
20 If this is the year of sale, enter the amount from line 17. Otherwise, enter -0-.	**20**	0.
21 Payments received during year (see instructions). **Do not** include interest, whether stated or unstated	**21**	15,000.
22 Add lines 20 and 21.	**22**	15,000.
23 Payments received in prior years (see instructions). **Do not** include interest, whether stated or unstated. **23**		
24 **Installment sale income.** Multiply line 22 by line 19.	**24**	12,455.
25 Enter the part of line 24 that is ordinary income under recapture rules (see instructions).	**25**	
26 Subtract line 25 from line 24. Enter here and on Schedule D or Form 4797 (see instructions).	**26**	12,455.

Part III   **Related Party Installment Sale Income.** Do not complete if you received the final payment this tax year.

27 Name, address, and taxpayer identifying number of related party _____

28 Did the related party resell or dispose of the property ('second disposition') during this tax year? .... ☐ Yes   ☐ No

29 **If the answer to question 28 is 'Yes,' complete lines 30 through 37 below unless one of the following conditions is met.
Check the box that applies.**

   a ☐ The second disposition was more than 2 years after the first disposition (other than dispositions of marketable securities). If this box is checked, enter the date of disposition (month, day, year) .... ►_____

   b ☐ The first disposition was a sale or exchange of stock to the issuing corporation.

   c ☐ The second disposition was an involuntary conversion and the threat of conversion occurred after the first disposition.

   d ☐ The second disposition occurred after the death of the original seller or buyer.

   e ☐ It can be established to the satisfaction of the Internal Revenue Service that tax avoidance was not a principal purpose for either of the dispositions. If this box is checked, attach an explanation (see instructions).

30 Selling price of property sold by related party.	**30**	
31 Enter contract price from line 18 for year of first sale.	**31**	
32 Enter the **smaller** of line 30 or line 31.	**32**	
33 Total payments received by the end of your 2001 tax year (see instructions).	**33**	
34 Subtract line 33 from line 32. If zero or less, enter -0-.	**34**	
35 Multiply line 34 by the gross profit percentage on line 19 for year of first sale.	**35**	
36 Enter the part of line 35 that is ordinary income under recapture rules (see instructions).	**36**	
37 Subtract line 36 from line 35. Enter here and on Schedule D or Form 4797 (see instructions).	**37**	

Form **6252**

Source: Tax Form Courtesy of Matthew Crammer, Crammer Accountancy, Downey, CA, 562-923-9436

CHAPTER ELEVEN

Combining a 1031 Exchange with an Installment Sale

By combining a 1031 exchange with an installment sale, a property investor can accomplish the following:

- Step down to a smaller property investment and still defer capital gains.

- Diversify investing by splitting funds between real estate and a trust deed.

- Create an enhanced stream of income from the carryback investment.

- Favorably reallocate the basis on the replacement property.

THE BEST OF BOTH WORLDS

Sometimes, to meet your objectives the best alternative is to combine two or more of the tax-deferral or elimination tools to meet your specific needs. One of the more common combinations is the 1031 exchange used in conjunction with an installment sale. Two of the main reasons for using this combination of tools are to reduce the level of real estate investment as a whole and to reduce an owner/manager's workload but maintain a stream of income into the foreseeable future.

The most common reason by far for a hands-on investor to combine a 1031 exchange with an installment sale is retirement. Most find the idea of lightening the workload and maintaining a stream of income from the tax-deferred profit very appealing. Others see the combination as a flexible and manageable exit strategy from being a landlord altogether. Whatever the reasons, the 1031 exchange combined with an installment sale is an effective tool and has been getting much more popular in recent years.

LEGAL STATUS AND POSSIBLE COMPLICATIONS

Under the Internal Revenue Code, a taxpayer may combine the two tax-deferral methods to completely defer capital gains taxes. However, certain less-than-intuitive rules must be taken into consideration.

When combining an exchange with an installment sale note, the IRS requires that the following three rules apply:

1. The contract price is reduced by the fair market value of the like-kind property received in the trade.

2. The gross profit is reduced by any gain on the trade that can be postponed.

3. Like-kind property received in the trade is not considered payment on the installment obligation.

The net effect of these rules is to shift more of the capital gain into the installment sale portion of the transaction. The following is based on an example provided by IRS Publication 537.

Example: In 2001, George Brown trades property with an installment sale basis of $400,000 for like-kind property having a fair market value of $200,000. He also receives an installment note for $800,000 in the trade. Under the terms of the note, he is to receive $100,000 (plus interest) in 2002 and the balance of $700,000 (plus interest) in 2003. George's selling price is $1 million ($800,000 installment note + $200,000 fair market value of like-kind property received). His gross profit is $600,000 ($1,000,000 − $400,000 installment sale basis). The contract price is $800,000 ($1,000,000 − $200,000). The gross profit percentage is 75 percent ($600,000 ÷ $800,000). He reports no gain in 2001 because the like-kind property he receives is not treated as a payment for figuring gain. He reports $75,000 gain for 2002 (75 percent of $100,000 payment received) and $525,000 gain for 2003 (75 percent of $700,000 payment received).

As you can see, the first rule—the contract price is reduced by the fair market value of the like-kind property received in the trade—acts to effectively increase the gross profit percentage on the installment note payments. If the property had been sold by installment sale alone, the gross profit percentage would have been 60 percent ($600,000 ÷ $1,000,000). On the other hand, if the exchange property had a fair market value of $400,000, the gross profit percentage would be 100 percent ($600,000 ÷ $600,000). Does it really matter? Yes, if you are trying to plan what your yearly capital gains taxes will be from the installment sale payments.

Presumably, the IRS created this shifting or reallocation rule to set the tax payments in motion for receipt sooner rather than later. After all, an installment sale has set payments and a foreseeable repayment schedule, so the higher the gross profit ratio, the faster the gain is received and the taxes become due. On the other hand, the reallocation rule forced an additional adjusted basis to the replacement property (up to its fair market value) and thereby minimizing the gain that would have qualified for the indefinite deferral of an exchange. In the IRS's example above, the basis exceeded the fair market value of the property received, so no portion of the gain is allocated to the exchange replacement property, and thus no gain is being "indefinitely" deferred by the like-kind exchange portion of the split. Score one for the IRS? Maybe. Let's change the facts a little to see how the taxpayer might come out ahead (changes italicized).

Example: In December 2001, George Brown trades property with an installment sale basis of $400,000 for like-kind property having a fair market value of *$400,000*. He also receives an installment note for *$600,000* in the trade. Under the terms of the note, he is to receive *regular amortized payments with a balloon due in ten years (30 due in 10)*. George's selling price is $1 million (*$600,000* installment note + *$400,000* fair market value of like-kind property received). His gross profit is $600,000 ($1,000,000 − $400,000 installment sale basis). The contract price is *$600,000 ($1,000,000 − $400,000)*. The gross profit percentage is *100 percent ($600,000 ÷ $600,000)*. He reports no gain in 2001 because the like-kind property he receives is not treated as a payment for figuring gain. He reports *100 percent of the principal repayment as gain as he receives the future payments*.

The main change made in the example was that we made George's replacement property equal to the adjusted basis ("installment sale basis") of the relinquished property. Now, after applying the IRS's reallocating rules, the entire adjusted basis of the relinquished property is assigned to the replacement property, and the gross profit ratio on the installment sale portion is now 100 percent. (See Figure 11.1.)

FIGURE 11.1   Reallocation of Basis

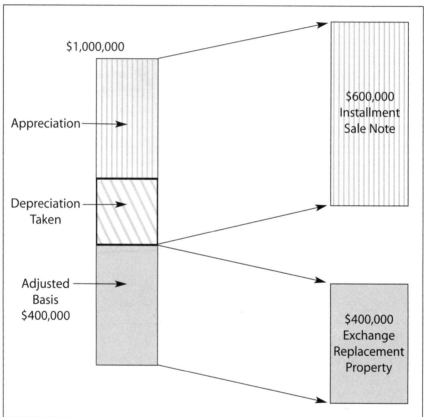

At first glance, this outcome doesn't seem desirable. George's replacement property is not deferring *any* of the capital gain and the installment sale principal payments received in the future have to be reported as 100 percent taxable. However, there is a bright side for George.

Looking at these results from a different perspective, George might find his position *very* desirable. First, consider the fact that the installment note has a secure 60 percent loan-to-value ratio ($600,000 note on a $1 million property). Normally, to get that type of a loan-to-value ratio, George would have had to receive $400,000 cash as the down payment—all of which would have been immediately taxable. George saved $60,000 to $100,000 in immediate capital gains taxes depending on his state tax rate (15 percent for federal plus his state tax rate). Second, and perhaps more important, George succeeded in doing something most investors are always trying to accomplish: he separated his original investment from his profit. George has a $600,000 installment note made up of all tax-deferred profit and a $400,000 property with a $400,000 adjusted basis.

Interestingly, if George were to hold the replacement property received in the exchange portion of this scenario a few years and then sell it outright, he would have minimal taxes on the sale. Remember, the allocation-shifting rules forced the full basis of the relinquished property to the replacement property. Also remember that a capital gain is the difference between sales price and the adjusted basis. So in George's case, if the market value of his $400,000 replacement property remained constant, there would be very little or no gain on a subsequent sale of the property.

Keep in mind that the IRS will disallow the exchange portion of George's 1031 exchange combined with an installment sale if it was his "intent" at the time of the exchange to sell off the replacement property and cash out. However, if George intended to hold the property for use in business or as an investment, but some unforeseeable circumstance arose and George needed to cash out, he could do so without triggering significant taxes. Also, if the replacement property were held for a sufficient time before being sold, the exchange would not usually be questioned. How long is a "sufficient" time? There is no firm answer. The conventional wisdom is that two years is long enough, but the IRS has resisted confirming or disputing any definite period.

One additional potential issue arises when combining 1031 exchanges with installment sales. If the properties involved have existing mortgages, there are mortgage over basis considerations and mortgage boot issues that must be taken into account. The mere fact that there are existing mortgages should not discourage you, but it does complicate the analysis enough to necessitate getting expert advice from a qualified tax professional or real estate tax attorney.

12

Private Annuity Trusts

PROPOSED REGULATION WARNING
Proposed REG-141-901-05

As this book went to print, the IRS shook up the tax-planning community with an announcement giving notice of proposed new rule-making and notice of a public hearing on private annuity trusts. If the new regulations are adopted as proposed, they will *eliminate any tax deferral benefits* of private annuity trusts. The IRS announcement was made on October 18, 2006, and specifically stated that if adopted after the public hearing, they would apply to any private annuity trust arrangements created after October 18, 2006. The proposed regulations do not affect existing private annuity trusts created before that date.

The scheduled public hearing for these proposed new regulations is set for February 16, 2007. At that time, feedback from the public and the tax-planning community may change the IRS's position and private annuity trusts may survive in some form as a tax-planning tool.

If you are considering a private annuity trust, be sure to get the latest information on these proposed regulations before you act. You can find the latest information at *www.privateannuitytrusts.com*.

By using a private annuity trust, the owner of an appreciated property can accomplish the following:

- Defer capital gains taxes on the sale of a property

- Defer the tax on recapture of depreciation

- Create a lifetime stream of income for an individual or jointly for both spouses

- Defer receipt of the annuity payments (*and taxes*) until retirement

- Create a family investment trust with the remainder going to the owner's family or heirs

- Provide a financing vehicle for family members

- Remove the asset from the owner's taxable estate

PRIVATE ANNUITY TRUSTS HAVE BECOME MAINSTREAM

At the time I wrote the first edition of this book, the private annuity trust (PAT) concept was considered a unique and sophisticated tax planning technique. Few people had even heard of private annuity trusts let alone understood how they worked. However, as of the writing of this second edition, private annuity trusts have become much more mainstream and are embraced by the real estate investment community. It seems like everyone is touting the benefits of PATs—lawyers, accountants, financial planners, and real estate brokers.

HOW PRIVATE ANNUITY TRUSTS WORK

A private annuity trust is a vehicle by which a property owner can sell appreciated real estate, create a stream of income for life, and defer the capital gains taxes. The concept stems, but is quite different, from the commonly known insurance company annuities. The annuity structure is basically the same, but a private annuity, as the name suggests, is between private parties. In most cases, private annuities are between parents and children, although that is not a requirement. A private annuity describes a situation in which one person (the *annuitant*) gives another person or entity (the *obligor*) a lump sum of money or an asset in exchange for the promise to provide a stream of payments in the future (an *annuity contract*).

A *private annuity* trust is simply a specially designed trust set up to give structure and formality to a private annuity contract. The assets used to create this private annuity trust can be almost anything, including appreciated real estate. Most important, when appreciated real estate is exchanged for a private annuity contract, no capital gains taxes are triggered. The tax liability works much like an installment sale—the obligation to pay the capital gains tax and recapture of depreciation is deferred until the future payments are actually received by the annuitant (seller). But unlike installment sales, there are no risks of foreclosure or the buyer paying off the note early and triggering the full and immediate capital gains tax liability.

Another significant advantage of the private annuity trust is the seller's ability to defer receipt of the payments. Because it is an annuity, the IRS allows you to defer receiving payments for any length of time up to the age of 70½. Because no tax is due until you start to receive payments, deferring payments results in deferring the tax liability. This is where private annuity trusts really shine as a tax-planning device. The fact that you can defer payment of the capital gain allows the trust to invest and earn income from funds that otherwise would have gone to the government.

Example: Don and Julie are a married couple who own an apartment building they bought for $100,000 15 years ago. The apartment building has a present value of $500,000 and an adjusted basis of $50,000. The couple would like to sell the building but know they face state and federal taxes of approximately $135,000. As expected, they are not excited about paying the taxes and are looking for an alternative. They no longer wish to be landlords, so they have ruled out a 1031 exchange, and they are uncomfortable with the risks associated with an installment sale. Don and Julie are both 55 years old and have two adult children. They intend to retire at 65 and are presently financially secure with no immediate need for the money from the sale of the property. Don and Julie decided to create a private annuity trust and make their two adult children the co-trustees and beneficiaries. They then transferred the apartment building to the trust in exchange for a private annuity contract with a present value of $500,000 and the beginning payment deferred until they reach 65. Once the property was transferred to the trust, the trustees (the children) authorized the sale, sold the property, and placed the proceeds from the sale in a trust investment account, where the trust principal will continue to grow until Don and Julie reach 65. At that time the trust will begin making the scheduled annuity payments to Don and Julie according to the terms of the annuity contract. Once the annuity payments begin, Don and Julie will have to recognize, report, and pay the capital gains tax on a portion of each payment received.

This simplified summary of how a private annuity trust works shows how such trusts are commonly used. Private annuity trusts are sophisticated tax and estate planning devices; and in the right situations they are excellent tax-deferral and investment tools. Unlike an installment sale and a 1031 exchange, a private annuity trust is one deferment tool that requires you to get professional assistance and strictly adhere to IRS rules.

Why Private Annuity Trusts Were Not Well Known

Private annuity trusts have been around for some time but are just becoming well known. Many major investment houses have used private annuity for clients' tax and estate planning. In addition, some estate planning attorneys and sophisticated financial planners are also aware of private annuity trusts, but most people don't seek out attorneys or financial planners when considering the sale of property. Instead, the primary source of information and advice on tax deferment options usually comes from a local real estate professional. Unfortunately, few real estate professionals are aware of private annuity trusts or understand how they work. Unlike installment sales and 1031 exchanges, the real estate community has not caught on to this option for tax deferral. The primary reason real estate professionals failed to embrace the use of private annuity trusts a long time ago is probably its level of complexity, the need to bring in an additional advisor or advisors, and the formalities required. Nevertheless, as more and more baby boomers reach retirement age and look for stream-of-income alternatives, real estate professionals are now getting up to speed on private annuity trusts, or at least the savvier ones are.

Given the right circumstances and investor objectives, a private annuity trust can be one of the most useful tax and planning vehicles available.

The Different Names by Which They're Known

The foundation of a private annuity trust is simply a contractual annuity agreement and an irrevocable trust to provide structure. Some of the organizations that specialize in financial and estate planning products have tried to bestow a proprietary feel to private annuity trusts by giving then slightly different names. Recently, I have seen a lot of marketing material about "deferred sale trusts" that look a lot like PATs to me. In addition, you may find advisors who want to combine private annuity contracts with other types of planning devices, some of which can be quite extravagant, such as off-shore trusts or international business companies. In recent years, anything that sounds like an "off-shore" or "international" tax planning strategy has drawn the immediate attention of the IRS. (A word to the wise: stay away from this kind of stuff and anyone who touts it.) There has also been a lot of press about combining a PAT with specialty life insurance. Again, the IRS has taken a dim view on these types of strategies. Although there may be valid reasons for these types of extravagant tax and estate planning strategies, they are too fancy (and questionable) for my liking. I tend to discourage clients from getting too complicated. On a tax planning complexity scale from 1 to 10, a basic private annuity trust is somewhere around the 4 to 5 range, making it not too difficult for the average investor to understand.

Although you may find private annuity trusts called by different names, the main structure always includes the basic components of a private annuity contract and an irrevocable trust.

A DUAL PLANNING ADVANTAGE

Private annuity trusts have estate planning as well as tax deferral advantages. A private annuity trust accomplishes capital gains tax deferral on real estate transactions—a primary focus of this book—but, it would be appropriate here to also mention its estate planning benefits.

If capital gains taxes are considered bad, then estate taxes are worse. At the time of this writing, the estate tax exemption amount is $2 million rising incrementally over the next five years and then set to revert to $1,000,000 in 2011. The $2 million exemption sounds like a lot, but anyone who has a home and a couple of investment properties arrives at that level pretty fast and is probably facing some estate tax. For those people, the tax on assets above the exemption amount starts at 37 percent and quickly moves up to 50 percent. If that's not enough of a motivation to engage in estate planning, then consider the additional 55 percent generation-skipping tax that applies to estates passing directly to grandchildren. That means $1 million of estate-taxable assets passing from parents to children incur between $370,000 to $500,000 in taxes. Those same assets passing to grandchildren will, in essence, be taxed again under the application of the generation-skipping tax with the end result being that the tax can eat up approximately 75 percent of the total value. There are exemptions, exclusions, and the like, but once you use those up, the remaining estate faces hefty taxation.

Example: Mary is a 60-year-old widow with one child, Don. Mary's longtime home and her stock investments together equal approximately $2 million. In addition, about 20 years ago Mary inherited an investment property currently valued at $1 million that has an adjusted basis of $200,000. If Mary were to pass away in a year when the exemption amount was $2 million and her son were to inherit the whole estate, the end result would look something like this:

Home and stock	$2,000,000
Investment property	$1,000,000
Total estate	$3,000,000
Less estate tax exemption	($2,000,000)
Net taxable estate	$1,000,000
Less approximate estate tax	($399,000)
After-tax estate	$2,601,000

A private annuity trust can significantly reduce estate tax liability by removing an asset from your estate. By transferring the asset into a private annuity trust in exchange for a private annuity contract, you have sold the property. Thus, you no longer own the asset, so it will not be considered a part of your estate for taxation purposes. The private annuity contract you received in exchange for the property is set only for lifetime payments; it has no value on your death, so again it is not counted as part of your estate.

As you can see, the estate taxes would be approximately $399,000. If, instead, Mary had transferred the investment property into a private annuity trust with her son as the trustee and beneficiary, the estate would have had *no* estate tax due because the $2 million value in Mary's home and stock investments would have been protected by the $2 million exemption, and the investment property would no longer be in the estate at all. The investment property would pass outside the estate to her son as the beneficiary of the trust. There would still be a reckoning for the deferred capital gains tax, but the tax savings overall would be significant.

The estate tax saving is certainly a consideration, but most people creating private annuity trusts do so to defer capital gains and generate a stream of income. Using Mary's situation, the stream of income generated from the private annuity trust for Mary would be projected at $7,492 per month for life. The following is how Mary's situation would appear in a financial illustration:

Proposed transfer date	12/2007
Projected §7520 rate	6.00%
FMV of property	$1,000,000
Client's basis	$200,000
Payment period	Monthly
Payment timing	End
Number of annuitants	1
Mary's age	60
Annuity factor	10.8279
Payout frequency factor	1.0272
Annual payout	$89,909
Monthly payment	$7,492
Single life expectancy	24.2 years
Life exp. adj. factor	0.0
Tax-free portion	$8,264
Capital gain portion	$33,058
Ordinary income portion	$48,586

Illustration courtesy of NumberCruncher (www.leimberg.com); 610-924-0515.

THE MECHANICS OF PRIVATE ANNUITY TRUSTS

Structure

A private annuity trust is an irrevocable nongrantor trust, which means that once it is set up and funded, it is difficult and costly to change. The trust itself has to be established for the benefit of someone other than the property seller, usually the seller's children or family, and there are specific rules and IRS requirements that must be followed. Once the trust is established, the seller transfers ("sells") the property to the trust in exchange for a private lifetime annuity contract. The seller now becomes an annuitant, that is, the seller is due annuity payments—and the trust becomes the obligor—that is, the trust is now obligated to make the annuity payments. No tax is due on the transfer of the property into the trust because the tax is deferred much like an installment sale.

The trustee of the trust has all the responsibility and authority for the property thereafter; the trustee then sells the property. No tax is due on the trust sale of the property because what the trust paid for the property (the present value of the annuity contract) and the amount of the market sale will be equal, so there is no gain to be taxed. The proceeds from the sale then go into the trust investment accounts or other investment vehicles established by the trust. The trustee then has the responsibility to manage the investments and to make the annuity payments to the annuitant at the predetermined times.

The annuity payments are for the lifetime of the annuitant, and when the annuitant dies, the trustee has the responsibility of distributing the remaining trust assets and money to the predetermined beneficiaries, who are usually (but not necessarily) family members. The IRS requires the lifetime annuity payments for a person younger than 70 to be based on the average life span of 85 years of age. The annuity payments can be set for an individual life span or, in the case of a husband and wife, can be set to make payments until both die. See Figure 12.1 for an illustration of how a private annuity trust works.

The first step is to get knowledgeable legal and tax advice. A qualified advisor is able to give you the pros and cons of a private annuity trust in terms of how it will have an impact on your specific situation. Don't rely on financial advisors who would like to manage the trust money. Don't rely on companies that want to sell you a bunch of different planning and financial tools. And don't rely on the general descriptions and examples given in this book. Each person's situation is

FIGURE 12.1   How a Private Annuity Trust Works

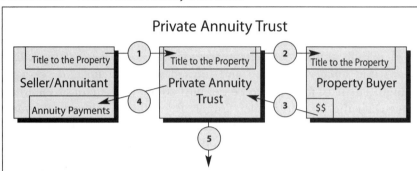

1. The property is transferred to the trust in exchange for an annuity contract.
2. The property is sold by the trust.
3. The proceeds from the sale go back into the trust for investment.
4. The private annuity trust makes the scheduled annuity payments.
5. On the death of the annuitant, the balance of the trust assets go to the heirs.

different, and there is no substitute for good *situation-specific* legal and tax advice. With that said, the establishment of a private annuity trust is fairly straightforward after getting the appropriate advice.

Your advisor should be able to provide you with financial illustrations of exactly how your private annuity contract would work for you. Once you approve the financials, you'll need a private annuity-trust-knowledgeable attorney to create the trust structure. Then you and your selected trustee will have to execute and notarize the appropriate documents. Once that is done, the trust will exist, and the property can be transferred to it in exchange for an "estimated" private annuity contract.

The contract is merely estimated because the trust sale of the property has not yet occurred, so the actual net proceeds from the sale can only be estimated until the sale is completed. On the completion of the sale, the trust issues a replacement private annuity contract based on the actual confirmed net proceeds. At that point, the establishment of the private annuity trust is complete, and the trustee is now responsible for managing the proceeds from the sale.

TRANSFER AND SALE OF THE PROPERTY

If you have time, it is usually best that the property not be listed for sale or under a contract for sale prior to being transferred to the trust. Why? The conventional wisdom is that the IRS is okay with private annuity trusts as planning tools but less as last-minute tax-avoidance tools. Therefore, one of many factors considered if the IRS scrutinizes your private annuity trust is whether the property was already in the process of a sale. Some advisors say this is easy to get around; that may be true, but why not just do it right to begin with? If you are already listed or under contract to sell, talk to your advisor. The best sequence of transfer and sale would be as follows:

1. The seller establishes the trust.

2. The seller transfers the property to the trust in exchange for the annuity contract.

3. The trustee (not the seller) then lists the property for sale.

4. The trustee (not the seller) executes the contract for sale and all escrow and closing documents.

5. The escrow or closing agent must issue the closing proceeds in the name of the private annuity trust, and the proceeds become trust funds.

Thereafter, the trustee is responsible for the management of the trust funds and making the annuity payments as prearranged in the trust and annuity contract.

What if the property is already in escrow before the PAT is implemented? That's a good question that lacks a solid answer. There are two schools of thought here. Everyone agrees that a PAT cannot be implemented *after* the property is sold. It's the word *sold* that causes the problem.

One school of thought comes from the real estate community. Anyone who comes from a real estate background will tell you that a property is not "sold" until the closing has occurred. To the real estate community, a property is not sold until a deed conveys it to the buyer. You can say the property is in escrow or under contract, but it is not sold until the transaction is completed. There would seem to be significant support for this perspective. For example, it is well established that a seller can decide to defer taxes by implementing a 1031 exchange anytime before closing. Likewise, it is well established that a seller can decide to defer taxes by implementing an installment note anytime up to the closing. With this in mind, it seems logical that a seller would be able to defer taxes by implementing a PAT up until the property has closed. Everyone agrees that neither a 1031 or an installment sale is allowed after the property has closed (been sold).

The other school of thought says that once a property is under contract to be sold it is in fact "sold." There is some authority for this position as well. The conventional view of the legal community is that charitable remainder planning (discussed in Chapter 13) is not allowed after a property is under contract; therefore by extension, this school of thought says private annuity planning is not allowed either.

Who's right? I don't know of any legal authority one-way or the other that specifically addresses this issue. There are cases that have been decided where one of the factors the court looked at was whether the property was transferred into the trust right before it was deeded to the buyer. However, none of those courts invalidated the private annuity trust solely on that issue. So what should you do if you want to implement a PAT and your property is already in escrow? I guess that depends on how *you* and your PAT advisor define "sold."

THE MAGIC OF DEFERRING PAYMENTS.

One of the most valuable characteristics of a private annuity trust is the annuitant's ability to defer payments, meaning the person establishing the private annuity trust can legally defer receipt of any payments up to age 70½. If you are 50 at the time you establish the private annuity trust, you can defer the payments for 20½ years. This is an amazing feature when you recall that capital gains taxes are deferred until the annuitant actually starts receiving payments. That means that assuming you were 50, the trustee you selected would *invest the entire proceeds of the sale (now trust funds) for the benefit of the trust for 20 years before having to pay out one dollar in annuity payments.*

If a light bulb didn't go off in your head, you should stop, back up, and reread the last paragraph. Okay, let's see what could happen based on a 20-year deferral.

> **Example:** Don is 50 years old. He owns an apartment building valued at $725,000, still owes $300,000 on the mortgage, and has an adjusted basis of $300,000. He establishes a private annuity trust and transfers the apartment building to the trust in exchange for a private annuity contract. The private annuity contract specifies that the lifetime payments be deferred until he reaches age 70. The trustee of the

trust sells the property and after selling expenses (hypothetically $25,000) and paying off the mortgage ($300,000), the net proceeds that go into the trust are $400,000. All capital gains taxes are deferred until Don starts receiving payments. The trust now wisely invests the money and over the 20-year deferral period is able to earn an average after-tax 10 percent return per year. That means when Don starts receiving his private annuity payments, the trust principal could have grown to approximately $2,931,229.45.

That's the magic of deferring payments and compound interest. Although this sounds too good to be true, it's not. A private annuity trust can be structured to work just like an IRA or other retirement investment vehicle. In fact, one of the more common advantages for starting a private annuity trust is to catch up on, or supplement, retirement planning. The rate of return built into the previous example is not unrealistic for long-term investments; many commonly traded mutual funds are expected to exceed this average over ten-year periods. However, the trust is not locked into mutual fund investing and has great flexibility for investment options.

TRUST INVESTING: WHATEVER YOU CAN IMAGINE—WELL, ALMOST

The structure of a private annuity trust is just that—private. So however the trust invests is up to the trustee and the directions drafted into the trust at inception. The fact that your trustee has the freedom to choose how the money is invested is one really good reason you must be able to rely absolutely on the person you choose as trustee. Most people choose a family member, usually a son or daughter who will be the beneficiary of the trust if the annuitant dies. The person you choose as trustee is up to you. If your children are not as financially savvy or responsible as you'd like, you can always choose a professional trustee or a combination of family member and professional trustee to act jointly as co-trustees. Whomever you choose has a fiduciary responsibility to invest the funds prudently, but "prudently" still leaves a great deal of flexibility. All of the traditional investments, such as stocks, bonds, and mutual funds, are okay, but the trust can also buy commercial annuities, real estate, and just about anything else you can imagine.

Private Annuity Trusts Investing in Commercial Annuities

One of the best ways to invest money within a private annuity trust is to buy commercial annuities or appreciable assets. Remember, the private annuity trust structure, like all business and investment entities, requires yearly tax filings and payment of taxes on the yearly income earned. So for ease of management, security, and maximum tax deferral, a commercial annuity offers advantages. Commercial annuities don't offer the growth potential of other types of investments, but they do provide security and additional tax deferral.

Example: Carl, who is 55 years old, has a large piece of vacant land he bought 20 years ago for $100,000. A developer has been urging him for some time to sell the land, which has a current market value of $500,000. Carl plans to retire in ten years and feels the market for the property is strong now but may not be in ten years. Carl decides to establish a private annuity trust and transfers the land to the trust in exchange for a private annuity contract with the lifetime annuity payments deferred until he is 65. The trust sells the land to the developer and uses the $500,000 proceeds to buy a commercial annuity with its payments also deferred for ten years. Now, when Carl retires at 65, the commercial annuity will start making payments to the private annuity trust that will in turn make the private annuity payments to Carl. Carl has deferred his capital gains taxes on the sale of the land by selling it to the trust in exchange for the private annuity contract. And because the trust bought a deferred commercial annuity, there is no taxable income for the trust to report until the commercial annuity begins making payments to the trust.

Is this legal? Yes; taxes are not being eliminated, only deferred. The trust will have to pay taxes on the investment income when the payments start, and Carl will have to pay the capital gains taxes and interest income tax when the private annuity payments begin. The IRS has not lost any money. It will get the capital gains and interest income taxes from you eventually. After all, it is probably safe to assume that the IRS will still be here after both you and I are gone.

INSTALLMENT SALES WITHIN PRIVATE ANNUITY TRUSTS

In most cases, a private annuity trust is considered an alternative to an installment sale as both provide a stream of income that allows you to defer capital gains tax liability over a period. However, in certain situations a person may want to establish a private annuity trust, transfer the property to it in exchange for the private annuity contract, and then have the private annuity trust sell the property with installment sale terms. Why? Because the two big drawbacks associated with installment sales are thus eliminated: *the risk of early payoff (triggering immediate tax) and the taxes due on the down payment.*

Example: Tom Smith owns a small shopping center he inherited from his parents 15 years ago. The current basis on the property is $300,000. He wants to sell it, but the available financing for the property is tight, and he knows that to get full value he will have to offer seller financing. Tom doesn't mind financing the property so long as the loan-to-value ratio is sufficient to reduce the risk of having to foreclose. The property is currently valued at $1 million, and Tom wants at least 30 percent down to feel comfortable with the risk. Under an installment sale, however, according to Tom's accountant, approximately $100,000 in taxes will be due (state and federal) on the $300,000 down and the buyer may refinance or sell the property in a few years, pay off the note, and trigger an immediate capital gain situation for Tom. Tom decides to establish a private annuity trust (the Smith Family Trust) and transfer the property to it in exchange for a private annuity contract deferring his taxes until the annuity payments start. The trust then sells the property to a buyer for the 30 percent down and 70 percent owner (now the trust) financing. The trust realizes no gain on the sale because what it paid for the property—the value of the annuity contract—and what it sold it for are the same. The trust now has the full $300,000 in cash to invest and a note for the other $700,000. All capital gains taxes are deferred until Tom starts receiving the annuity payments from the private annuity trust. Moreover, even if the buyer subsequently sells or refinances the property and pays off the $700,000 note, no triggering of capital gains will ensue because no gain is attributable to the sale by the trust.

As you can see, a private annuity trust combined with an installment sale does have advantages. However, each situation must be thought through carefully, because using this structure may create a second layer of taxation on the interest earned. There are ways to avoid this second layer of taxation, but you should discuss it at length with your tax advisor or attorney to make sure a private annuity would work for you.

PRIVATE ANNUITY TRUST AS A FAMILY FINANCIAL TOOL

One of the more interesting aspects of establishing a private annuity trust is that it becomes a family investment tool. Because the trustee can be flexible about the choice of investments, interesting advantages for family members, or friends for that matter, can be created.

> **Example:** Using the previous example, let's say Tom deferred the annuity payments for ten years, which gives the Smith Family Trust (the private annuity trust) at least that much time to invest the funds. Let's also say that Tom has two adult children, one of whom owns his own home and has a $150,000 mortgage with the local bank. The other child is about to purchase her first home. The Smith Family Trust can provide financing for the child about to buy a home and offer to refinance the mortgage on the other child's home. The trust simply acts as any lender would in structuring the notes and interest at market rates. The end result is that both children have their homes financed though the Smith Family Trust, and all interest accumulating on the mortgages is paid into the Smith Family Trust instead of the local bank. All homeowner mortgage deductions for the children remain exactly as they would if a commercial lender had made the loans. The notes can be structured to require both children to refinance their homes to pay off the notes in ten years so that the Smith Family Trust can start making annuity payments to the annuitant (Tom Smith). However, the children may not have to refinance their homes at the ten-year point as long as the payments they make and the other assets of the trust are sufficient to make the monthly annuity payments to Tom.

This is a really great way to help out children or grandchildren who are buying a home. It is also a good way to control the return on the trust investments and keep it in the family. Family home mortgages are but one possibility. The Smith Family Trust could help the family in many ways: It could provide financing for a family member to start a business, provide a down payment on an apartment building, finance (by loan) the cost of medical school, or finance almost anything else you can imagine.

Whatever investments the trust makes, the goal is to have the funds available to make the annuity payment to the annuitant when they come due. The investments, therefore, should always be economically and financially reasonable so that the trust can meet its obligations.

LEGAL FORMALITIES AND REQUIREMENTS

Now that I've covered the potential benefits of establishing a private annuity trust, you may be thinking . . . what's the catch? Common sense warns us: anything that sounds too good to be true usually is. Up to this point, you have been shown the positive features, potential for growth, and other opportunities associated with a private annuity trust. Now it's time to explore the less-than-desirable aspects.

Seller Cannot Be the Trustee

In the case of a private annuity, the annuity, by definition, must be an unsecured promise to make lifetime payments in exchange for a lump sum payment. For the purpose of this book, that lump sum payment is made in the form of appreciated real estate instead of cash. The IRS has determined that if the promise to make lifetime payments is in any way secured, then the promise to make the payments is more like a financing agreement than an annuity. As such, the agreement would not qualify for the tax treatments afforded annuities under the law. In simple terms, if the seller retains any interest in, or control over, the property, the IRS disallows the private annuity tax advantages. It thus becomes obvious why the person who establishes the private annuity trust (the annuitant) cannot be a trustee or a named beneficiary of the trust agreement.

The requirement that private annuities be unsecured basically means that the annuitant has to give up all ownership and control over the property and how the trust assets are invested after the property is sold. The trustees selected to manage the trust have to be absolutely trustworthy, which is why private annuity trusts are usually intra-family planning tools. In most cases, private annuity trusts are created by parents and managed by their adult children, although that isn't a requirement. Another option is to have the trust managed by a professional corporate trustee. And some people opt for having cotrustees by choosing both a family member and a professional trustee to serve jointly. The only rule is that the trustee cannot be the annuitant, the spouse of the annuitant, or the fiduciary of an annuitant.

Annuity Contract Must Be Unsecured

By definition, a private annuity is a lifetime series of payments under an unsecured contract. In the situation where real estate is given in exchange for an annuity, it is especially important to differentiate a private annuity from an installment sale for tax purposes. Both have tax deferral characteristics, but only an annuity has payment deferral options and alternative investment opportunities. A private annuity also acts to remove an asset from your estate for estate tax purposes, whereas an installment sale note would still be an estate asset subject to estate taxes.

The requirement that a private annuity be unsecured is somewhat discomforting to many property owners because it means a loss of control over their asset. The structure of a private annuity trust requires the trustee to have control over the trust assets, and the annuitant cannot have any overt control over the trustee. This seems like a fiction because most private annuity trusts have a family member or professional trustee, so some ability to influence the actions of the trustee exists whether it is acknowledged or not.

Strict Guidelines and Formalities

To qualify for the benefits of a private annuity trust, the trust structure and annuity contract must conform to IRS requirements. I've already discussed a few of these in preceding sections: The annuity must be unsecured; the annuitant cannot be the trustee; the property should be transferred to the trust before it is sold; and so on. However, the list of requirements is long and includes items I haven't yet discussed. The following are other requirements that need to be considered:

- The annuity interest rate must be set at an amount equal to the federally set rate (section 7520 rate) at the time the annuity contract is created. The federal rate changes each month.

- Payments may be deferred but must start by age 70½. An annuitant may structure the annuity contract so that scheduled payments are deferred for any period but has to follow the minimal distribution rules providing that payments must begin by age 70½.

- The trust must have independent economic viability. This means that some portion of the fair market value of the asset (usually 7 percent) must be excluded from the annuity calculation and "gifted" to the trust beneficiaries but retained by the trust. By doing this, the trust has an independent economic substance beyond annuity. You may have to pay capital gains taxes on the portion gifted to the beneficiaries and in the case of very large PATs, the gifting may reduce the annuitant's available estate tax exemption (discuss this with your PAT advisor).

- Payments must be calculated on the life expectancy of the annuitant as determined by actuary tables. In the case of a joint husband and wife annuity, the payments are based on the life expectancy of the younger, but the limit on the deferral period is based on the age of the older.

- The trust is it's own taxable entity and will have to pay taxes on the yearly investment earnings. The annuity payments made to the annuitant(s) is not an expense deductible to the trust so proper investment strategies, accounting, and tax planning at the trust level become very important.

- The annuitant cannot control or influence the financial investment decisions of the trustee. Attempts to exert any control or influence and the arrangement will be seen as the annuitant retaining control over the assets, and the annuity trust will fail.

- A private annuity with scheduled payments equaling less than the IRS's required present market value is treated as a partial gift for tax purposes.

Costs to Create and Manage a Private Annuity Trust

Every method of deferring capital gains taxes has costs associated with its implementation. The private annuity trust is probably the most expensive because its structure is irrevocable and usually lasts many years, if not decades. Most of the costs are in the creation, but ongoing yearly tasks are associated with properly maintaining the trust and filing annual tax returns. Many of the fees for these tasks can be reduced or eliminated if your chosen trustee is competent and willing to personally perform the tasks. The following are the three main areas where expenses are incurred:

1. *Creation of the trust and annuity contract.* Private annuity trusts are not for the do-it-yourselfer. You will need an attorney to set up your trust and draft the annuity contract. The attorney's fees should be in the $3,000 to $5,000 range and include drafting/executing the trust and annuity contract as well as preparing and recording the deed transferring the property to the trust. Finding a knowledgeable attorney is the real trick. Tax and estate planning attorneys are your best bet, but understand that this area of law is very specialized. Even an experienced tax or estate planning attorney may have never been asked to do a private annuity trust. Don't let some new attorney use you as a training tool; hire only someone who has specific experience with private annuity trusts.

2. *Cost of managing trust assets.* If you are going to use an adult child to manage the day-to-day affairs of the trust, you will be able to keep costs here at a minimum. If not, a professional trustee charges a set fee based on the value of the trust assets. The fees are commonly around 1 to 1.5 percent for money manager–type duties but may be a higher percentage on smaller trusts or a slightly lower percentage on trusts of over $1 million. Professional trustees that do more than merely perform money management duties usually charge a flat yearly fee based on the size of the trust and an hourly fee for services performed. As previously mentioned, these fees may be partially avoided if your chosen trustee is an adult child who is able (and trustworthy) to handle and competently invest the money. If not, the fees charged by professional trustees are well worth the expense and will let you sleep better at night.

3. *Accounting expenses.* This is another area where professional help is necessary. Trust accounting, especially private annuity trust accounting, is a specialty. Your local tax preparer won't understand how the yearly tax returns must be handled. Get appropriate help to avoid trouble in this area. Trust tax returns will cost a few hundred dollars a year or more depending on the complexity of the trust investment activities.

COMPARISON WITH INSTALLMENT SALES

A private annuity trust is similar to an installment sale in that both create a stream of income from the tax-deferred sale of a property. Likewise, they are similar in how taxes are eventually paid. In both a private annuity sale and an installment sale, the capital gains taxes on the disposal of the property are deferred or spread out until the payments are actually received. In both cases, the monthly payments received are divided into three components: a percentage representing interest income; a percentage representing capital gain; and a nontaxable percentage representing recovery of the initial investment or basis. These percentages are established up front and don't change. In the years thereafter, the taxpayer reports the amount of interest income and gain on his or her tax returns for payments received during that tax year.

Even though the preceding paragraph may seem to imply the two are alike, the similarities end there. They both defer the payment of taxes, but the risks and costs associated with each are significantly different. For example, installment sales are generally easier and less expensive to implement, but come with the risks associated with lending money and the possibility of an early payoff triggering taxes. Private annuity trusts resolve both of those risks but are more complicated and have a higher start-up cost and slightly higher yearly tax-filing expenses. In addition, each of these deferral methods is significantly different in its legal formalities, structure, estate planning applicability, and flexibility. Which method is better for you depends on how well the tool meets your specific objectives.

FREQUENTLY ASKED QUESTIONS

By creating a private annuity trust, you can sell appreciated property to the trust in exchange for a private annuity contract. The trust can then sell the property and reinvest the funds. Neither the transfer of the property to the trust nor the subsequent sale of the property by the trust triggers immediate capital gains tax liability. The trust then makes lifetime payments to you, and any remaining assets in the trust will pass to your heirs on your death.

Private annuity trusts are a bit more complex than the other deferral methods we've looked at so far. The fact that they are slightly more complicated is exactly why the real estate community as a whole has been slow to embrace them. However, that is changing because the average investor is becoming more sophisticated. Although there are significant pros and cons to consider, the private annuity trust is sure to grow into one of the more favored real estate exit strategies in the future.

This chapter has provided an overview of private annuity trusts but is far from comprehensive. There is no substitute for getting good one-on-one advice, but the following are some of the more frequently asked questions about private annuity trusts:

Q. *How come I have never heard of private annuity trusts?*

A. *Private annuities are not highly touted in the real estate community because of their relative complexity. However, finding a knowledgeable attorney or accountant should be fairly easy. Also, you can find a lot of information on the Internet by going to www.privateannuitytrusts.com.*

Q. *Why aren't the taxes triggered when I sell the property to the trust?*

A. *You are receiving a lifetime annuity contract from the trust as payment. There is no way to accurately determine how many payments will be made during your lifetime, so the IRS has decided it is better to tax you as the payments are received. The way you are taxed is a lot like an installment sale–you are taxed when the payments are received.*

Q. *What happens if the trust runs out of money before I die?*

A. *You would have the option to sue the trust for breach of the annuity contract. But if the trust has exhausted its assets, there would be no point.*

Q. *What happens if I die younger than the (85-year-old) life expectancy used in calculating the annuity payments?*

A. *The existing trust assets pass to your heirs as you arranged in the trust. The unpaid portion of the deferred capital gains taxes would become due at that time.*

Q. *Can I have the trust pay the annuity to both my spouse and me?*

A. *Yes, second-to-die or joint annuities for spouses are common.*

Q. *Who should be the trustee?*

A. *Typically, the trustee is one of your children or one of the beneficiaries of the trust. You may also choose a professional trustee, an accountant, an attorney, or a combination of professionals and/or children. However, neither you nor your spouse can act as trustee.*

Q. *How much does it cost to set up a private annuity trust?*

A. *Fees vary, but in the neighborhood of $3,000 to $ 5,000 should be expected.*

Q. *How long does it take to get the trust established and ready to go?*

A. *That would depend on how busy your attorney is, but you should usually plan on about 10 to 20 days.*

Q. *If my property is already on the market, can I still do a private annuity trust?*

A. *Yes, but see your advisor for more information.*

Q. *Are there any rules governing how the trust has to invest the proceeds from the sale of the property?*

A. *Yes, but there is a great deal of flexibility. For example, investments in stocks, bonds, mutual funds, real estate, mortgage notes, certificates of deposit, commercial annuities, and more are all allowed.*

Q. *Does the trust have to pay taxes on the income from investments?*

A. *Yes, and the tax rates are generally higher than the rates for personal income. For this reason, financial and tax planning is important to minimize or eliminate taxes at the trust level.*

Q. *If I don't need the monthly annuity payments now, can I defer them?*

A. *Yes. Private annuity payment deferral options follow some of the same rules as retirement accounts. You may defer receipt of payments (and the tax liability that goes along with them) up to the age of 70½.*

Q. *If I own more than one property, can I add additional properties to the private annuity trust at a later date?*

A. *Yes. The private annuity trust "pays" you for each property by means of an annuity contract. In some situations, a single annuity contract may cover more than one property if the properties are sold within the same calander month of each other. However, to add a property at a later date, an additional annuity contract must be created for the new property or properties. Each annuity contract stands on its own and may set different deferral periods for each subsequent annuity contract.*

Q. *What if I change my mind and want to change the deferral period after the original annuity contract is created?*

A. *You can amend to receive payments sooner, but you cannot change the annuity contract to defer the payments for a later date.*

Q. *I like the idea of the private annuity trust, but I wanted some cash out of the sale. Can I do that?*

A. *Yes. You can allocate a fractional portion of the property to the private annuity trust with the remaining portion paid out to you at the closing. However, keep in mind that you will have to pay taxes on any capital gain not deferred. Along those same lines, you can also combine a private annuity trust and a 1031 exchange by allocating a portion of the property you are selling for each purpose. See your advisor.*

WHERE TO GET MORE INFORMATION ABOUT PRIVATE ANNUITY TRUSTS

Private annuity trusts are one of the lesser-known tax-deferral devices described in this book. You can find more information on the Internet at *www.privateannuitytrusts.com.*

CHAPTER THIRTEEN

Charitable Remainder Trusts

A charitable remainder trust is a tax-deferral and estate planning device that offers taxpayers a way to sell appreciated real estate (or other assets) and accomplishes all of the following:

- Eliminates capital gains tax

- Creates a reliable stream of income to one or more persons during their lifetime

- Provides an immediate income tax charitable deduction

- Avoids future taxes at the estate level

- Supports a person's choice of a worthwhile charity

Charitable remainder trusts are generally associated more with estate planning than they are with real estate sales. For that reason, charitable remainder trusts are commonly, and mistakenly, overlooked as a capital gains tax alternative.

A charitable remainder trust is simply an irrevocable trust you create that specifies you (or you and your spouse) as the income beneficiary for life and a charity as the remainder beneficiary on your death. This allows you to receive all the income generated from the trust, and on your death the remaining assets pass to your charity of choice.

Many people don't understand the advantages of charitable remainder trusts. In fact, a common initial reaction is, "Why would I want to give my property away?" This type of negative response is why many real estate advisors don't even bother to discuss the option. That's unfortunate because sometimes a charitable remainder trust is the perfect tool to meet a property investor's objectives.

ADVANTAGES
Financial Advantages

I've already noted that a charitable remainder trust allows you to defer taxes, create a stream of income, and receive an immediate income tax deduction. Nevertheless, it is hard to understand the trust's advantages without looking at financial projections of its impact. Each situation is different, and your own financial projections of the impact need to be analyzed for you by a qualified advisor. The next sections illustrate stream-of-income and income tax deduction advantages to give you a general idea of how charitable remainder trusts are financially beneficial.

Stream-of-income and deduction examples. The starting place for anyone considering a charitable remainder trust is to obtain a picture of how the financial and tax benefits will work. Most charitable and financial advisors have computer software that can show you a detailed analysis of the financial impact. Figure 13.1 is a sample financial illustration based on the following situation.

Example: A married couple, ages 60 and 59, are considering transferring a $500,000 apartment building to a charitable remainder annuity trust. The apartment building has an adjusted basis of $75,000. The couple's current yearly combined income (prior to the trust) is $80,000, and they want the charitable remainder annuity trust to pay out based on their joint lifetime. Their combined federal and state capital gains tax rate is 25 percent, and the tax code's section 7520 rate is 6 percent.

Although the information in Figure 13.1 looks complicated, it really isn't. In sum, the couple in this illustration would receive a monthly income of $2,713.33 from the charitable remainder annuity trust for as long as either of them lives. They would be able to take a charitable gift income tax deduction of $40,000 in the first year, saving them $6,923 in income taxes. In the second year they would get another charitable gift income tax deduction of $31,789, saving an additional $5,272. Their total capital gains tax savings would be $106,250.

FIGURE 13.1   Charitable Remainder Annuity Trust

Inputs

Calculation Type:	Life
Transfer Date:	12/2003
§ 7520 Rate:	6.00%
FMV of Trust:	$500,000.00
Percentage Payout:	6.512%
Payment Period:	12
Payment Timing:	End
Ages:	60, 59

Summary

Rev. Rul. 77-374 Prob. Test: 3.94%, 40 yrs.; Char. Ded is ALLOWABLE

Monthly Payment:	$2,713.33
Amount of Annuity:	$32,560.00
Two Life Annuity Factor:	12.8032
Payout Frequency Factor:	1.0272
Present Value of Annuity = Annual Payout x Factors:	$428,211.12
Charitable Remainder = FMV of Trust less PV of Annuity:	$71,788.88
Charitable Deduction for Remainder Interest:	$71,788.88
Donor's Deduction as Percentage of Amount Transferred:	14.357%

Deduction as Percentage of Amount Transferred

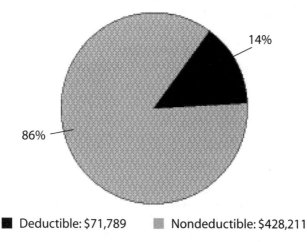

14%

86%

■ Deductible: $71,789   ▨ Nondeductible: $428,211

(continued)

FIGURE 13.1   Charitable Remainder Annuity Trust, continued

Income Tax

Adjusted Gross Income:	$80,000.00
Deductions:	$40,000.00
Adjusted Personal Exemptions:	$6,100.00
Taxable Income:	$33,900.00

2003 Tax Due: **$4,485.00**

Regular Standard Deduction:	$8,050.00
Additional Elderly Deduction:	$0.00
Standard Deduction:	$8,050.00
Itemized Deductions:	$0.00
Charitable Deduction:	$40,000.00
Deduction Phaseout:	$0.00
Adjusted Itemized Deductions:	$40,000.00
Personal Exemptions:	$6,100.00
Personal Exemption Phaseout:	$0.00
Adjusted Personal Exemptions:	$6,100.00
Average Tax Rate:	5.61%
Marginal Tax Rate:	15.00%

Tax Due as Percentage of Gross Income

6%

94%

■ Tax Due   ▨ After-Tax

Tax Savings

Value of Property:	$500,000.00
Cost Basis:	$75,000.00
Capital Gains Rate:	25.00%
Capital Gains Tax Savings:	**$106,250.00**
Charity Type:	50%

Income Tax

Bar chart with y-axis from $0 to $10,000 in $2,000 increments. Categories: 2003, 2004. Legend: ■ Without Deduction ▨ With Deduction

Year	Deduction Taken	Remaining Deduction	Tax If No Deduction	Tax If Deduction	Tax Savings
2003	$40,000	$31,789	$11,408	$4,485	**$6,923**
2004	$31,789	$0	$10,959	$5,687	**$5,272**

Source: Illustration courtesy of Charitable Gift Planner (www.leimberg.com), 601-924-0515.

Income tax charitable gift deduction. As noted in the previous section, you are able to take a charitable gift income tax deduction that can be used to reduce your immediate income tax liability. The amount of the income tax deduction and the actual benefit depends on two factors: the estimated value to the charity and the type of charity.

The total amount of the income tax deduction allowed is based on the projected value of the remainder interest of the property donated to the trust. Specific formulas are used to determine the deduction you get. Basically, in a lifetime annuity trust the younger you are, the lower the charitable deduction because it is anticipated that the trust will have to make more lifetime payments to you, thereby reducing the amount that eventually goes to the charity.

The amount of the income tax deduction also depends on the type of charity you choose as the donee. Most public charities are classified as 50 percent charities, and you may deduct charitable contributions to the extent they do not exceed 50 percent of your adjusted gross income. Certain organizations (such as veterans groups, fraternal orders, and private foundations) are classified as 30 percent charities. When making contributions to these charities, you may deduct gifts to the extent they do not exceed 30 percent of your adjusted gross income. Any unused part of the deduction can be carried forward for up to five years.

Philanthropic Advantages

It's always nice to come out ahead financially, but many times the true motivation for a charitable remainder trust is to support a favorite charity, university, or religious institution. If your motivation is primarily philanthropic, the best part of a charitable remainder trust is the ability to benefit from the asset while you are still alive and can make a current commitment to give. Many charities rely on this type of gifting to survive, and your charitable gesture will be appreciated.

HOW CHARITABLE REMAINDER TRUSTS WORK

Figure 13.2 shows how the property title transfer and money flow in a typical charitable remainder trust. As you will see, the structural characteristics are fairly easy to understand. The subtopics following Figure 13.2 take a closer and basic look at how charitable remainder trusts work.

FIGURE 13.2   How a Charitable Remainder Trust Works

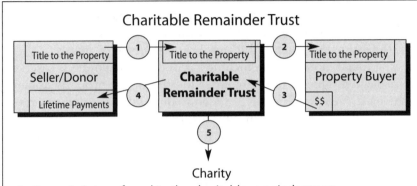

Charitable Remainder Trust

1. Property is transferred to the charitable remainder trust.
2. Charitable remainder trust sells the property.
3. Proceeds from the sale go back into the trust for investment.
4. The trust pays seller-donor the scheduled lifetime payments.
5. On the death of the seller-donor, the balance of the trust assets go to the selected charitable organization(s).

Structure of the Trust

As the name implies, a charitable remainder trust is a *trust*, and a trust is simply an entity created to hold and manage assets. The legal specifics are beyond the scope of this book, so you would be well advised to let an attorney properly draft the required documents for you. Don't let the legal side of this discourage you, however, as charitable remainder trusts are considered fairly commonplace for trust and estate planning attorneys.

Unlike commonly known and used revocable living trusts, a charitable remainder trust is irrevocable, which means that once it is created and in operation, you cannot change your mind. For that reason, it is prudent to get good advice and make sound decisions up front.

Once the trust itself has been created, you transfer the property into the trust. It is important not to put the property on the market or begin the process of selling until the trust has been created and the property transferred into the trust. Nevertheless, if you have already started the sale process, it is possible to back up and create the necessary structure and documentation; although, strictly speaking, you are not supposed to. If you have already sold the property and the escrow has closed, it is too late to use a charitable remainder trust to defer the taxes.

Sale of the Property

Once the property has been transferred to the trust, the trust owns it. It is the trustee you selected (usually you are the trustee) who has to sign the listing agreement, sale contract, escrow and/or closing instructions, and any other transactional documents on behalf of the trust. When the sale is completed, the proceeds from the sale must go to the trust for investment and management under the terms of the trust. When the trust sells the assets, there will be no capital gains taxes because a charitable remainder trust is exempt from any capital gains tax.

Investment of Funds

Once the asset has been sold, the trustee reinvests the proceeds for growth and to provide the lifetime income stream(s) established by terms of the trust. The amount and type of payment you receive depends on the choices you made at the time you set up the trust.

Many charitable organizations will act as trustee of a charitable remainder trust if named as a beneficiary. In fact, most want to control designing the trust, selling the property, investing the funds, and making the lifetime payments to you. There is no requirement, however, that you must have a charitable organization act in any of those capacities. You may choose almost anyone you want, including yourself, to act as trustee and administer the trust's affairs.

Income for Life

Once the property is sold and the sale proceeds are invested by the trust, the trust will be responsible for paying you and any co-payee named in the scheduled payments. How you structure the payments is a matter of your preference. Depending on your choice of payment options, your charitable remainder trust will be either a charitable remainder unitrust (CRUT), which has variable payments calculated as a percentage of the trust assets, or a charitable remainder annuity trust (CRAT), which has fixed payments regardless of the trust's investment performance. I look more closely at both CRUTs and CRATs later.

Remainder to the Charity

The end result of a charitable remainder trust is that the remaining assets of the trust eventually go to your chosen charity when the person or persons receiving lifetime income payments die.

TYPES OF CHARITABLE REMAINDER TRUSTS

Charitable remainder trusts have been around for a long time and are more common than most people think. These trusts can have two basic structures: an annuity trust or a unitrust. For charitable remainder trusts to be valid, regulations require that they be either an annuity trust or a unitrust, not a hybrid or blending of the two. As you will see, the basic difference between these two is how the stream of income for the donor is calculated.

Charitable Remainder Annuity Trust (CRAT)

A charitable remainder annuity trust is structured to pay the donor a *fixed* amount each year for the donor's lifetime or for a term of years, with the property remaining in the trust passing to the charity on the donor's death. The payments can be set up to pay the donor and spouse during their joint lifetimes and can even go to other persons, such as children or grandchildren.

The annuity payments can initially be set as a fixed amount of the initial value of the assets in the trust or can be set as a fixed sum. The annual payments must be set no lower than 5 percent and no higher than 50 percent. As a practical matter, most CRAT payments are set at an annual payout of somewhere in the range of 5 to 15 percent. Once set, the payments can't be changed regardless of future inflation or investment performance of the trust.

Charitable Remainder Unitrust (CRUT)

A charitable remainder unitrust is structured to pay the donor a *percentage* of the fair market value of the trust assets each year for the donor's lifetime or for a term of years, with the property remaining in the trust passing to the charity on the donor's death. Here again, the payments can be set up to pay the donor and spouse during their joint lifetimes and can go to other persons, such as children or grandchildren.

At least four variations are possible for structuring how a CRUT pays out:

1. *Type I*—Standard (CRUT). A standard CRUT pays a flat fixed percentage of the net fair market value of trust assets. The payments are made regardless of trust earnings and are usually intended to come from income but will be made from trust principal when necessary.

2. *Type II*—Net Income or Income Only (NICRUT). This is a simple variation of the standard charitable remainder unitrust. The "net income" or "income only" simply means that the payout is limited to the lesser of the standard unitrust specified percentage or the actual trust income. Unlike the standard unitrust, a NICRUT must have income to make payments; no invasion of principal is allowed. Trust income is usually defined as interest, dividends, rents, and royalties but would preclude annual payments being made from capital gain or trust principal. This payout structure is commonly referred to as an income-only, net income, or Type II unitrust.

3. *Type III*—Net Income with Makeup (NIMCRUT). The NIMCRUT structure works just like the NICRUT, except that the trust may make payments from trust income in excess of the standard unitrust specified percentage to make up for deficiencies in prior years. This payout structure is referred to as a net income with makeup or Type III unitrust.

4. *Type IV*—FLIP CRUT. The FLIP CRUT is generally used for a gift of property that will not generate any income until it is sold, such as vacant land. Like a NICRUT, the FLIP CRUT is initially structured for payments of the lesser of the net income or standard unitrust specified percentage. The result is that during the period before the sale, the income-only provision eliminates the need for the trust to make payments if no cash and/or income is available. On some established triggering event, usually the sale of the property, the income-only provision ceases and the unitrust payout structure changes or "flips" to set itself to the specified payout percentage exactly like a standard CRUT.

Are you confused yet? If so, don't worry about it. The main difference between the CRAT and the four variations of a CRUT are simply how the payout is structured. Just remember that the CRAT structure pays the donor a *fixed* amount each year, regardless of inflation or changes in the value of trust assets. The various CRUT structures pay out a set *percentage* of the annually determined fair market value of the trust assets.

Which is better? It depends on what you want. The annuity structure provides the security of fixed payments in a declining market but risks the depletion of the trust's assets. The unitrust structure provides a hedge against inflation but risks lower payments if the total value of trust assets goes down.

CHARITABLE REMAINDER TRUST REQUIREMENTS

It is important to follow the IRS requirements for structure and form of charitable remainder trusts. If you are going to do a charitable remainder trust, in all likelihood you will be using either your own attorney or one provided by the charity to draft the necessary documents and advise you. This is an area of tax planning and law that needs careful attention to detail and full consideration before you act. Most advisors are able to walk you through the issues that affect you specifically, but the following are considerations common in most charitable remainder trusts.

Irrevocability

All charitable remainder trusts are required to be irrevocable, which means that once the trust is created and the property transferred to the trust, there is no going back. It is possible to seek court-assisted modifications to the structure of the trust, but there has to be a good reason, and the costs associated with making changes are usually prohibitive.

Mortgage Issues

If you have an existing mortgage on the property being considered for a charitable remainder trust, you may not be able to use it. The IRS has taken the position that mortgaged property does not qualify for charitable remainder trust tax treatment. Why? At first, this rule doesn't seem to make sense because in most cases the property being transferred into the trust is going to be sold anyway. So why not just calculate the value of the charitable remainder trust (and gift) on the net proceeds after the mortgage is paid off? Seems to make sense, but here's the problem.

> **Example:** Bob has an eight-unit apartment building he is thinking about selling. He bought it a long time ago, and its current adjusted basis is $100,000. The property has a fair market value of $400,000, and Bob has calculated his capital gains taxes if he sells outright at about $100,000. The building is currently owned free and clear. Bob decides to take out a 75 percent loan-to-value mortgage on the property and put the proceeds ($300,000) from the mortgage in his bank. Bob now plans to gift the property to a charitable remainder trust.

If there were no rule against mortgaged properties in charitable remainder trusts, Bob's trust would have a net value of $100,000 ($400,000 sales price less the mortgage payoff of $300,000), and Bob would receive the stream of income from the trust for his lifetime, with the remainder going to the designated charity. What has really happened here is that Bob has been able to pull out $300,000 of tax-free money (the loan proceeds) and then donate the property's remaining equity, which would have otherwise been tax dollars, to charity. Obviously, the IRS caught on to this creative planning pretty fast and put a stop to it by not allowing mortgaged property to qualify.

If you do have mortgaged property that you would like to use for a charitable remainder trust, speak to an attorney specializing in this type of trust or one of the larger charities in your area. Depending on the value of the asset and the amount of the mortgage, there are still ways to get around no-mortgage rules. Also, you may want to consider the alternative of a private annuity trust with a charitable beneficiary; private annuity trusts don't have a no-mortgage restriction.

Seller as Trustee

For the purposes of this book, the function of a charitable remainder trust is to hold and invest the tax-free proceeds from the sale of a property and pay the lifetime stream of income to the seller-donor. In most cases, the seller-donor will want to retain some control over how those sale proceeds are invested. The person granted the authority to manage the trust investments—the trustee—can typically be any person, including the donor, a donor's relative, a financial advisor, accountant, attorney, and so on. Cotrustees—for example, a husband and wife, a parent and child, or any relative and a professional advisor—can also manage the investments.

Certain trustee powers, if retained, will cause problems with how the IRS views the tax-exempt status of the trust. These issues usually don't arise in the garden-variety situation of the trust simply selling the property and investing the proceeds. Your charitable remainder trust advisor can tell if your specific situation will create any restrictions on your being the trustee.

Payment and Term Restrictions

Usually the person starting the charitable remainder trust wants to maximize the stream of income from the trust and the immediately available charitable deduction from the gift. Many factors come into play in calculating just how to maximize the benefits. The income stream—who gets it and for how long—is up to you, but there are limits and controlling factors. Whether you choose the annuity format or one of the various unitrust structures, every charitable remainder trust has the following four restrictions in common:

1. *Minimum and maximum distributions.* In structuring the income stream for an annuity format, the annual distribution has to be no less than 5 percent, or no more than 50 percent, of the fair market value of the assets initially transferred to the trust. Similarly, for a unitrust the annual distribution must be no less than 5 percent, or no more than 50 percent, of the total trust assets valued annually.

2. *Stream-of-income duration restrictions.* Both annuity and unitrusts can be set up to create a stream of income for the lifetime of any person living at the time the trust is created, which would include the joint lifetimes of husband and wife. A charitable remainder trust may also be structured to create a stream of income for a set term of years rather than being based on a lifetime. If structured for a set term, the period may not exceed 20 years. Instead of paying to an individual, the stream of income from a charitable remainder trust may go to another trust, a partnership, or a corporation but only under a set-term structure and not exceeding 20 years.

3. *Projected benefit to charity.* Every charitable remainder trust must be structured from the outset to provide that after all the anticipated stream-of-income payments are made, a minimum of 10 percent of the fair market value of the initial trust assets will still go to the charity. This is an initial projection only, so the trust

will not fail in later years if the investment performance fails to keep pace. The rule governing the projected benefit to charity is based on payment amounts and actuary tables.

4. *Probability of exhaustion.* No charitable remainder trust may be structured in a way that results in a greater than 5 percent chance that the trust will run out of money before making the remainder gift to the charity. This rule applies to both trust structures but is more applicable to lifetime payments under an annuity format. The probability-of-exhaustion rule limits the risk that the donor will outlive his, her, or their actuarial life expectancies.

The first rule states that the annual payout can be set anywhere from a minimum of 5 percent to a maximum of 50 percent, which seems to provide a tremendous amount of leeway. In reality, however, the other rules limit the payout by requiring that an amount still be available for the charity when all is said and done. When the payments are set for life, the age of the donor is the most significant limiting factor.

DISADVANTAGES OF CHARITABLE REMAINDER TRUSTS

Irrevocability

The concept of a charitable remainder trust is basically that a donor makes a present or completed gift to a charity, but retains a lifetime benefit from the asset before the charity actually receives it. The key words here are "present or completed gift," meaning that once you transfer the asset to the trust, you cannot take it back or change your mind. Only a present or completed gift qualifies for the charitable deduction and other tax advantages already explored. For the IRS to treat the transfer into the trust as a "present or completed gift," the trust itself cannot be amendable or revocable.

This requirement of irrevocability applies primarily to the financial structure of the trust and the gift itself. A donor may retain the right to remove a bad trustee and even to change the ultimate charitable recipient of the gift. It is usual for people to like the idea of charitable remainder gifts but be unsure which charity they want to have ultimately benefit. The possibility also exists that a named charity might cease to function or change its philanthropic purposes to something different than those the charitable remainder gift donor had in mind. For these reasons, a charitable remainder trust may contain provisions allowing the donor to amend it to change the charity or charities. However, other than these few exceptions, the trust must be irrevocable.

Family Inheritance Considerations

Another of the distinct disadvantages of a charitable remainder trust is that the trust assets go to a charity on the donor's death rather than to the donor's children or family. This may not matter if the donor has sufficient other assets for inheritance purposes or has an overriding desire to benefit the charity. But for many people, family inheritance considerations discourage the use of charitable remainder trusts.

Charities have always faced this issue and have come up with a few ways for you to either soften the blow or completely replace the asset for heirs. In the following sections I examine the two primary methods of making the gift *and* leaving something for your heirs.

REPLACING THE ASSET FOR FAMILY INHERITANCE

The most crucial disadvantage of charitable remainder trusts is that the principal of the trust (the remainder) will ultimately go to charity rather than to the donor's family or children. To overcome this disadvantage or to lessen its impact, planners have come up with two possible ways to replace the donated asset.

Wealth Replacement Trusts

One possible solution is to create a wealth replacement trust, a trust basically designed to purchase and continue paying the premiums on a life insurance policy that will pay a set amount on the death of the donor or on the last to survive in the case of couples. The idea is that you use some of the income from the tax savings and perhaps a portion of the monthly income from the charitable remainder trust to purchase the insurance. The death benefit of the life insurance goes directly to the heirs as a replacement for the value of the asset transferred to the charitable remainder trust. (See Figure 13.3.)

The fact that the insurance death benefit goes *directly* to the heirs is of significant planning importance, because it means it will not be included in the donor's estate at death and is therefore not exposed to estate taxes. For a person with an estate in excess of the estate tax exemption, this type of planning can be an extremely smart move.

Example: Bob has a piece of vacant land left to him by his father 25 years ago. The basis on the land is about $100,000 and the current market value is approximately $500,000. Bob is 55 years old and his net worth or estate is approximately $2 million and his yearly income $100,000. Bob would like to make a donation to his university for needy students. To accomplish that, he has decided to create a charitable remainder trust and donate the land to the trust. He also wants to leave his estate to his two children, so he has decided to create a wealth replacement trust to purchase a $500,000 life insurance policy. Bob intends to fund the wealth replacement trust with the immediate income tax savings he will receive as a result of the charitable remainder gift. He has worked out all the legalities and has put his plan in motion.

FIGURE 13.3 How a Wealth Replacement Trust Works

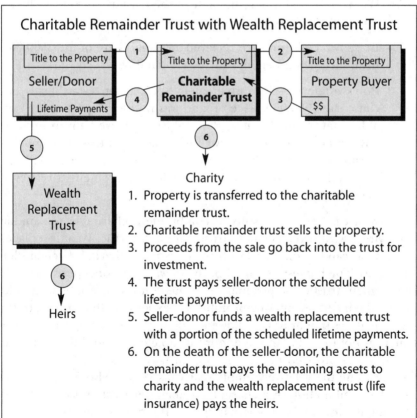

Charitable Remainder Trust with Wealth Replacement Trust

1. Property is transferred to the charitable remainder trust.
2. Charitable remainder trust sells the property.
3. Proceeds from the sale go back into the trust for investment.
4. The trust pays seller-donor the scheduled lifetime payments.
5. Seller-donor funds a wealth replacement trust with a portion of the scheduled lifetime payments.
6. On the death of the seller-donor, the charitable remainder trust pays the remaining assets to charity and the wealth replacement trust (life insurance) pays the heirs.

In this example, Bob has accomplished a lot through a fairly straightforward plan. Let's say Bob is killed in an automobile accident two years later. Let's also assume the estate tax exemption at the time of his death is $1 million. Given this scenario, Bob's plan would accomplish the following:

- Bob's transfer of the land into the charitable remainder trust netted him an immediate $30,000 income tax deduction in each of the two years he lived.

- Bob, as trustee of his charitable remainder trust, sold the land on receipt and paid no capital gains tax. By doing so, Bob was able to turn a nonproducing asset into cash that could be invested to generate income for the charitable remainder trust, which would in turn make the scheduled payment to Bob.

- Bob was able to receive two years of scheduled lifetime income from the trust—approximately $59,500.

- When Bob died, the remainder of the trust assets went to Bob's university to fund scholarships for needy students.

- Bob's two children each received an equal share of the $500,000 insurance death benefit with no tax liability.

- Bob's estate saved approximately $225,000 in estate taxes because the $500,000 piece of land was no longer part of the taxable estate. And because the children received the insurance payment directly from the wealth replacement trust, their net inheritance was $225,000 *higher* than it would have been had the charitable remainder trust and wealth replacement trust never been created.

As you can see, the results of combining a charitable remainder trust with a wealth replacement trust can be dramatic. Wealth replacement trusts can be combined with any type of the charitable remainder structures. The biggest potential problem with the concept of a wealth replacement trust is the possibility that the donor may not be insurable or that the insurance may be prohibitively expensive. In addition, there are formalities that must be followed to be sure the life insurance death benefit is not included in the donor's taxable estate. And there are the attorney fees involved in setting up both trusts and yearly accounting fees for filing the relatively simple yearly tax returns. But despite all of this, the combination of a charitable remainder trust and a wealth replacement trust can be a powerful tool in the right situations.

Income Accumulation Accounts

The other possibility is the simple concept of setting the annual income from the charitable remainder trust aside for the benefit of heirs. If you have sufficient income and simply don't need more, you can set up an investment account with the idea that it will pass to your heirs on your death. You could also disburse a portion of the income to fund children's or grandchildren's college funds, retirement funds, or whatever.

FREQUENTLY ASKED QUESTIONS

Q. *Why would I want to give my property to charity instead of to my heirs?*

A. *You may not want to, but do the math and look at the benefits before you rule out the charitable remainder trust option. A knowledgeable advisor can do a financial "what if" analysis for your review. Even if the financial results are less than perfect, it's still great to hold off the IRS and at the same time support your favorite charity.*

Q. *Can more than one person receive lifetime payments?*

A. *Yes. IRS regulations require that no more than two annuitants are to receive payments. It is common for charitable reminder trusts to be structured for the life of both spouses, although no regulation requires that a spouse be the second person. You may structure a charitable remainder trust to have a child, sibling, parent, or significant other as the second lifetime (or term of years) payee. If other than a spouse is selected, though, there may be gift or estate tax considerations.*

Q. *What if I still owe money on the property?*

A. *As a general rule, the property should be free and clear for a charitable remainder trust. Some of the larger charities and universities, however, have programs that accept encumbered properties. Also, you may want to consider a private annuity trust with a charitable beneficiary as an alternative.*

Q. *What if I change my mind on which charity I want or if the charity I initially selected goes out of business?*

A. *You can name three choices initially and may even substitute a different charity later.*

Q. *Can I delay the start of the income until later, such as at my retirement, when my income is lower?*

A. *Not in a charitable remainder trust, but there are larger charities that offer charitable gift annuities or deferred gift annuities. Using a deferred gift annuity, the annuity earnings accumulate on a tax-deferred basis. The donor receives a tax deduction in the year the annuity is established, and deferred earnings increase the annuity's principal so that the deferred payment annuity grows in size and the income, when it starts at retirement, will be more per year. A private annuity trust may be a more suitable alternative.*

WHERE TO GET MORE INFORMATION ABOUT CHARITABLE REMAINDER TRUSTS

Many of the larger charities and most universities have fundraising departments that will be happy to provide any information you might want. However, many people prefer to retain some flexibility about where their remainder gift will ultimately go. In that case, you need to contact an attorney to draft your charitable remainder trust. If you are in the Long Beach, California, area or don't mind dealing with your attorney by phone and mail, you can reach my office at 562-961-1329.

CHAPTER FOURTEEN

Tax-Free Real Estate Investing in an IRA

How would you like to invest in real estate but never have to pay taxes on rental income or capital gains when you sell it? This may sound like nonsense, but it is possible. Although most people don't know it, you can structure your individual retirement account (IRA) so that you may buy and sell real estate through your IRA. And depending on the type of IRA, your capital gains and rental income on those investments will be either tax deferred or, in the case of a Roth IRA, completely tax free.

Many people today have an IRA, Roth IRA, or some type of other retirement plan (e.g., 401(k), 403(b)) that can be rolled over to an IRA or Roth IRA. In the case of employer-originated retirement plans, you won't be able to influence the types of investments made by the plan. But if you have the ability to shift or roll over your retirement funds from a company-originated plan to your own IRA, you can get a lot more control over how your money is invested.

Most IRAs are administered and invested by one of the big brand-name investment firms. If you have one of these accounts, the last few years have probably been discouraging. Both the New York Stock Exchange (NYSE) and the Nasdaq have been declining overall for the past few years, and no one but stockbrokers seem optimistic. Conventional wisdom says the stock market will come back; at least it always has in the past. Nevertheless, more and more, people are starting to look for ways to have better control over the performance of their investments. And while most stock portfolios have performed poorly in the last few years, real estate investments have been a shining star.

Most people are unaware they can use their IRAs to invest in real estate, much less that capital gains on those investments can be tax free. Although there is a lot of confusion on this subject—even some magazine and newspaper articles incorrectly state that IRA real estate investment is illegal—the fact is that an IRA *is* allowed to buy and sell real estate. Moreover, real estate investments along with the rents from the investments have the same tax-deferred or tax-free characteristics as do other types of investments within your IRA.

Real estate investing within IRAs seems to be one of the best-kept secrets around. If you ask a traditional stockbroker or financial advisor, especially ones from big-name investments firms, about using your IRA to invest in real estate, you'll probably get stunned silence or a "You can't do that." After all, the most profitable way for the big-name firms to make money from your money is to control it in the financial investment markets. The bottom line: they lose profits if you take money out of their hands and put it into real estate investments. It is therefore not surprising that the big-name investment firms completely ignore this option. What is surprising, however, is that the real estate industry seems to be missing a lucrative opportunity to promote the use of IRAs for real estate investment.

Today, with the increasing uncertainty of the stock market, investors are actively looking for investment alternatives. The seemingly endless headlines proclaiming corporate officers caught using illegal and fraudulent accounting techniques to mislead investors or outright stealing from companies have brought about a prevailing investor skepticism. The everyday investor's blind trust of big-name investment firm recommendations is changing, and many individual investors are practicing a more hands-on investment strategy that includes a growing real estate component.

IMAGINE THE POSSIBILITIES

The concept of tax-advantaged investments in an IRA is very exciting. Most people invest for the future, and in most cases the *future* means retirement or accumulated wealth to pass along to heirs. If this describes your situation, the concept of IRA real estate investments deserves a closer look. The following are three examples of how a person might benefit from this type of investment.

Example: Carl has a Roth IRA worth $50,000. His neighbor has a four-unit apartment building he is interested in selling for $400,000. The neighbor has offered it to Carl and is willing to provide 20-year financing on the building (the neighbor's goal is to defer the tax consequences on the sale and create a stream of income so an installment sale fits his needs). Carl and the neighbor agree on terms of $40,000 down and a 90 percent seller carryback (note). Carl moves his IRA from his current IRA administrator to one that allows him to self-direct the investments. He then instructs his new IRA administrator to purchase the property in the name of his IRA, using funds from his IRA account as the down payment. The IRA becomes the owner of the property. As the tenants make the rent payments to the IRA (through a management company), the IRA makes the mortgage payments. At the end of 20 years, the note is paid in full and Carl, through his IRA, owns the property free and clear. Because Carl used a Roth IRA for the property's purchase, all rental income after the note is paid off will go into the IRA account free of taxes. Likewise, if Carl decides to sell the property somewhere along the way, proceeds from the sale of the property and any resulting capital gain go into the IRA tax free. Most important, because this is a Roth IRA, the distributions to Carl during retirement are also tax free.

Example: Pat and Laura live in an area experiencing a tremendous amount of growth. They have an opportunity to buy a large parcel of land they feel is going to be in the path of development. Many new homes are being built in the area, and the parcel they are considering is perfect for subdividing and reselling as smaller parcels. Pat and Laura both have IRAs with enough funds to purchase and subdivide the parcel. From their self-directed IRA accounts, they instruct the administrator to buy the land and arrange the subdivision process with IRA funds. As the subdivided lots are sold in the future, all profits will go into their (regular) IRA accounts and continue to grow (shielded from taxes) until distributions begin in their retirement.

Example: Bob is a contractor who buys run-down houses, fixes them up, and resells them at a profit. He does about two to three houses a year and makes a good living at it. Lately, the market has been very hot, and he is sure he could do an additional house or two a year without much trouble. He has an IRA with sufficient funds to purchase and remodel a house or two per year. Bob converts his IRA to a self-directed IRA and instructs the administrator to purchase an appropriate house he has found. He remodels the house and resells it for a profit. Even though Bob usually pays ordinary income taxes on the profit from his resales, the house owned and resold by his IRA won't incur ordinary income taxes. All profits will go tax free into his IRA account and continue to grow for his retirement.

IRAS: TAX FREE VERSUS TAX DEFERRED

Before examining the mechanics of using IRAs for tax-free and tax-deferred real estate investing, it is important to understand the difference between the terms *tax deferred* and *tax free*.

Tax deferred. Most retirement accounts are tax-deferred vehicles that allow taxpayers to put away money each year for retirement planning. Yearly contributions to a tax-deferred account are made with pre-tax dollars, so they have the added advantage of reducing a taxpayer's income tax in the year the contribution is made. The tax-deferred characteristic in this case refers to the fact that the disbursements from the account made to the taxpayer during retirement is taxable income in the year it's made.

Tax free. Roth IRAs, on the other hand, are tax-free retirement accounts. Yearly contributions to Roth IRAs are made with after-tax dollars, so they offer no tax advantage in the year the contribution is made. But the big advantages of Roth IRAs are the tax-free investment growth of the retirement account and tax-free future disbursements during retirement.

Clearly, if you were selecting the type of retirement account for real estate investing now, you would choose the Roth IRA for its tax-free characteristics. But if you were like most others, including myself, you probably opted for up-front yearly tax benefits by contributing to a traditional IRA and are now in the tax-deferred investment category rather than the tax-free one. It is possible to cross over and convert a traditional IRA to a Roth IRA, but the taxes due at the time of the conversion are usually too high to stomach. Whether your IRA investments are tax deferred or tax free, real estate investments can be a very smart move.

The first step in using an IRA for tax-free or tax-deferred real estate investing is to set up your IRA to be self-directed.

THE SELF-DIRECTED IRA

The traditional problem faced by IRA owners is that the financial firm handling their IRA doesn't offer a way to use IRA funds to invest in real estate. Enter the self-directed IRA, which is simply one in which the investor has a greater control over how the IRA funds are invested. You can buy and sell investments, including real estate, within your self-directed IRA while deferring taxes. Today, literally hundreds of companies offer self-directed IRAs, but not all self-directed IRAs are alike. Some of the bigger investment firms have recently started offering *pseudo* self-directed IRAs that allow investors to choose from a number of preselected investment options. Many times the options offered are the same ones that were used by the firm before the repackaging and remarketing of their product as a "self-directed" IRA.

As previously mentioned, the investment firms are most profitable if they control your money, so the option for real estate investment will be unavailable. The dividing line between a pseudo self-directed IRA and a true self-directed IRA is usually whether the company is simply acting as a custodian of the account (your money) or acting more as the administrator. Custodians generally don't have the paperwork and accounting systems in place to facilitate real estate investments, but many IRA administrators now do.

A small but growing number of companies offering self-directed IRA administration services have started to spring up across the country. Likewise, many independent financial advisors who have begun to embrace the idea of diversifying their clients' IRA holdings to include a real estate component are looking to the true self-directed IRA.

The first step in moving toward an IRA with real estate investment ability is to move, or roll over, existing retirements accounts to one of the administrators offering the real estate investment option. Generally, any traditional IRA, Roth IRA, Simple, or Keogh type of retirement account can be converted into a self-directed IRA. Employer-sponsored plans can sometime also be converted. To find out the process, contact the IRA administrator of your choice for assistance.

HOW TO BUY REAL ESTATE WITH YOUR IRA

Once you have established your self-directed IRA, your administrator has a procedure for you to follow in directing funds to a property investment. The ordinary transactional process of offer and acceptance, escrow, title insurance, and so on is the same, but your IRA administrator is the purchasing (or selling) party on behalf of your IRA. Each of the various IRA administrators has his or her own specific process, but in each case you direct the administrator's actions through the use of a buy or sell order of some type. Charges and fees are associated with each transaction you make, so be sure to investigate the costs involved before you settle on a particular administrator.

There are also IRA advisors out there if you want more than just an administrator. IRA advisors generally provide a full range of assistance, including helping you find investments and showing you how to work with an administrator.

SELF-DEALING AND OTHER PROHIBITED TRANSACTIONS

Before you get too excited about the possibilities of using your self-directed IRA for real estate investing, you have to eliminate certain types of transactions and property uses from consideration. The following are transactions that will not qualify for IRA-advantaged tax treatment:

- The sale or exchange, or leasing, of any property between the IRA and a disqualified person

- Lending money or other extension of credit between the IRA and a disqualified person

- Furnishing goods, services, or facilities between the IRA and a disqualified person

- The transfer to, or use by or for the benefit of, a disqualified person of the income or assets of the IRA

- Any act by a disqualified person who is a fiduciary whereby that person deals with the income or assets of an IRA in his or her own interest or own account

- The receipt of any consideration for his or her own personal account by any disqualified person who is a fiduciary from any party dealing with the IRA in connection with the transaction involving the income or assets of the IRA

For purposes of the prohibited transaction rules, the definition of a "disqualified person" includes yourself and any persons or entities (corporations, trusts, estates, or partnerships) that stand in close relationship to you.

LEVERAGED PROPERTIES AND UBI

There is no dispute that an IRA may invest in real estate outright, but an issue arises when you leverage or finance property within your IRA. The best way to maximize IRA real estate investments is usually by leveraging the property, so this is an issue for most IRA real estate investors. The problem is that a somewhat obscure IRS rule regarding *unrelated business income* (UBI) comes into play. IRS Publication 598 defines UBI as:

The income from a trade or business that is regularly carried on by an exempt organization and that is not substantially related to the performance by the organization of its exempt purpose or function, except that the organization uses the profits derived from this activity.

In this case, the exempt organization referred to is your IRA. Income that would otherwise be tax free in your IRA may therefore be taxed if it is defined as UBI. The publication goes on to specifically state that income from *debt-financed* property is considered UBI.

Thus, if you own an asset in your retirement account that generates UBI, your account may be subject to taxation on that income. Generally, the rules state that IRAs receiving $1,000 or more of UBI during a single tax year must file a special form before the tax filing deadline and pay taxes on that amount of income. IRAs that receive less than $1,000 of UBI are not required to file.

As you can imagine, this UBI rule puts a bit of a damper on what would otherwise have been tax-deferred or tax-free income and investment. So if you are a leverage-minded investor (as most people are), the challenge becomes finding a way to have leveraged property in your IRA without its earning more than the yearly $1,000 UBI limit.

Of the two primary considerations here, the first is to structure the investment so that the available property depreciation and annual operation expenses offset the property's income. The second, less intuitive approach recommended by some self-directed IRA administrators is to *simply use any excess UBI to make a lump sum principal reduction on the debt each year.* Once the debt is paid off, the income from the investment is no longer considered UBI because the investment is no longer a debt-financed property. This seems a reasonable approach considering the IRA account holder will not have access to the funds until retirement anyway.

SUMMARY

Using your IRA for real estate investment seems as though it will be a large part of diversifying retirement funds in the future. Eventually, the real estate community will catch on to this potentially limitless source of investment funds. Once it does, the public will hear a lot more about it and many more IRA administrators will emerge to handle a growing number of these types of IRA investments.

A number of these companies can be located right now on the Internet with a simple search for "self-directed IRA." Names you are sure to find include Entrust Administration (*www.entrustadmin.com*), Sterling Trust Services (*www.Sterling-trust.com*), and Mid Ohio Securities (*www.midoh.com*). Each of these companies, especially Entrust Administration, has an extensive Web site with lots of helpful information.

CHAPTER FIFTEEN

Working with Advisors

One of the most common requests I get from new clients is to refer them to good advisors. No matter what you are considering doing in real estate, the best thing you can do is get advice from someone who has already "been there" or someone who regularly advises clients who have. Unfortunately, finding advice when you need it isn't always easy. With this in mind, I think some information on finding and working with advisors is necessary.

There are three primary advisors that are good to have in real estate transactions and capital gains tax planning: an attorney, an accountant, and a real estate broker. Each of these three professions will have differing perspectives on how to go about a particular transaction and it is usually necessary to work with all three to get the whole picture. The ideal situation is to have trusted advisors in all three professions who regularly interact with each other. However, in the real world it is rare that your accountant would be having conversations with your attorney and even more rare that your attorney and your real estate broker would be interacting. Still, if you are able to find advisors who will work together, you will be way ahead of the average real estate investor.

For some of the basic tax-planning techniques in this book— tax–planning techniques, installment sales, and 1031 exchanges—you probably don't need to talk to a lawyer. In those situations a conversation with a knowledgeable accountant and broker will keep you on the right track. However, as you start getting more sophisticated or start mixing in the idea of limited liability companies, corporations, or partnerships, your attorney becomes crucial.

ATTORNEYS

Although I am an attorney, I will be the first to admit that attorneys, as a whole, are a strange lot. The most important thing for you to understand is that the profession of law has become very specialized. There was a day when a single lawyer (a general practitioner) would take care of all your general legal needs. Those days are long gone. I often use this analogy to explain how specialized law has become: Picture a philharmonic orchestra on a stage. Everyone up there is a musician and everyone up there can read music, but the flutist cannot play the violin and the harpist cannot play the tuba. The same is true for attorneys—the corporate lawyer is usually not competent to draft trusts and the real estate lawyer can't advise you on family law issues. With that in mind, the first thing you must do when looking for an attorney is look for the right type of lawyer. For capital gains tax planning in real estate transactions, you will be looking for either a real estate attorney or a tax attorney. Generally, tax attorneys are *very expensive* and real estate attorneys are just *expensive*. Nevertheless, if the tax bill you are trying to avoid is big enough, the attorney fees will seem a bargain by comparison.

ACCOUNTANTS

I talk with my accountant at least a few times a month; sometimes it's more like a few times a week. It makes a good point: I am comfortable picking up the phone and calling him if I have a question. That is exactly the relationship you should look for with your accountant. What good is an accountant if you can only talk to him or her once a year at tax time?

Many people use the term *accountant* or *CPA* to describe all tax advisors, but there are actually different tax credentials. Here is how my own accountant puts it:

> *"Enrolled Agents (EAs), certified public accountants (CPAs), attorneys, commercial firms, and seasonal tax preparers are some popular choices for tax advisors. However, only Enrolled Agents, CPAs, and attorneys can represent you before the IRS. While the average client may never*

have the need to be represented in an audit or collection, it is still important to find a qualified tax professional to prepare and file your return. By bargain shopping during tax time, the money you might save by using an unqualified preparer will probably be overshadowed by the increased tax you may pay if the unqualified preparer is unfamiliar with current tax deductions and credits that are specific to your needs.

"There is no question that many CPAs and attorneys are tax advisors, but only Enrolled Agents are required to specialize in taxation. Enrolled Agents must demonstrate to the IRS their competence in matters of taxation before they may represent a taxpayer before the IRS. They do so in one of two ways. The first is by passing a comprehensive two-day examination given annually by the IRS. The test covers taxation of individuals, corporations, partnerships, estates, trusts, procedures, and ethics. The other way is that they can apply by being employed as an agent of the Internal Revenue Service for at least five years. During that time they must be regularly applying and interpreting the provisions of the Internal Revenue Code and regulations.

"Unlike CPAs, who may or may not choose to specialize in taxes, all Enrolled Agents are required to specialize in taxation. Enrolled Agents are the only taxpayer representatives who receive their right to practice from the U.S. government (CPAs and licensed preparers are licensed by the state). In addition, Enrolled Agents are required to earn 72 hours of continuing education every three years in order to maintain their status. Because of the difficulty in becoming enrolled and maintaining that enrollment, there are fewer than 34,000 Enrolled Agents in the United States. In contrast, there are about 375,000 CPAs nationwide. I would recommend that in searching for an appropriate tax advisor, whether it be a CPA, attorney, or licensed preparer, you always look for a person who holds the EA designation." (Source: Matthew Crammer, Crammer Accountancy, Downey, California, 562-923-9436)

Today there also seems to be a lot of crossover between tax advisors and financial planners; again, here is how my accountant explains these differences:

"The most important difference in financial advisors is commission-based advisors versus fee-based advisors. Ask the advisor how he or she gets paid. A commission-based advisor naturally gravitates toward those investment products that provide the best commission incentive. A *fee-based advisor, on the other hand, charges you a fee as a percentage of your total portfolio. In my opinion, a commission-based advisor has an inherent conflict of interest.*

"For example, let's say Jack, a commission-based advisor, is reviewing mutual funds he is going to recommend to you for your portfolio. On one hand, there is mutual fund X, which has performed moderately and has a 5.75 percent up-front commission and a 1.5 percent trail commission paid to the advisor. On the other hand, there is mutual fund Y, which has performed exceptionally but only has a 2 percent up-front commission and a 0.75 percent trail commission paid to the advisor. We all hope Jack would choose the exceptionally performing mutual fund for our portfolio, but the reality is he may choose to leave that one out of his recommendations because of the lack of commission.

"Here's another example. Gary, a fee-based advisor, has opened an account for you where he has a 1.5 percent fee for all your assets under management. Gary is reviewing funds for you as well. Gary is not receiving any commissions from any of the mutual funds he is choosing because his agreement is to charge you a percentage of your portfolio value. Gary has no hesitation in making sure you receive the funds with the best performance available because there are no other incentives involved. Gary's compensation is directly related to how well those funds perform. Essentially, Gary is a member of your team. If your investments perform well, Gary is going to get increased compensation. This gives Gary the incentive to offer the best recommendations he can find.

"You also can have the confidence that when a fee-based advisor calls to rearrange your assets under management, he is doing it because he feels it is in your best interest. Fee-based advisors earn the same paycheck regardless of what investments you buy. In contrast, when a commission-based advisor recommends you move investments, you always have the concern he or she may be doing it to generate another commission."

REAL ESTATE BROKERS

The most important thing you can do when selecting a real estate broker is make sure that broker actually has experience in the type of property you are buying or selling. If your are buying or selling an apartment building, only use a broker who specializes in apartment buildings.

Today, it seems like everyone has a real estate license. I understand that every agent has to start somewhere. However, you only should be looking for an experienced agent to handle your real estate transactions.

RECOMMENDED ADVISORS

Finding good advisors in the area of capital gains tax planning is difficult. Many real estate agents and accountants tend to steer you away from some types of tax-deferral devices simply because they don't understand them. Advice is only as good as the advisor you choose. Many of the tax strategies discussed here are unknown to your local real estate agents and tax preparers.

The following two people are recommended because of their knowledge and experience in handling investment properties and developing capital gains tax-planning strategies. Both of these advisors are located in Southern California.

Real estate broker and investment property specialist. Ed Dowd handles marketing and sales of Coldwell Banker investment properties anywhere in Los Angeles and Orange Counties. He has hands-on experience with every tax deferral strategy in this book.

Ed Dowd
5540 7th Street
Long Beach, CA 90804
562-961-1305

Accountant and financial planner. Matthew Crammer is a tax advisor and financial planner with an in-depth knowledge of the various capital gains tax strategies. He can provide all accounting services from filing tax returns to advising you about financial investments.

Matthew Crammer
Crammer Accountancy
8141 E. 2nd Street, Suite 340
Downey, CA 90241
562-923-9436

STATE CAPITAL GAINS TAX RATES

State	State Capital Gains Rate	Combined Capital Gains Rate	State	State Capital Gains Rate	Combined Capital Gains Rate
Alabama	5.00%	25.00%	Montana	10.00%	30.00%
Alaska	0.00%	20.00%	Nebraska	6.68%	26.68%
Arizona	3.74%	23.74%	Nevada	0.00%	20.00%
Arkansas	# 4.90%	24.90%	New Hampshire	0.00%	20.00%
California	9.23%	29.00%	New Jersey	2.45%	22.45%
Colorado	4.63%	24.63%	New Mexico	0.00%	20.00%
Connecticut	4.50%	24.50%	New York	6.85%	26.85%
Delaware	5.95%	25.95%	North Carolina	7.00%	27.00%
DC	9.50%	29.50%	Ohio	4.84%	24.84%
Florida	0.00%	20.00%	North Dakota	*	22.80%
Georgia	6.00%	26.00%	Oklahoma	6.75%	26.75%
Hawaii	7.25%	27.25%	Oregon	9.00%	29.00%
Idaho	8.10%	28.10%	Pennsylvania	2.80%	22.80%
Illinois	3.00%	23.00%	Rhode Island	**	25.20%
Indiana	3.40%	23.40%	South Carolina	7.00%	27.00%
Iowa	8.98%	28.98%	South Dakota	0.00%	20.00%
Kansas	6.45%	26.45%	Tennessee	0.00%	20.00%
Kentucky	6.00%	26.00%	Texas	0.00%	20.00%
Louisiana	4.00%	24.00%	Utah	7.00%	27.00%
Maine	8.50%	28.50%	Vermont	***	24.80%
Maryland	4.85%	24.85%	Virginia	5.75%	25.75%
Massachusetts	5.00%	25.00%	Washington	0.00%	20.00%
Michigan	4.20%	24.20%	West Virginia	6.50%	26.50%
Minnesota	7.05%	27.05%	Wisconsin	# 2.62%	22.62%
Mississippi	5.00%	25.00%	Wyoming	0.00%	20.00%
Missouri	6.00%	26.00%			
			Average		24.62%

Presumption = combined federal-state marginal individual capital gains tax rate based on married couple filing jointly with over $60,000 in annual income and capital gains over $20,000. Includes federal capital gains rate of 15 percent.

* 14% of the federal capital gains tax liability

** 26% of the federal capital gains tax liability

*** 24% of the federal capital gains tax liability

\# States that exclude a portion of the gain and tax the remainder at ordinary income tax rates

SAMPLE IDENTIFICATION OF REPLACEMENT PROPERTY

The taxpayer(s) identified below (hereinafter "Exchangors") are in the process of doing a like-kind exchange of property under the provisions of the Internal Revenue Code section 1031. In accordance with the 45-day replacement property requirements, the Exchangors hereby identify the following properties:

• Property 1 _____ Value _____

• Property 2 _____ Value _____

• Property 3 _____ Value _____

IDENTIFICATION REQUIREMENTS: Under the provisions of IRC section 1031, replacement property is identified only if it is designated as replacement property in a written document signed by the taxpayer and hand delivered, mailed, faxed, or otherwise sent before the end of the identification period to either (a) the person obligated to transfer the replacement property to the taxpayer (regardless of whether that person is a disqualified person), or (b) any other person involved in the exchange other than the taxpayer or a disqualified person.

ALTERNATIVE AND MULTIPLE PROPERTIES: The taxpayer may identify more than one replacement property. Regardless of the number of relinquished properties transferred by the taxpayer as part of the same deferred exchange, the maximum number of replacement properties that the taxpayer may identify is (a) three properties without regard to the fair market values of the properties (the "3-property rule"), or (b) any number of properties so long as their aggregate fair market value as of the end of the identification period does not exceed 200 percent of the aggregate fair market value of all the relinquished properties as of the date the relinquished properties were transferred by the taxpayer (the "200-percent rule"). If you intend to identify more than three properties, consult your qualified intermediary or exchange advisor before doing so.

IDENTIFICATION CANNOT BE MADE LATE: Identification must be made within the 45-day requirement. The IRS does not allow any extension for holidays or weekends. If the 45th day of your identification period falls on a holiday or a weekend, your identification must be properly made on the ordinary business day BEFORE the holiday or weekend.

Date_____

_____   _____

EXCHANGOR   EXCHANGOR

_____   _____

EXCHANGOR   EXCHANGOR

Source: Exchange agreement courtesy of Barrister Exchange Corporation, Long Beach, CA, 562-961-1329.

SAMPLE INSTALLMENT SALE MORTGAGE

THIS INDENTURE, made as of the _____ day of _____, 20___, by and between _____ ("Mortgagor") and _____ ("Mortgagee").

WITNESSETH:

AMOUNT OF LIEN: _____

WHEREAS, Mortgagor is justly indebted to Mortgagee in the sum of _____ DOLLARS ($ _____) in lawful money of the United States, and has agreed to pay the same, with interest thereon, according to the terms of a certain note (the "Note") given by Mortgagor to Mortgagee, bearing interest from the date herein.

DESCRIPTION OF PROPERTY SUBJECT TO LIEN: "PREMISES"

NOW, THEREFORE, in consideration of the premises and the sum hereinabove set forth, and to secure the payment of the Secured Indebtedness as defined herein, Mortgagor has granted, bargained, sold and conveyed, and by these presents does grant, bargain, sell and convey unto Mortgagee property situated in _____ County, _____, more particularly described in Exhibit "A" attached hereto and by this reference made a part hereof;

TOGETHER with all buildings, structures and other improvements now or hereafter located on, above or below the surface of the property herein before described, or any part and parcel thereof; and,

TOGETHER with all and singular the tenements, easements, riparian rights, and appurtenances thereunto belonging or in anywise appertaining, whether now owned or hereafter acquired by Mortgagor, including all rights of ingress and egress to and from adjoining property (whether such rights now exist or subsequently arise) together with the reversion or reversions, remainder and remainders, rents, issues and profits thereof; and also all the estate, right, title, interest, claim and demand whatsoever of Mortgagor of, in and to the same and of, in and to every part and parcel thereof; and,

TOGETHER with all machinery, apparatus, equipment, fittings, fixtures, whether actually or constructively attached to said property and including all trade, domestic and ornamental fixtures, and articles of personal property of every kind and nature whatsoever (hereinafter collectively called "Equipment"), now or hereafter located in, upon or under said property or any part thereof and used or usable in connection with any present or future operation of said property and now owned or hereafter acquired by Mortgagor; and,

TOGETHER with all the common elements appurtenant to any parcel, unit or Lot which is all or part of the Premises; and,

ALL the foregoing encumbered by this Mortgage being collectively referred to herein as the "Premises";

TO HAVE AND TO HOLD the Premises hereby granted to the use, benefit and behalf of the Mortgagee, forever.

U.C.C. SECURITY AGREEMENT - It is agreed that if any of the property herein mortgaged is of a nature so that a security interest therein can be perfected under the Uniform Commercial Code, this instrument shall constitute a Security Agreement and Mortgagor agrees to join with the Mortgagee in the execution of any financing statements and to execute any and all other instruments that may be required for the perfection or renewal of such security interest under the Uniform Commercial Code.

EQUITY OF REDEMPTION - Conditioned, however, that if Mortgagor shall promptly pay or cause to be paid to Mortgagee, at its address listed in the Note, or at such other place which may hereafter be designated by Mortgagee, its or their successors or assigns, with interest, the principal sum of _____ DOLLARS ($_____) with final maturity, if not sooner paid, as stated in said Note unless amended or extended according to the terms of the Note executed by Mortgagor and payable to the order of Mortgagee, then these presents shall cease and be void, otherwise these presents shall remain in full force and effect.

ARTICLE ONE COVENANTS OF MORTGAGOR

Mortgagor covenants and agrees with Mortgagee as follows:

Secured Indebtedness. This Mortgage is given as security for the Note and also as security for any and all other sums, indebtedness, obligations and liabilities of any and every kind arising, under the Note or this

Mortgage, as amended or modified or supplemented from time to time, and any and all renewals, modifications or extensions of any or all of the foregoing (all of which are collectively referred to herein as the "Secured Indebtedness"), the entire Secured Indebtedness being equally secured with and having the same priority as any amounts owed at the date hereof.

Performance of Note, Mortgage, et Cetera. Mortgagor shall perform, observe and comply with all provisions hereof and of the Note and shall promptly pay, in lawful money of the United States of America, to Mortgagee the Secured Indebtedness with interest thereon as provided in the Note, this Mortgage and all other documents constituting the Secured Indebtedness.

Extent of Payment Other Than Principal and Interest. Mortgagor shall pay, when due and payable, (1) all taxes, assessments, general or special, and other charges levied on, or assessed, placed or made against the Premises, this instrument or the Secured Indebtedness or any interest of the Mortgagee in the Premises or the obligations secured hereby; (2) premiums on policies of fire and other hazard insurance covering the Premises, as required herein; (3) ground rents or other lease rentals; and (4) other sums related to the Premises or the indebtedness secured hereby, if any, payable by Mortgagor.

Insurance. Mortgagor shall, at its sole cost and expense, keep the Premises insured against all hazards as is customary and reasonable for properties of similar type and nature located in _____ County, _____.

Care of Property. Mortgagor shall maintain the Premises in good condition and repair and shall not commit or suffer any material waste to the Premises.

Prior Mortgage. With regard to any Prior Mortgage, Mortgagor hereby agrees to: (i) Pay promptly, when due, all installments of principal and interest and all other sums and charges made payable by any Prior Mortgage; (ii) Promptly perform and observe all of the terms, covenants and conditions required to be performed and observed by Mortgagor under any Prior Mortgage, within the period provided in said Prior Mortgage; (iii) Promptly notify Mortgagee of any default, or notice claiming any event of default by Mortgagor in the performance or observance of any term, covenant or condition to be performed or observed by Mortgagor under any such Prior Mortgage. (iv) Mortgagor will not request nor will it accept any voluntary future advances under any Prior Mortgage without Mortgagee's prior written consent, which consent shall not be unreasonably withheld.

ARTICLE TWO DEFAULTS

Event of Default. The occurrence of any one of the following events which shall not be cured within _____ days after written notice of the occurrence of the event, if the default is monetary, or which shall not be cured within _____ days after written notice from Mortgagee, if the default is non-monetary, shall constitute an "Event of Default": (a) Mortgagor fails to pay the Secured Indebtedness, or any part thereof, or the taxes, insurance and other charges, as hereinbefore provided, when and as the same shall become due and payable; (b) Any material warranty of Mortgagor herein contained, or contained in the Note, proves untrue or misleading in any material respect; (c) Mortgagor materially fails to keep, observe, perform, carry out and execute the covenants, agreements, obligations and conditions set out in this Mortgage, or in the Note; (d) Foreclosure proceedings (whether judicial or otherwise) are instituted on any mortgage or any lien of any kind secured by any portion of the Premises and affecting the priority of this Mortgage.

Options of Mortgagee upon Event of Default. Upon the occurrence of any Event of Default, the Mortgagee may immediately do any one or more of the following: (a) Declare the total Secured Indebtedness, including without limitation all payments for taxes, assessments, insurance premiums, liens, costs, expenses and attorney's fees herein specified, without notice to Mortgagor (such notice being hereby expressly waived), to be due and collectible at once, by foreclosure or otherwise; (b) Pursue any and all remedies available under the Uniform Commercial Code; it being hereby agreed that ten (10) days' notice as to the time, date and place of any proposed sale shall be reasonable; (c) In the event that Mortgagee elects to accelerate the maturity of the Secured Indebtedness and declares the Secured Indebtedness to be due and payable in full at once as provided for in Paragraph 1.02(a) hereinabove, or as may be provided for in the Note, or any other provision or term of this Mortgage, then Mortgagee shall have the right to pursue all of Mortgagee's rights and remedies for the collection of such Secured Indebtedness, whether such rights and remedies are granted by this Mortgage, any other agreement, law, equity or otherwise, to include, without limitation, the institution of foreclosure proceedings against the Premises under the terms of this Mortgage and any applicable state or federal law.

ARTICLE THREE MISCELLANEOUS PROVISIONS

Prior Liens. Mortgagor shall keep the Premises free from all prior liens (except for those consented to by Mortgagee).

Notice, Demand and Request. Every provision for notice and demand or request shall be deemed fulfilled by written notice and demand or request delivered in accordance with the provisions of the Note relating to notice.

Meaning of Words. The words "Mortgagor" and "Mortgagee" whenever used herein shall include all individuals, corporations (and if a corporation, its officers, employees or agents), trusts and any and all other persons or entities, and the respective heirs, executors, administrators, legal representatives, successors and assigns of the parties hereto, and all those holding under either of them. The pronouns used herein shall include, when appropriate, gender and both singular and plural. The word "Note" shall also include one or more notes and the grammatical construction of sentences shall conform thereto.

Severability. If any provision of this Mortgage or any other Loan Document or the application thereof shall, for any reason and to any extent, be invalid or unenforceable, neither the remainder of the instrument in which such provision is contained, nor the application of the provision to other persons, entities or circumstances, nor any other instrument referred to hereinabove shall be affected thereby, but instead shall be enforced to the maximum extent permitted by law.

Governing Law. The terms and provisions of this Mortgage are to be governed by the laws of the State of _____. No payment of interest or in the nature of interest for any debt secured in part by this Mortgage shall exceed the maximum amount permitted by law. Any payment in excess of the maximum amount shall be applied or disbursed as provided in the Note in regard to such amounts that are paid by the Mortgagor or received by the Mortgagee.

Descriptive Headings. The descriptive headings used herein are for convenience of reference only, and they are not intended to have any effect whatsoever in determining the rights or obligations of the Mortgagor or Mortgagee and they shall not be used in the interpretation or construction hereof.

Attorneys' Fees. As used in this Mortgage, attorneys' fees shall include, but not be limited to, fees incurred in all matters of collection and enforcement, construction and interpretation, before, during and after suit, trial, proceedings and appeals. Attorneys' fees shall also include hourly charges for paralegals, law clerks and other staff members operating under the supervision of an attorney.

Exculpation. Notwithstanding anything contained herein to the contrary, the Note which this Mortgage secures is a non-recourse Note and such Note shall be enforced against Mortgagor only to the extent of Mortgagor's interest in the Premises as described herein and to the extent of Mortgagor's interest in any personalty as may be described herein.

IN WITNESS WHEREOF, the Mortgagor has caused this instrument to be duly executed as of the day and year first above written.

Witnesses: _____ _____

STATE OF _____ COUNTY OF _____

Notarization Area

SAMPLE PROMISSORY NOTE
SECURED BY DEED OF TRUST

_____, California _____, 20___

On _____, 20___, for value received, the undersigned (the "Borrower") promises to pay to _____ (the "Holder"), or order, at any other place designated in a writing submitted by Holder to Borrower, the principal sum of $ _____, plus interest on the unpaid principal balance according to the terms contained in this Note.

Interest on the unpaid principal balance of this Note shall be computed at the rate of _____ percent per annum, from _____, 20____, until the principal balance of this Note and all accrued interest on the Note are paid in full. Commencing on _____, 20____, and continuing each consecutive month thereafter until _____, 20____, Borrower shall pay principal and interest in monthly installments of $ _____ or more on the _____ day of each month. On _____, 20____, Borrower shall pay a final payment (the "Balloon Payment") of any unpaid principal and all accrued but unpaid interest on the same date.

Each monthly payment shall be credited first on interest then due and the remainder on principal. Immediately thereafter, interest shall cease on the principal so credited.

Principal and interest are payable in lawful money of the United States.

Should the Borrower default in any monthly payment of interest or principal when due, or in payment of the Balloon Payment when due, or in the performance of any of the agreements contained in the deed of trust securing this Note, the whole sum of principal and interest shall become immediately due and payable at Holder's option. Failure by Holder to exercise this option shall not constitute a waiver of the right to exercise it in the event of any subsequent default.

Whether or not suit is filed, Borrower agrees to pay all reasonable attorneys' fees, costs of collection, costs, and expenses incurred by Holder in connection with the enforcement or collection of this Note. Borrower further agrees to pay all costs of suit and the sum adjudged as attorneys' fees in any action to enforce payment of this Note or any part of it.

This note is secured by a Deed of Trust, dated _____, 20___, to _____ as Trustee, executed by Borrower in favor of Holder and is given as part of the purchase price for the real property described in that Deed of Trust.

_____

Borrower

SAMPLE DEED OF TRUST

RECORDING REQUESTED BY
AND WHEN RECORDED MAIL TO:

_____

_____

_____

A.P.N.

_____**SPACE ABOVE THIS LINE FOR RECORDER'S USE**_____

DEED OF TRUST

THIS DEED OF TRUST is made this ___ day of _____, 20__,
between _____ (the "Trustor"), whose address
is _____, and
_____ (the "Beneficiary"), whose address
is _____, and
_____ (the "Trustee"), whose address is
_____.

TRUSTOR HEREBY irrevocably grants, transfers, and assigns to Trustee,
in trust, with power of sale, all that property in the City of _____,
County of _____, State of _____, described as:

together with rents, issues, and profits of the Property, subject, however,
to the right, power, and authority given to and conferred upon Beneficiary to collect and apply these rents, issues, and profits.

FOR THE PURPOSE OF SECURING:
Payment of the indebtedness evidenced by a promissory note executed
by Trustor on _____, in the principal sum of
$ _____, and any renewal, extension, or modification of the
promissory note (the "Note"); any additional sums and interest that
may hereafter be loaned to the then record owner of the Property by
Beneficiary, when evidenced by another note or notes reciting that it or
they are so secured; and, the performance of each agreement contained in this Deed of Trust.

TO PROTECT THE SECURITY OF THIS DEED OF TRUST,
TRUSTOR AGREES:

Maintenance and Repair

To keep the Property in good condition and repair; not to remove or demolish any buildings on the Property; to complete or restore promptly and in good and workmanlike manner any building that may be constructed, damaged, or destroyed on the Property; to pay when due all claims for labor performed and materials furnished for the Property; to comply with all laws affecting the Property or requiring any alterations or improvements to be made on the Property; not to commit or permit waste of the Property; not to commit, suffer, or permit any act upon the Property in violation of law; and to cultivate, irrigate, fertilize, fumigate, prune, and do all other acts that from the character or use of the Property may be reasonably necessary.

Fire Insurance

To provide, maintain, and deliver to Beneficiary fire insurance satisfactory to and with loss payable to Beneficiary. The amount collected under any fire or other insurance policy may be applied by Beneficiary upon any indebtedness secured by this Deed of Trust and in any order determined by Beneficiary, or at the option of Beneficiary the entire amount so collected or any part of that amount may be released to Trustor. This application or release shall not cure or waive any default or notice of default under this Deed of Trust or invalidate any act done pursuant to such a notice.

Defense of Security

To appear in and defend any action or proceeding purporting to affect the security of this Deed of Trust or the rights or powers of Beneficiary or Trustee; and to pay all costs and expenses, including cost of evidence of title and attorneys' fees in a reasonable sum, in any such action or proceeding in which Beneficiary or Trustee may appear, and in any suit brought by Beneficiary to foreclose this Deed of Trust.

Payment of Liens and Taxes

To pay, before delinquency, all taxes and assessments affecting the Property, including assessments on appurtenant water stock; all encumbrances, charges, and liens, with interest, on the Property or any part of the Property, which appear to be prior or superior to this Deed of Trust; and all costs, fees, and expenses of this Trust. If Trustor fails to make any payment or to do any act as provided in this Deed of Trust, then Beneficiary or Trustee may (but is not obligated to) make the payment or do the act in the required manner and to the extent deemed necessary by Beneficiary or Trustee to protect the security of this Deed of Trust. The performance by Beneficiary or Trustee of such an act shall not require notice to or demand upon Trustor and shall not release Trustor from any obligation under this Deed of Trust. Beneficiary or Trustee shall also have the following related rights and powers: to enter upon the Property for the foregoing purposes; to appear in and defend any action or proceeding purporting to affect the security of this Deed of Trust or the rights or powers of Beneficiary or Trustee; to pay, purchase, contest, or compromise any encumbrance, charge, or lien that in the judgment of either appears to be prior or superior to this Deed of Trust; to employ counsel; and to pay necessary expenses and costs, including attorneys' fees.

Reimbursement of Costs

To pay immediately and without demand all sums expended by Beneficiary or Trustee pursuant to this Deed of Trust, with interest from date of expenditure at the amount allowed by law in effect at the date of this Deed of Trust, and to pay any amount demanded by Beneficiary (up to the maximum allowed by law at the time of the demand) for any statement regarding the obligation secured by this Deed of Trust.

THE PARTIES FURTHER AGREE THAT:

Condemnation Award

Any award of damages in connection with any taking or condemnation, or for injury to the Property by reason of public use, or for damages for private trespass or injury to the Property, is hereby assigned and shall be paid to Beneficiary as further security for all obligations secured by this Deed of Trust. Upon receipt of such proceeds, Beneficiary may hold the proceeds as further security, or apply or release them in the same manner and with the same effect as provided in this Deed of Trust for the disposition of proceeds of fire or other insurance.

Waiver of Late Payments

By accepting payment of any sum secured by this Deed of Trust after its due date, Beneficiary does not waive its right either to require prompt payment when due of all other sums so secured or to declare default for failure to pay any indebtedness secured by this Deed of Trust.

Trustee's Powers

Upon written request of Beneficiary and presentation of this Deed of Trust and the Note for endorsement, Trustee may (a) reconvey all or any part of the Property; (b) consent to the making and recording, or either, of any map or plat of all or any part of the Property; (c) join in granting any easement on the Property; or (d) join in or consent to any extension agreement or any agreement subordinating the lien, encumbrance, or charge of this Deed of Trust. Trustee need not provide Trustor with notice before taking any of the foregoing actions, and shall not be liable for the proper performance of the act. The exercise by Trustee of any of the foregoing powers shall not affect the personal liability of any person for payment of the indebtedness secured by this Deed of Trust, or the lien of this Deed of Trust on the remaining property as security for the repayment of the full amount secured by this Deed of Trust.

Full Reconveyance

Upon written request of Beneficiary stating that all sums secured by this Deed of Trust have been paid, surrender of this Deed of Trust, the Note, and any other notes secured by this Deed of Trust to the Trustee for cancellation and retention, and payment of Trustee's fees and charges, Trustee shall reconvey, without warranty, the Property then subject to this Deed of Trust. The recitals in the reconveyance shall be conclusive proof of the truthfulness of the recitals. The grantee in the reconveyance may be described as "the person or persons legally entitled thereto." Five years after issuance of the full reconveyance, Trustee may destroy the Note and this Deed, unless directed in the request to retain them.

Assignment of Rents

As additional security, Trustor hereby gives to and confers upon Beneficiary the right, power, and authority during the continuance of these Trusts, to collect the rents, issues, and profits of the Property, but reserves the right, prior to any default by Trustor in payment of any indebtedness secured by this Deed of Trust or in the performance of any agreement under this Deed of Trust, to collect and retain these rents, issues, and profits as they become due and payable. Upon any such default, Beneficiary may, without notice and without regard to the adequacy of the security for the indebtedness secured by this Deed of Trust, either personally or by agent or court-appointed receiver, do the following: enter upon and take possession of the Property or any part of the Property; sue for or otherwise collect all rents, issues, and profits, including those past due and unpaid; and apply these rents, issues, and profits, less costs and expenses of operation and collection (including reasonable attorneys' fees), upon any indebtedness secured by this Deed of Trust, in any order determined by Beneficiary. The exercise of the foregoing rights by Beneficiary shall not cure or waive any default or notice of default under this Deed of Trust or invalidate any act done pursuant to such a notice.

Default in Foreclosure

Upon default by Trustor in the payment of any indebtedness secured by this Deed of Trust or in the performance of any obligation under this Deed of Trust, Beneficiary may declare all sums secured by this Deed of Trust immediately due and payable by delivering to Trustee a written declaration of default and demand for sale and a written notice of default and election to sell the Property. Trustee shall cause the notice of default and election to sell to be recorded. Beneficiary also shall deposit with Trustee this Deed of Trust, the Note, and all documents evidencing any additional expenditures secured by this Deed of Trust.

After the required time period has lapsed following the recordation of the notice of default, and after notice of sale has been given as required by law, Trustee, without demand on Trustor, shall sell the Property at the time and place specified in the notice of sale, either as a whole or in separate parcels, and in any order determined by Trustee, at public auction to the highest bidder for cash in lawful money of the United States, payable at the time of sale. Trustee may postpone sale of all or any portion of the Property by public announcement at the time and place of sale, and from time to time thereafter may postpone the sale by public announcement at the time fixed by the preceding postponement. Trustee shall deliver to the purchaser at the auction its deed conveying the Property sold, but without any covenant or warranty, express or implied. The recital in the deed of any matter or fact shall be conclusive proof of the truthfulness of the recital. Any person, including Trustor, Trustee, or Beneficiary, may purchase at the sale.

After deducting all costs, fees, and expenses of Trustee and Beneficiary under this paragraph, including costs of procuring evidence of title incurred in connection with sale, Trustee shall apply the proceeds of sale to payment of: all sums expended under the terms of this Deed of Trust, not then repaid, with accrued interest at the amount allowed by law in effect at the date of this Deed of Trust; all other sums then secured by this Deed of Trust; and the remainder, if any, to the person or persons legally entitled to the remaining proceeds.

General Provisions

This Deed applies to, inures to the benefit of, and binds all parties to this Deed of Trust and their heirs, legatees, devisees, administrators, executors, successors, and assigns. The term "Beneficiary" shall mean the holder and owner, including pledgee, of the Note secured by this Deed of Trust, whether or not named as a beneficiary in this Deed of Trust, and the heirs, legatees, devisees, administrators, executors, successors, and assigns of any such person. In this Deed, whenever the context so requires, the masculine gender includes the feminine and/or neuter, and the singular number includes the plural.

Acceptance by Trustee

Trustee accepts this Trust when this Deed, duly executed and acknowledged, is made a public record as provided by law. Trustee is not obligated to notify any party to this Deed of Trust of pending sale under any other deed of trust or of any action or proceeding in which Trustor, Beneficiary, or Trustee shall be a party unless brought by Trustee.

Substitution of Trustees

Beneficiary, or any successor in ownership of any indebtedness secured by this Deed of Trust, may from time to time, by written instrument, substitute a successor or successors to any Trustee named in or acting under this Deed of Trust. The substitution instrument shall contain the name of the original Trustor, Trustee, and Beneficiary under this Deed of Trust, the book and page where this Deed is recorded, and the name and address of the new Trustee. When executed by Beneficiary and duly acknowledged and recorded in the office of the recorder of the county or counties where the Property is situated, the substitution instrument shall be conclusive proof of proper substitution of the successor Trustee or Trustees. Any successor Trustee or Trustees shall, without conveyance from the Trustee predecessor, succeed to all its title, estate, rights, powers, and duties.

Cumulative Powers and Remedies

The powers and remedies conferred in this Deed of Trust are concurrent and cumulative to all other rights and remedies provided in this Deed of Trust or given by law. These powers and remedies may be exercised singly, successively, or together, and as often as deemed necessary.

Conclusiveness of Recitals

The recitals contained in any reconveyance, trustee's deed, or any other instrument executed by the Trustee from time to time under the authority of this Deed of Trust or in the exercise of its powers or the performance of its duties under this Deed of Trust, shall be conclusive evidence of their truth, whether stated as specific and particular facts, or in general statements or conclusions. Further, the recitals shall be binding and conclusive upon the Trustor, _____ [his or her] heirs, executors, administrators, successors, and assigns, and all other persons.

Attorneys' Fees

If any action is brought for the foreclosure of this Deed of Trust or for the enforcement of any provision of this Deed of Trust (whether or not suit is filed), Trustor agrees to pay all costs and expenses of Beneficiary and Trustee, including reasonable attorneys' fees; and this Deed of Trust shall secure these sums.

Cotrustees

If two or more persons are designated as Trustee in this Deed of Trust, any, or all, power granted in this Deed of Trust to Trustee may be exercised by any of those persons, if the other person or persons are unable, for any reason, to act. Any recital of this inability in any instrument executed by any of those persons shall be conclusive against Trustor and Trustor's heirs and assigns.

TRUSTOR

_____

STATE OF _____)
COUNTY OF _____)

On _____, before me, the undersigned notary public, personally appeared _____, personally known to me (or proved to me on the basis of satisfactory evidence) to be the person whose name is subscribed to within this instrument, and acknowledged to me that he/she executed the same in his/her authorized capacity, and that by his/her signature on this instrument the person, or the entity upon behalf of which the person acted, executed the instrument.

WITNESS my hand and official seal.

_____
NOTARY PUBLIC

REVENUE PROCEDURE 2000-37—
REVERSE EXCHANGES

Exchange of property held for productive use or investment—treatment of deferred exchanges—"qualified exchange accommodation arrangement."

IRS won't challenge qualification of property as either "replacement property" or "relinquished property" for purposes of applying nonrecognition rules of Code Sec. 1031, or treatment of accommodation party as property owner, if property is held in qualified exchange accommodation arrangement (QEAA). Regs issued in 1991 didn't apply to exchanges where replacement property is acquired before relinquished property is transferred. Since regs were published, taxpayers engaged in various transactions to facilitate reverse like-kind exchanges, and IRS believed establishment of "safe harbor" would enable taxpayers who had genuine intent to accomplish like-kind exchanges to qualify. Requirements are specified for QEAAs, and permissible agreements, regardless of whether their terms result from arm's-length bargaining, were also provided. Safe harbor applies to QEAAs entered into by qualified exchange accommodation titleholder on or after 9/15/2000.

1. Purpose

This revenue procedure provides a safe harbor under which the Internal Revenue Service will not challenge (a) the qualification of property as either "replacement property" or "relinquished property" (as defined in section 1.1031(k)-1(a) of the Income Tax Regulations) for purposes of section 1031 of the Internal Revenue Code and the regulations thereunder or (b) the treatment of the "exchange accommodation titleholder" as the beneficial owner of such property for federal income tax purposes, if the property is held in a "qualified exchange accommodation arrangement" (QEAA), as defined in section 4.02 of this revenue procedure.

2. Background

.01 Section 1031(a)(1) provides that no gain or loss is recognized on the exchange of property held for productive use in a trade or business or for investment if the property is exchanged solely for property of like kind that is to be held either for productive use in a trade or business or for investment.

.02 Section 1031(a)(3) provides that property received by the taxpayer is not treated as like-kind property if it: (a) is not identified as property to be received in the exchange on or before the day that is 45 days after the date on which the taxpayer transfers the relinquished property; or (b) is received after the earlier of the date that is 180 days after the date on which the taxpayer transfers the relinquished property, or the due date (determined with regard to extension) for the transferor's federal income tax return for the year in which the transfer of the relinquished property occurs.

.03 Determining the owner of property for federal income tax purposes requires an analysis of all of the facts and circumstances. As a general rule, the party that bears the economic burdens and benefits of ownership will be considered the owner of property for federal income tax purposes. See Rev. Rul. 82-144, 1982-2 C.B. 34.

.04 On April 25, 1991, the Treasury Department and the Service promulgated final regulations under section 1.1031(k)-1 providing rules for deferred like-kind exchanges under section 1031(a)(3). The preamble to the final regulations states that the deferred exchange rules under section 1031(a)(3) do not apply to reverse-Starker exchanges (i.e., exchanges where the replacement property is acquired before the relinquished property is transferred) and consequently that the final regulations do not apply to such exchanges. T.D. 8346, 1991-1 C.B. 150, 151; see Starker v. United States, 602 F.2d 1341 (9th Cir. 1979). However, the preamble indicates that Treasury and the Service will continue to study the applicability of the general rule of section 1031(a)(1) to these transactions. T.D. 8346, 1991-1 C.B. 150, 151.

.05 Since the promulgation of the final regulations under section 1.1031(k)-1, taxpayers have engaged in a wide variety of transactions, including so-called "parking" transactions, to facilitate reverse like-kind exchanges. Parking transactions typically are designed to "park" the desired replacement property with an accommodation party until such time as the taxpayer arranges for the transfer of the relinquished property to the ultimate transferee in a simultaneous or deferred exchange. Once such a transfer is arranged, the taxpayer transfers the relinquished property to the accommodation party in exchange for the replacement property, and the accommodation party then transfers the relinquished property to the ultimate transferee. In other situations, an accommodation party may acquire the desired replacement property on behalf of the taxpayer and immediately exchange such property with the taxpayer for the relinquished property, thereafter holding the relinquished property until the taxpayer arranges for a transfer of such property to the ultimate transferee. In the parking arrangements, taxpayers attempt to arrange the transaction so that the accommodation party has enough of the benefits and burdens relating to the property so that the accommodation party will be treated as the owner for federal income tax purposes.

.06 Treasury and the Service have determined that it is in the best interest of sound tax administration to provide taxpayers with a workable means of qualifying their transactions under section 1031 in situations where the taxpayer has a genuine intent to accomplish a like-kind exchange at the time that it arranges for the acquisition of the replacement property and actually accomplishes the exchange within a short time thereafter. Accordingly, this revenue procedure provides a safe harbor that allows a taxpayer to treat the accommodation party as the owner of the property for federal income tax purposes, thereby enabling the taxpayer to accomplish a qualifying like-kind exchange.

3. Scope

.01 EXCLUSIVITY. This revenue procedure provides a safe harbor for the qualification under section 1031 of certain arrangements between taxpayers and exchange accommodation titleholders and provides for the treatment of the exchange accommodation titleholder as the beneficial owner of the property for federal income tax purposes. These provisions apply only in the limited context described in this revenue procedure. The principles set forth in this revenue procedure have no application to any federal income tax determinations other than determinations that involve arrangements qualifying for the safe harbor.

.02 NO INFERENCE. No inference is intended with respect to the federal income tax treatment of arrangements similar to those described in this revenue procedure that were entered into prior to the effective date of this revenue procedure. Further, the Service recognizes that "parking" transactions can be accomplished outside of the safe harbor provided in this revenue procedure. Accordingly, no inference is intended with respect to the federal income tax treatment of "parking" transactions that do not satisfy the terms of the safe harbor provided in this revenue procedure, whether entered into prior to or after the effective date of this revenue procedure.

.03 OTHER ISSUES. Services for the taxpayer in connection with a person's role as the exchange accommodation titleholder in a QEAA shall not be taken into account in determining whether that person or a related person is a disqualified person (as defined in section 1.1031(k)-1(k)). Even though property will not fail to be treated as being held in a QEAA as a result of one or more arrangements described in section 4.03 of this revenue procedure, the Service still may recast an amount paid pursuant to such an arrangement as a fee paid to the exchange accommodation titleholder for acting as an exchange accommodation titleholder to the extent necessary to reflect the true economic substance of the arrangement. Other federal income tax issues implicated, but not addressed, in this revenue procedure include the treatment, for federal income tax purposes, of payments described in section 4.03(7) and whether an exchange accommodation titleholder may be precluded from claiming depreciation deductions (e.g., as a dealer) with respect to the relinquished property or the replacement property.

.04 EFFECT OF NONCOMPLIANCE. If the requirements of this revenue procedure are not satisfied (for example, the property subject to a QEAA is not transferred within the time period provided), then this revenue procedure does not apply. Accordingly, the determination of whether the taxpayer or the exchange accommodation titleholder is the owner of the property for federal income tax purposes, and the proper treatment of any transactions entered into by or between the parties, will be made without regard to the provisions of this revenue procedure.

4. Qualified Exchange Accommodation Arrangements

.01 GENERALLY. The Service will not challenge the qualification of property as either "replacement property" or "relinquished property" (as defined in section 1.1031(k)-1(a)) for purposes of section 1031 and the regulations thereunder, or the treatment of the exchange accommodation titleholder as the beneficial owner of such property for federal income tax purposes, if the property is held in a QEAA.

.02 QUALIFIED EXCHANGE ACCOMMODATION ARRANGEMENTS. For purposes of this revenue procedure, property is held in a QEAA if all of the following requirements are met:

(1) Qualified indicia of ownership of the property is held by a person (the "exchange accommodation titleholder") who is not the taxpayer or a disqualified person and either such person is subject to federal income tax or, if such person is treated as a partnership or S corporation for federal income tax purposes, more than 90 percent of its interests or stock are owned by partners or shareholders who are subject to federal income tax. Such qualified indicia of ownership must be held by the exchange accommodation titleholder at all times from the date of acquisition by the exchange accommodation titleholder until the property is transferred as described in section 4.02(5) of this revenue procedure. For this purpose, "qualified indicia of ownership" means legal title to the property, other indicia of ownership of the property that are treated as beneficial ownership of the property under applicable principles of commercial law (e.g., a contract for deed), or interests in an entity that is disregarded as an entity separate from its owner for federal income tax purposes (e.g., a single member limited liability company) and that holds either legal title to the property or such other indicia of ownership;

(2) At the time the qualified indicia of ownership of the property is transferred to the exchange accommodation titleholder, it is the taxpayer's bona fide intent that the property held by the exchange accommodation titleholder represent either replacement property or relinquished property in an exchange that is intended to qualify for non-recognition of gain (in whole or in part) or loss under section 1031;

(3) No later than five business days after the transfer of qualified indicia of ownership of the property to the exchange accommodation titleholder, the taxpayer and the exchange accommodation titleholder enter into a written agreement (the "qualified exchange accommodation agreement") that provides that the exchange accommodation titleholder is holding the property for the benefit of the taxpayer in order to facilitate an exchange under section 1031 and this revenue procedure and that the taxpayer and the exchange accommodation titleholder agree to report the acquisition, holding, and disposition of the property as provided in this revenue procedure. The agreement must specify that the exchange accommodation titleholder will be treated as the beneficial owner of the property for all federal income tax purposes. Both parties must report the federal income tax attributes of the property on their federal income tax returns in a manner consistent with this agreement;

(4) No later than 45 days after the transfer of qualified indicia of ownership of the replacement property to the exchange accommodation titleholder, the relinquished property is properly identified. Identification must be made in a manner consistent with the principles described in section 1.1031(k)-1(c). For purposes of this section, the taxpayer may properly identify alternative and multiple properties, as described in section 1.1031(k)-1(c)(4);

(5) No later than 180 days after the transfer of qualified indicia of ownership of the property to the exchange accommodation titleholder, (a) the property is transferred (either directly or indirectly through a qualified intermediary (as defined in section 1.1031(k)-1(g)(4))) to the taxpayer as replacement property; or (b) the property is transferred to a person who is not the taxpayer or a disqualified person as relinquished property; and

(6) The combined time period that the relinquished property and the replacement property are held in a QEAA does not exceed 180 days.

.03 PERMISSIBLE AGREEMENTS. Property will not fail to be treated as being held in a QEAA as a result of any one or more of the following legal or contractual arrangements, regardless of whether such arrangements contain terms that typically would result from arm's-length bargaining between unrelated parties with respect to such arrangements:

(1) An exchange accommodation titleholder that satisfies the requirements of the qualified intermediary safe harbor set forth in section 1.1031(k)-1(g)(4) may enter into an exchange agreement with the taxpayer to serve as the qualified intermediary in a simultaneous or deferred exchange of the property under section 1031;

(2) The taxpayer or a disqualified person guarantees some or all of the obligations of the exchange accommodation titleholder, including secured or unsecured debt incurred to acquire the property, or indemnifies the exchange accommodation titleholder against costs and expenses;

(3) The taxpayer or a disqualified person loans or advances funds to the exchange accommodation titleholder or guarantees a loan or advance to the exchange accommodation titleholder;

(4) The property is leased by the exchange accommodation titleholder to the taxpayer or a disqualified person;

(5) The taxpayer or a disqualified person manages the property, supervises improvement of the property, acts as a contractor, or otherwise provides services to the exchange accommodation titleholder with respect to the property;

(6) The taxpayer and the exchange accommodation titleholder enter into agreements or arrangements relating to the purchase or sale of the property, including puts and calls at fixed or formula prices, effective for a period not in excess of 185 days from the date the property is acquired by the exchange accommodation titleholder; and

(7) The taxpayer and the exchange accommodation titleholder enter into agreements or arrangements providing that any variation in the value of a relinquished property from the estimated value on the date of the exchange accommodation titleholder's receipt of the property be taken into account upon the exchange accommodation titleholder's disposition of the relinquished property through the taxpayer's advance of funds to, or receipt of funds from, the exchange accommodation titleholder.

.04 PERMISSIBLE TREATMENT. Property will not fail to be treated as being held in a QEAA merely because the accounting, regulatory, or state, local, or foreign tax treatment of the arrangement between the taxpayer and the exchange accommodation titleholder is different from the treatment required by section 4.02(3) of this revenue procedure.

5. Effective Date

This revenue procedure is effective for QEAAs entered into with respect to an exchange accommodation titleholder that acquires qualified indicia of ownership of property on or after September 15, 2000.

acceleration clause A clause within the mortgage agreement or trust deed, commonly referred to as a "due-on-transfer" clause, that requires the buyer to pay off the note if the property is resold or transferred.

accommodator A person or company hired to facilitate a 1031 exchange by creating the necessary supporting documentation and holding the proceeds from the sale of the relinquished property on behalf of the exchanging taxpayer until the completion of the purchase of the replacement property. Also known as a qualified intermediary, middleman, or facilitator.

adjustable-rate mortgage (ARM) A mortgage whose interest rate changes in accordance with changes in a specified indicator like Treasury bills or the prime rate. For example an "ARM at 2 points over prime" would mean an adjustable-rate mortgage with interest at whatever the prime rate is plus two (if the prime rate is 5 percent the interest on the note would be 7 percent).

adjusted basis The adjusted basis on a property is usually equal to the acquisition cost plus any capital improvements and less any depreciation taken.

assumption clause A clause within the mortgage note that details the conditions under which another person may assume the note. In some cases, the seller may not want the note to be assumable at all. In that case, the note must be paid in full if the property is sold (if there is a due-on-transfer clause). A note should contain either an assumption clause or, in the alternative, a due-on-sale clause.

balloon payment A lump sum payment that is larger than regularly scheduled monthly loan payments. A balloon payment is usually used in a note to reduce some portion of the principal or for a required early payoff of the whole note.

basis Usually, the original acquisition cost on a property if the property was purchased. Gifts and inherited property, however, have an assumed, or stepped-up, basis. The word basis is commonly used interchangeably with adjusted basis, which usually refers to the original cost plus any capital improvements and less any depreciation taken.

boot In a like-kind exchange, any money or other nonqualifying property transferred or received by the taxpayer and taxable to the extent of the gain.

buyer in 1031 exchanges In exchange discussions, usually refers to the person buying the relinquished property, although the exchanger is commonly, and mistakenly, referred to as the buyer of the replacement property.

constructive receipt An exchanger is not allowed to have receipt of the sale proceeds at any time during the exchange process, or the exchange will fail. The proceeds are considered constructively received by the exchanger if at any time the exchanger has unfettered use of, or access to, them. Funds need to be transferred to the qualified intermediary and held there in trust for the exchanger's purchase of the replacement property.

deferred exchange A nonsimultaneous exchange of property under the tax deferral provisions of Internal Revenue Code section 1031.

direct deeding The IRS now allows the respective titleholders in an exchange to deed directly to the ultimate owner. Before direct deeding was approved, both properties had to first be deeded to the qualified intermediary and then from the qualified intermediary to the ultimate owner.

disqualified person A person who cannot act as an exchanger's intermediary.

disqualified person (as defined for IRA-prohibited transactions)

1. A fiduciary of the plan (IRA)
2. A person providing services to the plan
3. An employer, any of whose employees are covered by the plan
4. An employee organization, any of whose members are covered by the plan
5. Any direct or indirect owner of 50 percent or more of any of the following:
   a. The combined voting power of all classes of stock entitled to vote or the total value of shares of all classes of stock of a corporation that is an employer or employee organization described in (3) or (4)
   b. The capital interest or profit interest of a partnership that is an employer or employee organization described in (3) or (4)
   c. The beneficial interest of a trust or unincorporated enterprise that is an employer or an employee organization described in (3) or (4)

6. A member of the family of any individual described in (1), (2), (3), or (5) (A member of a family is the spouse, ancestor, lineal descendant, or any spouse of a lineal descendant.)

7. A corporation, partnership, trust, or estate of which (or in which) any direct or indirect owner described in (1) through (5) holds 50 percent or more of any of the following:

   a. The combined voting power of all classes of stock entitled to vote or the total value of shares of all classes of stock of a corporation

   b. The capital interest or profit interest of a partnership

   c. The beneficial interest of a trust or estate

8. An officer, director (or an individual having powers or responsibilities similar to those of officers or directors), a 10 percent or more shareholder, or a highly compensated employee (earning 10 percent or more of the yearly wages of an employer) of a person described in (3), (4), (5), or (7)

9. A 10 percent or more (in capital or profits) partner or joint venturer of a person described in (3), (4), (5), or (7)

downleg Out-of-date (slang) terminology referring to the sale of a relinquished property.

due-on-transfer clause or due-on-sale clause A clause within a mortgage agreement or note and deed of trust that requires the buyer to pay off the note if the property is resold or transferred; also commonly referred to as a "due-on-sale" or "acceleration" clause.

exchange accommodation titleholder (EAT) One who holds title to a property and acts as a parking entity during a reverse exchange.

exchange agreement The agreement between an exchanger and the qualified intermediary that sets out the duties and responsibilities of each; normally passed through the escrow or closing agent and supplements the escrow or closing instructions.

exchange period The 180 days allowed by IRC section 1031 to complete the acquisition of a replacement property; with the clock starting to run at the close of the sale on the relinquished property.

exchanger The taxpayer using the provisions of IRC section 1031 to exchange one property for another and at the same time deferring capital gains taxes.

45-day period Refers to the 45-day replacement property identification period. Under IRC section 1031, the exchanger has 45 days to identify, in writing, a suitable replacement property and 180 days total to complete the replacement property purchase.

four-way exchange The term used by many older exchange publications to describe the traditional and customary 1031 exchange with an intermediary.

identification notice The notice required under the terms of IRC section 1031 for the exchanger to identify the potential replacement properties in the exchange within 45 days. A replacement property is properly identified only if it is designated as replacement property in a written document signed by the taxpayer and hand delivered, mailed, telecopied, or otherwise sent to either (1) the person obligated to transfer the replacement property to the taxpayer, even if that person is a disqualified person, or (2) to any other person involved in the exchange other than the taxpayer or a disqualified person under Reg § 1.1031(k)-1(k), before the end of the 45-day identification period.

identification period The 45-day replacement property identification period specified in IRC section 1031; the exchanger must identify a replacement property within this period or risk a failed exchange.

interest-only note A note or mortgage that provides for monthly payments consisting only of the interest on the principal. This is usually done to lower the buyer's payments for a period to simplify the calculations for the seller when principal payments are made or payoff calculations are needed.

IRC section 1031 Internal Revenue Code section 1031 pertaining to like-kind exchanges.

like-kind exchange An exchange of properties under the tax deferral provisions of Internal Revenue Code section 1031.

like-kind property All real estate used for business or held for investment, an exception being foreign real estate, which is not considered like-kind to domestic real estate.

loan servicing A service offered by certain banks or financial institutions whereby they collect payments and maintain records on seller-financed notes on behalf of a seller.

loan-to-value ratio (LTV) A measure of the amount of total financing in relation to the fair market value or sales price of a property; a $160,000 loan on a $200,000 property, for example, has an 80 percent LTV.

mortgage boot A term that stems from one of the primary conditions to be met in a fully tax-deferred exchange—a mortgage on replacement property must be equal to or higher than the mortgage that existed on the relinquished property. The net mortgage relief is considered "mortgage boot" if this condition is not met and is taxed to the extent of the gain.

95 percent rule An alternative to the commonly followed three-property identification rule that allows exchangers to identify as many properties as they desire so long as 95 percent of those identified properties are ultimately acquired as replacement property.

180-day period The provisions of IRC section 1031 that allow the exchanger 180 days from the closing of the relinquished property to complete the acquisition of the replacement property.

Phase I property Synonymous term for relinquished property.

Phase II property Synonymous term for replacement property.

prepayment penalty A provision in a mortgage note that requires the borrower to pay a monetary penalty if the note is paid off before a specified amount of time. Each state has its own laws restricting the use of prepayment penalties. (See Chapter 10 for more information.)

qualified intermediary A person or company hired to facilitate a 1031 exchange by creating the necessary supporting documentation and holding the proceeds from the sale of the relinquished property on behalf of the exchanging taxpayer until completion of the purchase of the replacement property. Also known interchangeably as an accommodator, middleman, or facilitator.

realized gain The difference between the amounts received on the sale or other disposition of property and the adjusted basis of the property.

recognized gain The portion of realized gain or loss that is subject to income taxation.

related persons People to whom special rules apply in exchanges between them. Related persons generally include family members (siblings, spouse, ancestors, and lineal descendants) or entities (corporations, partnerships, estates, trusts, etc.) in which a family member owns more than 50 percent in value of the entity directly or indirectly.

relinquished property The property given up in an exchange.

replacement property The property received in an exchange.

reverse exchange An exchange of properties under the tax-deferral provisions of IRC section 1031, although the replacement property in a reverse exchange is acquired prior to the sale of the relinquished property.

safe harbor A method of doing something expressly approved by the IRS; in exchanges, refers to the use of a qualified intermediary; in reverse exchanges, refers to an exchange accommodation titleholder.

seller in 1031 exchanges In exchange discussions, usually refers to the person who owns the replacement property before the exchange occurs, although the exchanger is commonly, and mistakenly, referred to as the seller of the relinquished property.

sequential deeding The process of deeding title of exchange properties first to the qualified intermediary, who in turn deeds title to the respective new owners. Sequential deeding is rarely used in ordinary exchanges, as most exchanges now involve direct deeding.

simultaneous exchange A properly documented 1031 exchange of property in which the completion of sale of the relinquished property and the completion of the purchase of the replacement property occur concurrently.

Starker exchange The name of an exchange stemming from a landmark court case allowing a deferral period, or delay, between a relinquished property sale and the replacement property purchase. Prior to the Starker decision, all 1031 exchanges were thought to require simultaneous closings.

stepped-rate mortgage A mortgage that has an increasing (or decreasing) interest rate over time.

tax service A service that monitors property tax payments on a property and notifies a lender if the borrower fails to keep the taxes current.

tax-deferred exchange A properly documented 1031 exchange indicating that taxes will not be triggered, as would otherwise be the case in an ordinary sale and subsequent purchase.

tax-free exchange A properly documented 1031 exchange indicating that taxes will not be triggered, as would otherwise be the case in an ordinary sale and subsequent purchase.

1031 exchange An exchange of properties under the tax deferral provisions of IRC section 1031.

30 due in 7 A description of the amortization schedule and term of a mortgage note. Most mortgages are amortized over 30 years, which means the payments are calculated to pay the accumulated interest each month and gradually pay off the principal due in that period. In a case where a note is due sooner, a balloon payment is made for the outstanding balance. For example, a "30 due in 10" indicates that a note has monthly payments based on the 30-year amortization schedule, but a balloon payment is due in ten years to fully pay off the loan. Likewise, a "20 due in 5" is a note amortized over 20 years but due to be fully paid off in five years by a balloon payment. Any amortization schedule can be used, but the usual and customary method in seller financing is to amortize the note over 30 years and set the due date for five, seven, or ten years. These terms are completely negotiable between the buyer and seller.

three-property rule Reference to IRC section 1031 requirement that an exchanger identify a potential replacement property within 45 days after the closing of the relinquished property but is allowed to identify three potential properties, at least one of which must be acquired within the 180-day exchange period.

200 percent rule An alternative to the commonly followed three-property rule that permits an exchanger to identify more than three properties if the total value of all identified properties does not exceed 200 percent of the value of the relinquished property.

two-way exchange A like-kind exchange in which the exchanger is actually trading property for property with another exchanger; no accommodator is needed in this simultaneous exchange. A two-way exchange is rare because of the real-world difficulty of finding two people who actually want each other's property.

up-leg Out-of-date (slang) terminology referring to the purchase of a replacement property.

Share the message!

Bulk discounts
Discounts start at only 10 copies and range from 30% to 55% off retail price based on quantity.

Custom publishing
Private label a cover with your organization's name and logo. Or, tailor information to your needs with a custom pamphlet that highlights specific chapters.

Ancillaries
Workshop outlines, videos, and other products are available on select titles.

Dynamic speakers
Engaging authors are available to share their expertise and insight at your event.

Call Kaplan Publishing Corporate Sales at 1-800-621-9621, ext. 4444, or e-mail kaplanpubsales@kaplan.com

PUBLISHING